FRANK GAFFIKIN & MIKE MORRISSEY

THE NEW UNEMPLOYED

Joblessness and Poverty in the Market Economy

ZED BOOKS
LONDON & NEW JERSEY

The New Unemployed was first published by Zed Books Ltd,
57 Caledonian Road, London N1 9BU, UK and 165 First Avenue,
Atlantic Highlands, New Jersey 07716, USA, in 1992.

Cover designed by Andrew Corbett.
Laserset by Paul Kernan.
Printed and bound in the United Kingdom
by Biddles Ltd, Guildford and King's Lynn.

A catalogue record for this book is
available from the British Library.

ISBN 1 85649 067 X Hb
ISBN 1 85649 068 8 Pb

Contents

Tables

Figures

Acknowledgements

Our thanks go to Paul Kernan of CTRS and David Smyth of CITU for their invaluable help with the Desk-Top Publishing, and to Paul Teague for his critical comments on the contents. Any deficiencies in either respect are our own responsibility.

Frank Gaffikin
Mike Morrissey

Foreword

This book emerged from the European Community's second poverty programme when the Belfast Centre for the Unemployed was responsible for a project with the long-term unemployed. It was a chastening experience: the Belfast travel to work area had over 50,000 unemployed, over half of whom had been jobless for a year or more; despite the prevalence of ideas about high benefit levels preventing the unemployed from seeking work, we discovered appalling conditions of poverty; and worst of all, public policy appeared to have abandoned the unemployed - mass unemployment had become the norm. Contacts with other projects within the poverty programme revealed a depressing similarity in these conditions throughout Europe. The problem was not peculiar to Northern Ireland, merely more pronounced.

Since Mike and Frank were heavily involved in the work of the Unemployed Centre, we discussed the idea of a book to describe and analyse the international problem of unemployment. Two factors make its timing important. The collapse of communism has given a new legitimacy to the market economies which helps conceal the economic waste and social costs of unemployment. It is crucial that this problem does not slip off the agenda simply because the major challenge to capitalism was itself terribly flawed. In Britain for example the re-election of a Conservative government has been hailed as a renewed triumph of market supremacy but does not augur well for the millions of unemployed. Second, the 1990s have seen a worsening of unemployment across Europe and the US, while the new orthodoxies have no more effective solutions than in the 1980s. The debate about alternative policies must therefore be given a new impetus.

Finally, I would stress that this analysis is not just the product of an economic debate. It is firmly rooted in the struggle against unemployment.

Brendan Mackin
Co-ordinator, Belfast Centre for the Unemployed

1. The Rise and Rise of Unemployment

The economic collapse of the Soviet Union and Eastern Europe was greeted as a triumph by adherents of the market economies. They urged the former command economies to rapidly restructure along market lines although the resources required to do so, with appropriate compensation for the inevitable social costs, were not made available. Privatisation of land and capital was seen as the key step, followed by the encouragement of enterprise and finally, full currency conversion. Any attempt to suggest that such rapid restructuring would generate extremely negative costs, particularly in the form of mass unemployment, was regarded as an expression of outmoded ideology or bureaucratic inertia.

Thus the 1991 G7 London conference was sceptical about the lack of commitment to market forces and the lack of detail in the Gorbachev reform plan. Some have suggested that the unwillingness to offer large-scale support at that time helped to precipitate the Soviet coup, the fall of Gorbachev himself and the break-up of the Soviet Union. Only when the Soviet Union disintegrated, did offers of substantial help materialise. The international conference in January 1992 promised larger aid disbursements, though the announcement in March 1992 of a $30 billion support package from the G7 countries remained small relative to the enormity of the problem.

This confidence in the market system exhibited by the leading politicians of the market economies, was not depressed by the inability of the G7 London meeting to provide a detailed perspective on how the economic difficulties affecting its member states could be tackled. For most of 1991, the US economy remained stalled in recession. Its car industry lost $5 billion in the first nine months of the year. Unemployment continued to rise and the social infrastructure further decayed, while the trade and budgetary deficits showed no significant improvement. Accordingly, the apparently unassailable political standing of President Bush steadily declined to the point where the 1992 election campaign seemed a real contest again. The UK has wrestled with recession, and experienced negligible growth with the 1992 Budget statement predicting only 1 per cent growth for the year. Meanwhile, UK unemployment escalated with many estimates suggesting that it would near 3 million by 1993. An analysis of the German economy published in October 1991 remained sombre about the costs of integrating the former GDR, projecting gloomy prospects for inflation and growth.[1] Indeed in April 1992 the IMF had to revise downwards that year's growth estimates for most of the G7 economies.

Paradoxically, the economic supremacy of the West over the former Soviet Union occurred at a time when the Western economies themselves appeared fragile and seemed to have abandoned full employment. Unemployment continued to be large-scale even during periods of economic growth and, in most market economies, the unemployed became the biggest single group among the poor.

The focus of this book will be on unemployment both in the EC and the US. It will examine its relationship to poverty and an assessment will be made of the responses by individual states. The central question will be whether full employment is now possible or was merely a transitory phase in the development of the market economies. The comparative perspective is important because it emphasises the general nature of the economic forces responsible for, and the political responses to, unemployment. Thus trends and policy developments in the US and the EC, two of the three largest economic blocs, can be compared. At the same time, a more detailed focus is provided by analyses of the UK and Ireland, both of which suffered particular problems of unemployment in the 1980s.

Why Unemployment?

Following the oil shocks of the 1970s, governments' commitment to full employment policies declined as a result of their desire to curb inflation. In any case, the normal Keynesian remedy to unemployment, higher public expenditure, had been discredited in the face of the simultaneous growth of prices and unemployment. It became commonplace to suggest that unemployment had little to do with public policy except to the extent that the level of social security benefit acted as a work disincentive. Unemployment was regarded as a consequence of forces operating outside particular national economies or as a function of low labour productivities, which, in turn, led to industrial uncompetitiveness.[2]

Keynesian economics had tackled unemployment through macroeconomic intervention, while inflation was controlled at the microeconomic level. Thus fiscal policies determined the levels of aggregate demand, and

---

[1] See, for example, Peel, Q. (22/10/1991), 'Germany given recession warning,' *Financial Times*, or Elliot, L. and Kelly, R. (28/10/1991), 'Europe stands breathless as the German engine hits the buffers', *The Guardian*.

[2] See Worswick, G.D.N. (1991), *Unemployment: A problem of policy*, Cambridge University Press, Cambridge, part 3.

industrial relations policies attempted to keep pay bargaining in line with productivity. Under a new orthodoxy which emerged in the 1970s, the function of macroeconomic policies, through monetary policy, was to control inflation. At the same time, unemployment was treated at the micro level - improving the competitiveness, and hence the growth potential, of particular firms. In this last process, government had a role but little responsibility.

A new ideology was thus generated concerning unemployment. Goran Therborn has argued that the function of ideology is to say what exists, to describe what is possible and to prescribe what is good.[3] This aptly describes the ways in which governments have responded to unemployment. For example:

•   During the 1980s, the British government dramatically altered the definition of who was unemployed and how the rate of unemployment was calculated, indicating that unemployment only 'existed' as an official construction;[4]
•   Nearly all governments, faced with high levels of unemployment, argued that it was not 'possible' to maintain full employment policies in the face of hostile global circumstances. This explained the demise of the brief Keynesian experiment of the French Socialist government;
•   Finally, rising unemployment has been regarded as a necessary condition for eradicating inflation. In that sense, its growth can almost be interpreted as a positive indicator of success in purging inflationary pressures from the economy. The IMF has regularly demanded that Third World governments adopt austerity programmes to curb inflation, despite the manifest employment consequences for large sections of their populations.

Thus not only has unemployment been a central feature of the market economies since the end of the 1970s, but around it has grown a complex ideology designed to legitimate its existence and consequences. The central argument here is that unemployment remains a crucial measure of the health of an economic system and its complementary social structure:[5]

Unemployment is important because it is costly both to individuals and to society as a whole. Firstly, unemployment imposes costs upon society; labour is perishable and labour not utilised for production causes a permanent loss of output and therefore consumption. Secondly, unemployment imposes suffering upon individuals, not just in terms of forgone consumption, but the associated low self esteem often results in behavioural and physical health problems and family/marital instability.

If a recession lasts two years and GNP falls below potential by around 5 per

---

[3] Therborn, G. (1980), *The Ideology of Power and the Power of Ideology*, Verso, London.

[4] See *Unemployment Bulletin*, various issues.

[5] Adnett, N. (1989), *Labour Market Policy*, Longman, London, p.172.

cent, each family suffers an income loss of about £2,000. In 1981 the British government estimated that the cost in benefits and the loss in taxation for every 100,000 extra unemployed was £340 million. Socially, the unemployed suffer the material cost of reduced income and, psychologically, the stigma associated with their condition. Unemployment remains wasteful both in economic and human terms, whatever the means used to deny its severity or the rhetoric designed to conceal its costs.

Before Full Employment

The idea of full employment emerged only with industrialisation and urbanisation, when labour market activity came to be essential for subsistence. Marx's use of the term 'wage slavery' referred to the impossibility of making ends meet in the absence of paid labour. At the same time, the institution of compulsory schooling and the gradual exclusion of women from the labour market ensured that the monetary resources for physical reproduction came, almost completely, from male wages. Thus the unemployment of a single member had consequences for the entire family. Even in 1848, there were demands that the state should, 'fulfill its task of finding employment at a sufficient rate of wages' for those unable to do so themselves.[6]

However, it was not until the inter-war period that the idea acquired political urgency and economic feasibility. The recession following the Wall Street Crash of 1929 was the deepest, the most general and the longest suffered by the market economies. The crisis originated in the United States and there the repercussions were dramatic. GNP fell by 9.9 per cent in 1930, 7.7 per cent in 1931 and 14.8 per cent in 1932. In this last year, unemployment stood at 25 per cent of the labour force and industrial production was only 59 per cent of its 1929 level.[7] In Britain, unemployment rose to 22 per cent in 1932, with 3.75 million out of work in September of that year.[8] In Germany, when Adolf Hitler was appointed Chancellor in 1933, there were 6 million officially registered as unemployed and industrial production was 40 per cent below the 1929 level.[9] In France, the initial consequences were less severe, but the economy was stagnant for most of the decade.

Government responses to the crisis varied dramatically. The minority Labour administration in Britain promoted a rhetoric of socialist planning,

---

[6] Keane, J. & Owens, J. (1986), *After Full Employment*, Hutchinson, London, p.29.

[7] Bleaney, M. (1985), *The Rise and Fall of Keynesian Economics*, MacMillan, London, p.41.

[8] Keane, J. and Owens,J. (1986), *op.cit.*, p.29.

[9] Bleaney, M. (1985), *op.cit.*, p.65.

but practised fiscal prudence. Tawney characterised labour programmes as wanting to 'nationalise land, mines and banking in one sentence and abolish fox hunting in the next.'[10] Oswald Mosley suggested that the government was like the Salvation Army taking to its heels on the day of judgement.[11] In fact, only the Liberal party, relying on the ideas of Keynes, produced a constructive programme for unemployment. Even the radical Popular Front government, elected in France in 1935, failed to develop a set of policies capable of tackling the crisis. The intention was to enhance aggregate demand by increasing the purchasing power of the working class, and to create employment through public works programmes and the reduction of working hours. While these measures promoted growth, they also induced inflation and capital flight. Amid increasing political difficulties, the Popular Front fell after only two years in office.

The election of Roosevelt in the US signalled more vigorous efforts to combat the recession there. The New Deal package, represented by the National Industrial Recovery Act, the Agricultural Administration Act and the Public Works Administration, acted as a stimulus to recovery. In 1934 and 1935 GNP rose by nearly 20 per cent. At the same time, Roosevelt was not convinced of the efficacy of deficit budgeting to promote recovery. Indeed, only in 1931 and in 1936 was the federal budget in deficit.[12] Germany saw the most spectacularly successful counter-recessionary policies. Unemployment had fallen by 3 million in 1934. By 1938, unemployment had almost disappeared and production was 29 per cent above the 1929 level. The Nazi government was largely responsible, through public works schemes, compulsory labour service and emergency relief work. While this accomplishment undoubtedly contributed to its popularity, the implementation of such measures was facilitated by the elimination of communist, social democratic and trade union resistance.[13] By the end of the decade, renewed spending on armaments was the catalyst for economic growth in all of these economies.

The mass unemployment of the 1930s was significant not merely because it cast a shadow on traditional economic management, but also because other models of economic organisation appeared to demonstrate a superior capacity to recover from the crisis. Both the authoritarian corporatism of Germany and Italy, and the establishment of a command economy in the Soviet Union, were lauded by right and left as appropriate models for economic planning. The former two had weathered the crisis, while, apparently, the Soviet Union's 1928 five-year plan made it irrelevant.

---

[10] Eatwell, R. (1979), *The 1945-1951 Labour Governments*, Batsford, London, p.25.

[11] Deakin, N. (1987), *The Politics of Welfare*, Methuen, London, p.37.

[12] Galbraith. J. (1988), *The Great Crash 1929*, Penguin, Middlesex, & Bleaney,M. (1985), op.cit.

[13] Bleaney, M. (1985), *op. cit.*, p.69.

However, both Italy and Germany sustained economic growth through military expansionism, while collectivisation and rapid industrialisation in the Soviet Union were accompanied by widespread deprivation, the elimination of political opposition and, indeed, famine.[14]

Nevertheless, the prevalence of capitalist recession generated hope within the Comintern that a world socialist system was a practical possibility. Capitalism appeared to be exhausted, while fascism was first viewed as a consequence of economic backwardness (Italy), and then as the end phase of capitalism, where monopoly rule and bourgeois democratic politics had become incompatible (Germany). The Sixth Congress of the Comintern (1928) correctly predicted the forthcoming global economic crisis but saw it as 'catastrophic and final'.[15]

Yet, the market economies endured the 1930s, survived the Second World War and subsequently experienced their most rapid, long-term period of growth. For much of this time, they also enjoyed full employment.

The Post-war Boom and Full Employment

With the exception of the United States, the Western economies emerged exhausted from the Second World War. Plant and equipment had been working at full capacity for over five years. Millions of military personnel had to be reintegrated into civilian life. Overseas assets had been consumed and public debt had escalated. In addition, war damage had significantly reduced capital stock.[16] It appeared that the post-war period would be a re-run of that following World War I, with considerable economic instability. In the first instance, that was prevented by Marshall Aid.

With no military damage and a booming economy, the United States was in a position to transfer substantial resources for European reconstruction. The rapid regeneration of the European economies would not only provide a market for US goods and a location for the investment of surplus capital, but would also act as a bulwark against the Eastern Bloc, newly created by the westward advance of the Soviet army. In addition, communist parties had become politically influential in France and Italy and were regarded as a danger to 'Western democracy'. These considerations prevented any return to US isolationism.

The extent of US support both to former allies and enemies can be gauged

---

[14] For accounts of the latter, see Cliff,T. (1974), *State Capitalism in Russia*, Pluto, London. For different perspectives, see Bettleheim, C. (1978), *Class Struggles in the USSR, 1923-1930*, The Harvester Press, Sussex, and Deacon, B. (1983), *Social Policy and Socialism*, Pluto Press, London.

[15] Poulantzas, N. (1979), *Fascism and Dictatorship*, Verso, London, p.46.

[16] Armstrong, P. Glyn, A. and Harrison, J. (1984), *Capitalism Since World War II*, Fontana, London, p.26.

from table 1.1. This very substantial level of subsidy pump-primed post-war recovery. In turn, the preparedness of governments to embrace Keynesian economics in order to manage aggregate demand is usually seen as the source of the sustained growth that followed the initial surge.

Table 1.1 US Non-military Grants and Government Long-term Capital, 1946-50					
$ million per year					
	UK	France	Germany	Italy	Japan
1946-47	1,722	984	371	474	419
1948-50	857	668	847	378	373
Source: Armstrong *et al.* (1984), p.119					

Keynes' publication of *The General Theory of Employment, Interest and Money* in 1936[17] was an attempt to rescue neoclassical economics from its failure to account for the long-term recession and mass unemployment. While neoclassical economics accepted the possibility of recession, it anticipated that flexibility in wages and prices would soon recreate conditions for profitable investment and, hence, new employment opportunities. The continuance of recession could, therefore, only be understood by rigidities in the price mechanism. Keynes demonstrated that even if money wages fell, falling prices would reduce the decline of real wages. As a further consequence, effective demand would be reduced, thus creating a situation of demand deficiency in the whole economy.

Moreover, Keynes regarded savings as a function of the level of income rather than of the rate of interest. Decreasing income would depress savings which, in turn, would lead to a decline in investment. An economy could suffer low output and high unemployment with no necessary tendency for self-correction. In such conditions of demand deficiency, government could 'top up' aggregate demand through public spending. This could be accomplished by deficit budgeting even when the tax base was too restricted to finance such expenditure. However, economic policy tended to embrace both neoclassical and Keynesian precepts. While fiscal policies were used to maintain aggregate demand, industrial relations policies were designed to ensure that wage costs did not rise faster than productivity. The latter was little more that an attempt to contain the real value of wages and could thus be directly related to neoclassical imperatives.

Nevertheless, it appeared that the means existed to permanently manage a full employment economy. Such optimism persisted for over 30 years. In 1973, just before the first oil shock, Nobel prize winning economist, Paul Samuelson, declared:[18]

---

[17] Keynes, J.M. (1983 edition), *The General Theory of Employment, Interest and Money*, Volume VII of The Collected Writings of John Maynard Keynes, MacMillan, London.

[18] Samuelson, P. (1973), *Economics*, 9th edition, McGraw Hill, New York.

Everywhere in the western world governments and central banks have shown they can win the battle of the slump. They have the weapons of fiscal policy (expenditure and taxes) and of monetary policy (open market operations, discount rate policy, legal reserve-ratio policy), to shift the various schedules that determine national income and employment. Just as we no longer meekly accept disease, we no longer need accept mass unemployment.

Certainly, the patterns of post war growth were impressive. Even the slow-growing countries achieved an annual increase in production of around 3 per cent. Italy and West Germany demonstrated remarkable capacities for post-war recovery with production increases of over 10 per cent per year. Armstrong et al. demonstrate that, by 1973, output in the advanced capitalist countries was 180 per cent higher than in 1950, and claim that more was produced in that quarter of a century than the previous three quarters. During this period, output per head of population in these countries rose by an average of 3.8 per cent per year compared to 1.2 per cent between 1913 and 1950.[19]

Table 1.2   Percentage Change in Industrial Production (excluding gas and oil), 1951-66

Belgium	51
France	127
Italy	227
Sweden	103
West Germany	185
UK	57

Source: Rowthorn,B.(1983), 'The past strikes back, in Hall,S. and Jacques,M. (eds.), *The Politics of Thatcherism*, Lawrence & Wishart, London, p.69

The consequences for unemployment were equally impressive. With the exceptions of Germany and Italy, unemployment rates in the market economies had remained in double figures for most of the 1930s. In 1939, the unemployment rates in the US and Britain were 17.2 and 11.7 per cent respectively.[20] Two decades later, the comparable rates were 5.7 and 2.9 per cent. Between 1959 and 1973, unemployment in West Germany never rose above 2 per cent, in France it remained below 2.5 per cent and, with the exception of 1959, was never above 4 per cent in Italy.[21]

---

[19] Armstrong, P. Glyn, A. and Harrison, J. (1984), *op.cit.*, p.167.

[20] Ashton, D.N. (1986), *Unemployment under Capitalism*, Wheatsheaf Books, Brighton, p.32.

[21] Sorrentino, C. (1981), 'Unemployment in International Perspective', in Sinfield,A. and Showler, B. (eds.), *The Workless State*, Martin Robertson, Oxford, p.170.

The significance of Keynesian theory in promoting these changes was considerable. When unemployment seemed the most pressing economic problem, a theory claiming to have found the secret of permanent full employment was inevitably popular. Conversely, when inflation overshadowed unemployment, neoclassical economics in the form of monetarism was reinstated.

Keynes, however, did not specify what form of public expenditure would be required to catalyse growth. He approved of the economic consequences of both pyramid and cathedral building. In the modern economy, the equivalent form is military spending:[22]

Military spending keeps the capital goods industry operating near full capacity without raising the economy's productive capacity as rapidly as would be the case if they provided capital goods for industry. Demand does not tend to drop below supply as persistently as it formerly did; military spending increases demand without increasing productivity.

The US is generally regarded as having applied 'military Keynesianism' most consistently. On one estimate, military related expenditure as a percentage of GNP rose from 1.2 per cent to 6.7 per cent between 1927 and 1973.[23] Other estimates are as high as 15 per cent.[24] For Britain, the decline of empire and its reduced global military role after Suez meant that military expenditure grew more slowly than social expenditure. For example, military spending fell from 34 per cent of civil expenditure in 1953 to 13 per cent in 1973.[25] In this period, other European countries also tended to invest more in physical and social infrastructure than armaments.

Some commentators argue that Keynesian policies were only one factor amidst a series of changes which generated the boom. Murray, for example, suggests that the post-war period was characterised by the wide-scale implementation of a new system of production, Fordism, in which conditions of mass consumption had to be created to match the new mass production.[26] Henry Ford first developed this system for car manufacture. It involved the standardisation of products on mechanised, flow-line assembly operations, where worker tasks were organised according to time-and-motion principles. The high fixed costs of setting up the system were more than offset by its low variable costs (achieved through higher labour productivity), provided

---

[22] Hunt, E.K. and Sherman, H.J. (1986), *Economics: An Introduction to Traditional and Radical Views*, 5th edition, Harper & Row, New York, p.161.

[23] Green, F. and Sutcliffe, B. (1987), *The Profit System*, Penguin, Middlesex, p.196.

[24] Hunt, E.K. and Sherman, H.J. (1986), *op.cit.*

[25] Rowthorn, B. (1980), *Capitalism, Conflict and Inflation*, Lawrence & Wishart, London, p.111.

[26] Murray, R. (1989), 'Fordism and post-Fordism', in Hall,S. and Jacques,M. (eds.), *New Times*, Lawrence and Wishart, London.

the market for the product was sufficiently large to permit long production runs. Ford's Model T was only one-tenth the price of craft-built cars and, in 1916, he captured 50 per cent of the US car market. The post-war period saw these methods used in the production of a wide range of consumption goods, whose prices fell in real terms over time. Advertising generated the desire for such products, while Keynesianism and credit expansion created the necessary demand. From this perspective, Keynesianism was a necessary, but not a sufficient, condition for the post-war boom and full employment.

Faire also contends that a more general set of factors accounted for full employment.[27] These included technological innovations during the war which led to new product development and enhanced labour productivity, the social organisation of production, the favourable terms of trade enjoyed by the advanced economies with respect to primary producers, and the expenditure on armaments sustained by the Cold War. This approach is congruent with the 'long wave theory' of industrial development where specific 'triggering' factors increase the rate of profit and, hence, induce long-term accumulation (the major cycle) within which minor fluctuations of economic activity occur.[28] From this perspective, the rise in unemployment in the mid-1970s was more than just a crisis for Keynesianism: it represented the end of a complete phase of industrialisation.

The long post-war boom was undoubtedly the result of a set of complex factors:

• transfers from the US first enabled the market economies to take advantage of the technological advances which had occurred during the war;

• a new system of production and the social organisation of demand permitted the rapid growth of consumption and employment; and

• a constant supply of cheap primary products, to the disadvantage of developing countries, helped maintain low production costs.

Crisis in the 1970s

By the 1970s, the three essential foundations of the post-war social democratic order - Keynesianism, welfarism and Fordism - were each in a precarious state, thereby threatening the very basis of the pledge to full employment. The problem of sustaining faith in Keynesian solutions to economic disequilibrium became evident in the late 1960s. In the UK, Wilson's Labour government effectively conceded political ground on the defence of full employment. As Townsend has noted, in 1967:[29]

---

[27] Faire, A. (1983), 'Ten Years of Crisis for the Advanced Capitalist Economies', in *World View 1983*, Pluto Press, London.

[28] See Mandel, E. (1978), *Late Capitalism*, Verso, London, ch.4.

[29] Townsend, P. (1978), 'The Problem: An Overview', in Barrett Brown, M. et al. (eds.),

the average number of unemployed rose to over a half a million without Labour Ministers being visibly alarmed or mortified. On the contrary, people were nursed into accepting a temporary higher level of unemployment as a necessary condition of economic recovery.

At the global level, one of the first clear signals of a looming crisis appeared in 1971 with the abandonment of the Bretton Woods Agreement, which had been in place since 1945 as a system to maintain exchange rate stability. Implicitly, it was a reluctant recognition on the part of the US that its best hope of improving its international competitiveness lay in devaluation.

Further instability followed the decision of the main oil-producing countries to hike up the price of oil in 1973, plunging the industrial economies of the West into deficit, while accentuating the pauperism of many Third World countries. The surplus petro-dollars at the disposal of OPEC were eventually re-circulated to Western banks. The latter, partly in response to depressed economic conditions in Western countries, made some injudicious loans to newly industrialising economies (NIEs) keen to maintain their development momentum. The NIEs expected to repay these loans by boosting exports and thereby increasing their foreign-exchange earnings. Such plans were dashed by the depressed global trading environment, prompted by the deflationary response of many advanced economies to the oil crisis. Aggravated by the high interest regimes of Western banking in the early 1980s, this situation would eventually deteriorate into an international debt crisis.

Monetary volatility was a reflection of the widening gap in global competitiveness:[30]

> During the 1970s the growth in productivity was again very unevenly distributed, with growth in the USA down to only 0.2 per cent as opposed to 3.2 per cent in Germany and 3.4 per cent in Japan.

The impact of these changes on the UK was acute. A decision taken by the Heath government in 1972 to adopt a floating exchange rate pressured the Labour government in its 1975 budget, to respond to an overseas deficit with a deflationary strategy, designed to secure the confidence of the international money markets:[31]

> The Budget statement forecast correctly that unemployment would rise above one million as a result of the proposals it contained. In this way the government explicitly signalled the rupture with the commitment to full employment given in 1944 and since shared by governments of both major political parties.

Full Employment, Spokesman, London.

[30] Glynn, A., *op. cit.,* p.221.

[31] Hudson, R. and Williams, A. (1986), *The United Kingdom,* Harper & Row, London, p.25.

This augured an austerity programme in advance of the formal intervention of the IMF in 1976, which further legitimated the primacy given to the defeat of inflation and the restoration of healthy trading balances over goals of full employment. Ormerod[32] recounts how public spending in the UK was restrained: by 1978-79, there would have been £4.7 billion more spent on capital expenditure and £3.1 billion more on current expenditure if the 1975-76 share of public spending had been maintained. This curb on the 'social wage' was applied at the same time as a 'social contract' with trade union leaders helped to secure a fall in average real wages of 8 per cent between 1975 and 1977. The seminal acknowledgement of the new revisionism was contained in the 1976 speech to the Labour party conference by Prime Minister Callaghan:[33]

> We used to think that you could just spend your way out of a recession and increase employment by cutting taxes and boosting government spending. I tell you in all candour that that option no longer exists, and that insofar as it ever did exist, it worked by injecting inflation into the economy. And each time that has happened the average level of unemployment has risen.

The result of this policy was a qualified success in its own terms. The trading deficit of £1 billion in 1976 was converted into a surplus of about the same amount by 1978, while inflation over the same period nearly halved from 16.5 per cent to 8.3 per cent. However, excluding the onset of the effects of oil and gas output, growth remained sluggish.[34] This failure to reverse growth trends compromised the arrangement with the trade union movement to enhance social consumption as a trade-off for a reduction in personal consumption.

Ultimately, it fomented the 'winter of discontent' in 1979, when low-paid workers risked the new discipline of unemployment to mount a series of strikes which were to contribute to a climate of popular disapproval of union power, successfully exploited by the 'New Right'.

By the late 1970s, before the ascendency of Reaganomics and Thatcherism, governments in the Western industrial economies were keen to dilute tenets of the post-war consensus such as full employment, without completely ditching corporatism in the process. In this respect, there was a conflict between the economic agenda of applying fiscal strictures and wage controls to prevent a reflated aggregate demand producing hyperinflation,

---

[32] Omerod, P. (1980), 'The Economic Record', in Bosanquet, N. and Townsend, P. (eds.), *Labour and Equality*, Heinemann, London.

[33] Caves, R. and Krause, J. (1980), *Britain's Economic Performance*, Brooking's Institute, Washington, p.75.

[34] Brett, E.A. (1985), *The World Economy Since the War: The Politics of Uneven Development*, MacMillan, London.

and the political imperative to sustain corporatism by containing unemployment. As Schott observed:[35]

> Ultimately Keynesian policy was replaced because in its accepted form, it could not deal with changes in the economy at the same time as overcoming or defusing the conflicts within society.

A key element in the crisis of Keynesianism was the increased pressure on state expenditure. In the 1950s, government spending as a proportion of GDP was quite stable in most traditional industrial countries, though there was considerable variation among them. The figure for Japan, at 15 per cent, was half or less that of its Western competitors. The composition of this expenditure changed over the decade. The share allocated to civil spending, such as education and health, rose while the military component of the budget declined, due to decolonialisation in Britain amongst other countries and the de-escalation of military engagement following the end of the Korean war, in the US.

Table 1.3	Proportions of State Expenditure in GDP (percentages), 1953-73			
	1953	1958	1963	1973
USA	27.5	29.1	29.2	32.7
UK	35.6	32.3	34.3	40.4
France	32.9	33.2	35.6	37.2
W.Germany	30.9	34.5	34.5	38.4
Italy	25.9	28.8	30.4	40.2
Japan	15.7	15.0	13.9	15.7
Note:	The 1973 figure for France is not compatible with previous figures and Japan's figures exclude gross fixed capital formation.			
Source:	OECD National Accounts 1950-1968, 1962-1973, abstracted from Rowthom, B. (1980), *op.cit.* p.111			

In the 1960s, the problem loomed of how to accommodate the rising costs of social reproduction, while also responding to the demand for increased military spending, such as, in the case of the US, in Vietnam. Essentially, the military share either rose or at least did not fall sufficiently to compensate for the continued growth of civil spending. As the table 1.3 shows, in most of the large capitalist countries this resulted in significant growth in the share of GDP taken by the state.

Coping With Stagflation

The capacity of government to prevent demand-deficient unemployment lay

---

[35] Schott, K. (1985), 'The Rise of Keynesian Economics: Britain 1940-1964', in Held, D. et al., (eds.), *States and Societies*, Blackwell, Open University, Oxford, p.346.

in its effective management of aggregate effective demand. This was supposedly assisted by its ability to predict with reasonable accuracy the opportunity cost of inflation in attaining a specific unemployment target. The problem of containing excess demand which could produce an inflationary gap was considered surmountable, particularly by the late 1950s, when the statistical device of the Phillips curve was available.

This contended that there was a calculable relationship between the rates of unemployment and those of wage inflation, to a point of deduction that zero inflation was achievable with an unemployment rate of around 2.5 per cent. But, critically, this was not a linear relationship. So, for example, there was a certain ceiling of unemployment, below which further reductions could only be achieved with the costs of progressively higher rates of inflation.

Despite these apparently more sophisticated understandings about fine-tuning demand management, there remained a contentious debate about whether inflation was fundamentally a supply-side or a demand-side problem. The 'cost-push' explanation suggested that inflationary pressures could emerge without the presence of excess demand. Rather, prices could spiral because of supply-side features such as high rates of unionisation, whereby workers were collectively organised into labour monopolies, capable of extracting wage increases which were not justified by productivity improvements. Such behaviour could persist for some time, because the corrective signals and disciplines of the market were muted by the political commitment to full employment.

Only market remuneration of skills could deliver efficient allocation of human capital. The political power of trade unions under corporatism essentially meant that wages were politically fixed. A 'proper' price structure in labour supply required the revocation of union immunities.

Moreover, in a situation of national pay bargaining and the growth of monopoly firms, microeconomic determinants were less and less applicable. Accordingly, a wage increase in a particular firm enjoying considerable productivity gains could become standard for all firms in the same industry, regardless of the differential rates of productivity they experienced. But in the long run, this could only lead either to government conceding an expansion of the money supply - which would merely invite further inflation - or to a profit and subsequent investment squeeze by business, with disastrous consequences for unemployment. This perspective was eagerly appropriated by sections of the popular media to propagate a view of unemployment as originating in the avarice of certain groups of workers, and the flawed leadership of trade union 'barons'. In populist terms, one person's 'unearned' pay increase was represented as an expensive price for another person's job.

A different interpretation was given by Marxist analysts. Rowthorn attributed the profit and investment containments of mature capitalism in the traditional industrial economies to the political pressures for rising state expenditures and the maintenance of full employment. Addressing the circumstances of the mid 1970s, he noted:[36]

> The industrial reserve army is, indeed, capitalism's own specific means of labour discipline. Its depletion by the nineteen-sixties was partly responsible for ending the expansionary phase of the long wave. Sustained accumulation will be very difficult unless this reserve army can be reconstituted in some way.

The dilemma for capitalism, in his view, was that to avoid stagnation either there could be investment in labour-saving technologies, which would involve an acute and costly rise in the organic composition of capital, or an absorption of the reserve army, thereby strengthening labour's capacity to curb capital's share of surplus value.

The question of how successful labour actually was in raising wage costs per unit of output in the case of Britain - often cited as a particularly clear example of union militancy - is contested by other Marxist critics. Harris contends that between 1960 and 1970, UK profit rates declined despite the fact that productivity rose relatively fast and pay rose relatively slowly.[37]

Between the monetarists and the Marxists, there were still voices which had not abandoned faith in Keynesian prescriptions. But they increasingly recognised that its applicability in the new era required a co-ordinated international reflation. One version of this agenda came from the proponents of a New International Economic Order, articulated in the Brandt Report which called for global development, and access to trade and capital for the poorer countries of the South. This programme was not sold on the basis of piety or altruism: it argued that boosting the economic opportunities of the South would enhance its spending power to purchase goods from the North, which increasingly required the stimulation of greater world trade to rescue it from sluggish growth. But, to be democratic, 'development' demanded redistribution as well as reflation, and was premised on the imperative to link recovery to disarmament.[38] One of the follow-up reports related the disparities between the rich and poor worlds to the increasing inequalities within societies. In each country the rich were developing stronger economic links with the rich in other countries than with the poor in their own societies. The transnational facet of this 'structural dualism' demanded that governments act in concert to counter-balance this private power. In this respect, the strategy must venture beyond Keynes and reflation, to also tackle restructuring and redistribution.[39]

---

[36] Rowthorn, B. (1980), *op. cit.*, p.108.

[37] Harris, L.(1985),'British capital: manufacturing,finance,and multinational corporations', in Coates D. Johnston, G. and Bush, R. (eds.), *A Socialist Anatomy of Britain*, Polity, London.

[38] Brandt Report (1980), *North-South: A Programme for Survival*, Pan Books, London.

[39] Manley Report (1985), *Global Challenge: From crisis to cooperation: breaking the north-south stalemate*, Pan Books, London.

The Crisis in Welfare

Central to the political and economic disturbances of the 1970s, were the contesting legitimacies of welfarism and capitalism. The objectives espoused by welfarism included those of a social solidarity derivative of common citizenship; social need redressed by collective provision; equality of opportunity, which often demanded positive discrimination; and full employment, which relied on state intervention. These credos were at odds with the imperatives of capitalism. Its successful operation was contingent on the facility for competitive individualism; the primacy of want, as expressed in market demand, over that of need as generously defined by empire-building welfare bureaucracies; and inequality, properly reflected in the preferential status accorded the risk-taking and industrious entrepreneur. The intriguing aspect of this conflict of values was that it was to a significant degree shared by both left and right. They differed more in prognosis than diagnosis.

The left believed that welfarism and capitalism were in disharmonious co-existence because the former was forever at the discretion of the latter. Wealth creation, inspired pre-eminently by private profit and capital accumulation, was destined to confine the public sphere to a poorly-funded casualty station for the individual and industrial victims of the economic system. Always the poor relation, the public sector constantly risked being simultaneously marginal to economic policy-making, while being blamed for, and financially penalised by, its failures. The objectives most cherished by welfarism could only be securely and adequately attained subsequent to the achievement of socialism.

Whereas the left bemoaned the dilution of welfarism by capitalism, the right maintained the converse was true: 'public' values had trespassed too far into the preserve of the 'private'. Capitalism had been severely compromised by the dislocation caused by welfarism in the relationship between effort, achievement and reward. The post-war social democratic consensus was supposed to combine the ladder of opportunity for the ambitious and successful with the safety net of welfare for the dependent and less fortunate.

In fact, the net became a featherbed for the undeserving poor, purchased by a punitive tax burden on the hard-working and enterprising. This, in turn, had caused an economic crisis, whereby both work ethic and profit motive had been eroded. The private citizen, confronted by an intrusive and rapacious state, was over-regulated and over-taxed, entirely because the state over-spent. But for the right, the malaise existed not only at the cultural and ideological levels: there were also crises in the fiscal and planning spheres. The rate of growth in the costs of social reproduction had pressured government to extend its revenue base, not only by means of tax increases but also through borrowing and/or printing money. Extra state borrowing tended to reduce the supply, and raise the cost, of money for the private sector.

Consequently, investment potential was curtailed and employment maintenance and creation in the private sector were obstructed. The ultimate fall-out was greater unemployment and poverty, which demanded yet more welfare, but, more welfare simply reinforced the circuitous pattern of extra government spending leading to less investment and employment.

Apart from the fiscal bind of how to finance welfare, there was also the problem of how to plan and administer its delivery. In the US and UK, two 'monopoly' parties competed with each other in a political market, demand-led by an electorate, whose rising expectations were stimulated by inflated promises of social consumption. The result was 'government overload'. The law of diminishing returns determined that the more government assumed responsibility, the less competently it accomplished any particular task, a process destined to bring planning into disrepute, and prompt public disenchantment with the political process. It was this so-called 'crisis of governability' in the UK that Thatcherism was particularly keen to confront. In its view, the resourcefulness of the industrious was being stifled by an effete landed gentry, accustomed to compromise in protection of its inherited privilege, and a militant working class emboldened through its experience of a faint-hearted opposition.

This pressure was not an exclusive British experience. Elsewhere, full employment was attained at the cost of government reflation, which was ultimately judged by the right to be bought at the price of inflation and budget deficits. Ironically, the current axiom of the right, that free markets and free politics are inextricably linked, was contested by some early challengers to Keynesian orthodoxies. Peter Jay remarked:[40]

> ....the operation of free democracy appears to force governments into positions (the commitment to full employment) that prevent them from taking steps (fiscal and monetary restraint) that are necessary to arrest the menace (accelerating inflation) that threatens to undermine the condition (stable prosperity) on which political stability and therefore liberal democracy depend.

According to some, the particular severity of this crisis in Britain was attributable to the impasse produced by a class stalemate.[41] Specifically, the working class had been defensively organised to resist the pressures from the capitalist class, but was too politically conservative to impose a socialist alternative. Meanwhile, a deteriorating economic performance, exacerbated by the recessionary trends that followed the 1973 oil crisis, could not sustain welfarist demands, thereby straining the corporatist structures. The very lack

---

[40] Jay, P. (1986), 'Englanditis', in Coates, D. and Hillard, J. (eds.), *The Economic Decline of Modern Britain*, Wheatsheaf Books, Brighton, p.122.

[41] Aaronovitch, S., Smith, R., Gardiner, J. and Moore, R. (1981), *The Political Economy of British Capitalism: A Marxist analysis*. McGraw Hill, London.

of competitiveness made workers resistant to the rationale of economic restructuring, since changes in production seemed inevitably to bode ill for job prospects. Yet, this 'bolshie' attitude was taken as further evidence of a workforce shielded from the realities of massive 'hidden unemployment' and supported in that deception by government collusion.

The Collapse of Fordism?

The emergence of Fordism as the pre-eminent form of production in the new growth sectors of the post-war period was a critical contribution to governments' capacity to deliver full employment. Involving, as it did, mass assembly lines producing standardised goods at an economy of scale both demanded and supplied by the new consumer society, it offered numerous, reasonably secure and remunerated labour opportunities. By the 1970s, the durability of this system was in question.

Some characterised the manufacturing job drain at this time in blanket terms of 'de-industrialisation'.[42] But some, like Massey and Meegan,[43] were convinced that it was a significantly differentiated process, requiring disaggregation at two levels. First, job loss was an outcome of changes in output and/or productivity. Second, industry's drive to improve international competitiveness could assume three distinct forms - rationalisation, intensification and technical innovation - each 'justifying' labour shedding. Rationalisation involved a cut in total capacity. Intensification was designed to extract productivity improvements without significant new investment or production reorganisation, while the application of technical change often entailed both these latter features.

By the late 1970s, it was widely acknowledged that the structural effect of the new micro-technology on employment would be significant and long-lasting.[44] While some were apprehensive about the job consequences, others lamented industry's hesitant embrace of the new opportunities available.[45] The optimists foresaw positive scope for job creation in the enlarged market for new products which the new technologies would generate.

Recognition that the new information-based society demanded an

---

[42] Blackaby, F. (ed.) (1979), *De-industrialisation*, National Institute of Economic and Social Research and Heinemann, London.

[43] Massey, D. and Meegan, R. (1982), *The Anatomy of Job Loss: The how, why and where of employment decline*, Methuen, London.

[44] Counter Information Services Report No.23 (1978), *The New Technology*, and The Advisory Council for Applied Research and Development, *The Application of Semi-Conductor Technology*, HMSO, London.

[45] ACARD (1979), *Joining and Assembly: The impact of robots and automation*, HMSO, London, and Policy Studies Institute (1981), *Micro-Electronics in Industry: the extent of use*, PSI, London.

integrated social and economic strategy was evident in some official reports. According to a 1978 French government report, the continued job losses in Fordist manufacturing would parallel:[46]

.....a fermenting cauldron of small economically viable enterprises on which the responsibility of innovation and the creation of economic wealth in international markets will fall, and on the other hand a mass of socially oriented organisations concerned more with providing employment and cultural or social purposes than with making profits.

By the early 1980s, as the pace and scale of economic restructuring became apparent, pessimisism over reversing mass unemployment grew. The Labour Movement in Britain proposed an 'Alternative Economic Strategy', in opposition to the fatalism of a revisionism which suggested that full employment was no longer a feasible objective:'The number of unemployed is the central manifestation of the economic crisis and any alternative strategy for resolving the crisis must offer some prospect of moving the economy back to full employment.'[47]

Some, not unsympathetic to the principles inherent in such optimism, nevertheless contended that any credible programme would have to accommodate a reappraisal of the work ethic and a new appreciation of leisure opportunities. Jenkins and Sherman argued that a transitory adjustment phase in the micro-computer age would require government intervention to mollify and cushion the effects of job displacement. They projected that the surplus generated by the new technologies could finance a generous social compensation for the negative fall-out: 'Technological unemployment will be based on high growth, high profits and returns, a highly competitive manufacturing and service base and high incomes, and these enable constructive policies to be adequately funded.'[48]

---

[46] *The Nora-Minc Report* (1978), quoted in, 'The next french revolution', New Scientist, June.

[47] CSE London Working Group (1980), *The Alternative Economic Strategy: A labour movement response to the economic crisis*, CSE Books, London, p.49.

[48] Jenkins, C. and Sherman, B. (1979), *The Collapse of Work*, Methuen, London, p.176.

The Challenge from the Command Economies

While its pre-war predictions of capitalist collapse did not materialise, the Soviet Union continued to assert the superiority of socialist planning for full employment, and still regarded the relatively low unemployment rates in the West as excessive. This confidence was exemplified in 1961 by Khruschev's speech at the 21st Congress of the Communist Party of the Soviet Union (CPSU) when he unveiled an ambitious 20-year plan to effect the transition from socialism to communism. He anticipated that, during that period, the Soviet Union would overtake the US in the production of a wide range of capital goods as well as increase its output of consumer goods. However, his subsequent removal on grounds of 'adventurism' meant the end of imaginative economic reforms for 20 years.[49] Recent evidence has pointed to considerable underemployment, inefficient production and the existence of hidden unemployment in the Soviet Union for much of the post-war period. For example, a study in Lithuania, in the mid-1960s, on labour turnover, found that:[50]

....only 11.3% of those who changed their place of work did so without a break in employment. One fourth (24.6%) of those who changed jobs were out of work for a week, while slightly more (25.4%) were unemployed for a period of one week to one month. An even larger number (29.7%), were without jobs for periods varying between one month and a year. 9% were unemployed for more than a year.

Even after the policies of *perestroika* and *glasnost* had been officially declared, there remained a marked reluctance to recognize the severity of the economic difficulties facing the Soviet Union. For example, in the introduction of a booklet designed to popularise *perestroika*, Zemlyanoi affirmed the:[51]

....creative impulse and significance of the October revolution...which give the contemporary world its uniqueness. And, of course, this is demonstrated above all by the steady economic, social and cultural growth of the collectivist society born of the October Revolution....

Yet today, in what is the former Soviet Union, privatisation and marketisation are regarded as both inevitable and desirable, while escalating unemployment is deemed necessary to the transition to a market economy. At least one commentator is worried that the mounting social costs of this

---

[49] George,V. and Manning, N. (1980), *Socialism. Social Welfare and the Soviet Union*, Routledge & Kegan Paul, London, pp.18-23.

[50] *Ibid.*, p.57.

[51] Abalkin, L. (1988), *USSR: Reorganisation and Renewal*, Progress Publishers, Moscow, p.6.

transition are being visited on the poorest sections of society.[52] Certainly, the pretence that the command economies could out-perform the market economies with respect to employment can no longer be sustained. The New Right regards this as unsurprising. The real cost of artificially maintained full employment is economic inefficiency in terms of a rigid labour market, incapable of responding to the challenges of new technology and restructuring. This raises the issue of whether any form of economic organisation can guarantee full employment.

No Return to Full Employment?

Since the oil shocks of the 1970s, employment has been fragile within the market economies. The average levels of unemployment have been substantially higher than they were in the 1950s and 1960s. Moreover, there has been greater divergence among the unemployment rates of different countries. The 1986-87 United Nations Economic Survey of Europe commented:[53]

> In spite of some improvement in recent years, unemployment remains a major problem for the industrialised countries. Unemployment rates in 1986 were close to or in excess of 10 per cent in seven of the 15 market economies, these seven accounting for nearly 40 per cent of the total labour force of the 15 countries. However, unemployment rates vary considerably among countries. They are very low in Norway, Sweden and Switzerland (between approximately 1 and 3 per cent), but in Belgium, the Netherlands and Ireland, they range between 11 and nearly 18 per cent.

In some cases, the very low rates are more a reflection of policies towards the unemployed than healthy economies. In Sweden, for example, the unemployed must accept a state-funded community job after a year without work. This affects the calculation of unemployment rates. Differences in unemployment rates over time can be observed in the table 1.4. The general trend is of steadily rising unemployment after the 1973-74 oil shock, reaching a peak in 1983. Although unemployment was declining from the mid-1980s, it had not fallen to its 1973 figure by 1989. The subsequent rise, related to the recession in the early 1990s, reversed this decline, putting unemployment rates once again substantially above those in the 1970s. Even with West Germany's almost non-existent unemployment in 1973, the difference between the lowest and highest national rates was 5.9 percentage points. By 1983, the difference was 9.8 points and in 1989, 8.6 points.

---

[52] Ascherson, N. (3/11/1991), 'Punishment for the poor, not the apparatchiks', *The Independent on Sunday*.

[53] United Nations Organisation, Secretariat of the Economic Commission for Europe (1987), *Economic Survey of Europe. 1986-87*, Geneva, p.40.

Table 1.4	Standardised Unemployment Rates in the G7 Economies (percentage of total labour force), Selected Years					
	1973	1975	1979	1983	1985	1989
USA	4.8	8.3	5.8	9.5	7.1	5.2
Japan	1.3	1.9	2.1	2.6	2.6	2.3
West Gem.	0.8	3.6	3.2	7.7	7.2	5.6
France	2.7	4.0	5.9	8.3	10.2	9.4
Italy	6.2	5.8	7.6	8.8	9.6	10.9
UK	3.0	4.3	5.0	12.4	11.2	7.1
Canada	5.5	6.9	7.4	11.8	10.4	7.5
G7 Avg.	3.4	5.4	4.9	8.1	7.2	5.7
Source:	OECD, *Economic Outlook*, No.49, July 1991, table R.18					

Such developments, together with the economic decline of the command economies, pose the critical question of whether full employment remains an achievable objective in the rapidly changing contemporary economies. From a variety of perspectives, the answer to this question has been no. Some point to a New International Division of Labour which has shifted the dynamic of the global economy. From this viewpoint, deindustrialisation was partly attributable to an internationalisation of production. The opportunity existed to decompose the production process so that its most labour-intensive elements were allocated to countries with low labour costs. This was facilitated by technologies which permitted the segmentation of production and improved information flow, enabling continued central management and co-ordination. The relative decline of transportation relative to production costs, meant that spatially disaggregated manufacturing was economically feasible. The new conditions of comparative advantage prompted the core economies to shake out 'uncompetitive' labour and to relocate in newly industrialising countries. As a consequence, 'surplus' blue collar labour grew as a proportion of the workforce.

Associated with the above process, was a shift in the global axis of production from the Atlantic to the Pacific. This realignment was led by Japan and the 'Asian Tigers'. Within the US, the most buoyant sectors moved West, concentrating in states like California. Some argue that this transformation is permanent, with the older economies burdened by declining industry and its consequent social costs. Others see it as more transitory: after a decade of the discipline of supply-side economics, particularly in economies like the US and UK, leaner and fitter industrial sectors can once again compete. This is reinforced by the argument that Japanese and other Asian workers will want to increase personal consumption, hence absorbing a greater share of production domestically and undermining export-led growth. In addition, there are those who query whether the loss of manufacturing is significant, pointing to the increasing proportion of financial and other tradeable services in GDP. In these circumstances, it is argued, certain countries will be able to exploit a new comparative advantage in tradeable financial services and remain internationally competitive, even if they have experienced an irreversible contraction of their manufacturing base.

The capacity of national governments to respond to such phenomena may be inhibited in two respects:

• Much of this change has been driven by the decisions of multinational corporations which, by their nature, are less amenable to national control. Ironically, many governments in the 1980s put great store by supply-side economics as the basis for regeneration. Yet this particular form of microeconomics has been dismissed as irrelevant to the understanding of the operations of multinational companies. Microeconomics tends to assume conditions of competition, whereas such companies not only control significant market share, but are in a fluid state of mergers and take-overs.

• Secondly, in Europe at least, supranational political structures are being developed to oversee the construction of an economic union. While this has created many tensions over issues of national sovereignty, the process of political integration appears irreversible. This simultaneously demotes the capacity of national governments to decide independently on economic priorities such as full employment, but has the potential of creating an international political structure more capable of engaging with big capital.

Even for those committed to reattaining full employment, the early 1990s have seen less optimism compared with the early 1980s. Then, the Socialist government in France intended to achieve full employment by national reflation. Equally, the Labour opposition in the UK articulated an Alternative Economic Strategy, which put job creation at the top of its agenda. Neither survived the 1980s. In the US, full employment had been a stated policy goal since the 1946 Full Employment Act. However, this was to be achieved largely through the 'trickle down' effect of general economic progress. While West German unemployment levels remained comparatively low in the 1980s, the economic costs of reunification have included a sharp rise in unemployment, for which the Kohl government has admitted no easy solution exists. Even Sweden, regarded for decades as having achieved the right balance between economic growth and social infrastructure, has experienced relative decline and the fall of its social democratic government. Few, if any, policy makers in the 1990s promise full employment.

There is increasing concentration on the supply-side sources of unemployment in terms of demographic growth, increasing participation rates, skills mismatches and apathy among the unemployed. From this perspective, augmenting the demand for labour will have little effect on unemployment rates. Jobs will be taken by those who are not in the ranks of the registered unemployed, while the unemployed will be inhibited in job uptake owing to their lack of skills or motivation. The key to tackling unemployment thus lies in supply-side interventions: improved education and training, the development of 'motivation' programmes, and reductions in the real level of benefits to restore monetary work incentives.

All of these developments have affected the structure and functioning of labour markets. The ability of national economies to respond to global shifts is seen as being dependent on the flexibility of their labour markets.[54] In response to the oil shocks, the UK was regarded as having high real wage rigidity, the US high money wage rigidity, while Japan had flexibility in both real and money wages. In Japan, the combination of the high proportion of bonus payments in wages, the flexibility of working hours, and the relative weakness of trade unions, allowed rapid wage adjustment to international recession. This was facilitated by the low proportion of permanent employees in the non-agricultural workforce (40%) and the high proportions of self -employed (30%) and temporary workers (30%). In turn, this sustained conditions of profitability and protected new investment, so that unemployment was not the primary consequence of structural shifts or downturns in global demand. While many industries in the US have a system of long-term contracts, they tend to deal with recession by temporary lay offs, generating a flexibility in real wages.

In contrast, UK real wages have been maintained or even increased in recessions. The adjustment mechanism consisted of increasing levels of unemployment for the most vulnerable groups in the labour market. Because of labour market segmentation, higher unemployment for many did not prevent some workers from making real wage gains. Labour market flexibility is thus seen as a key ingredient to international competitiveness and a guarantor against mass unemployment.

This has provoked a series of analyses suggesting that labour markets are in a process of transition towards high levels of flexibility.[55] Indeed, flexibility has become an increasing feature of labour markets in general. Britain experienced employment growth of over 1 million workers between 1983 and 1987 and a further million between 1988 and 1990.[56] In both periods, however, the most substantial element of the growth was in part-time employment. At the same time, numbers of self-employed and temporary workers also increased significantly. Thus it could be argued that the structure of the British labour market is becoming more like that of Japan.

A flexible labour force may also be created within the firm. Atkinson and

---

[54] Adnett, N. (1989), *op.cit.*, p.49.

[55] See Hakim, C. (1987), 'Trends in the Flexible Workforce', *Employment Gazette*, London, November.

[56] McLaughlin, E. (1991), 'Work and welfare benefits: social security, employment and unemployment in the 1990s', *Journal of Social Policy*, Vol. 20, Part 4, October, pp.485-508.

Gregory argue that firms are increasingly creating core and peripheral groups among their workers.[57] Core workers are permanent, full-time employees with high earnings and job security. They are knowledge-intensive or multi-skilled and are thus functionally flexible with respect to the increasingly differentiated tasks of post-Fordist production. Peripheral workers consist of several groups: semi-skilled workers who are full-time but vulnerable to labour shedding during recessions or restructuring; part-time and temporary workers; and external workers dependent on subcontracting specialist or routine tasks. Such workers are numerically flexible in that they can be disposed of in response to rapid economic change. They are therefore more vulnerable to unemployment and, in some instances, once out of work tend to remain unemployed for substantial periods.

Such theories have been challenged on the grounds that they are not sustained by empirical evidence. It is also argued that the observable trends reflect more the transition from manufacturing to services than any qualitative transformation of the labour market. Service industries are required to match working hours to customer demand which may fluctuate on a daily or weekly, as well as seasonal, basis. This generates a requirement for part-time and temporary work which, although frequently described as 'atypical labour', is increasingly becoming normal as services take up an increasingly large proportion of total employment.[58]

However, if flexibility is to become the dominant characteristic of the labour market, the implications for full employment are serious. In the first place, frictional and cyclical unemployment should increase as a proportion of all unemployment. Peripheral workers are liable to experience many bouts of unemployment, punctuated by periods of employment, since numerical flexibility is designed to allow firms to hire and fire in response to market conditions. Secondly, some groups of workers may lack the skills to fill core places and the capacity (through domestic responsibilities or other reasons) to engage in part-time or temporary work. They would then gravitate towards the ranks of the long-term unemployed. For example, older workers suffering redundancy or ill health may find little alternative to long-term unemployment. Other workers from declining industries may be occupationally downgraded, moving first to unskilled occupations and then unemployment. Certainly, in nearly all of the market economies, long-term unemployment grew as a proportion of all unemployment during the 1980s.[59]

Policy responses may exacerbate rather than resolve the problem. As

---

[57] Atkinson, J. and Gregory, D. (1986), 'A flexible future: Britain's dual labour force', *Marxism Today*, London, April, pp. 12-17.

[58] Allen, J. (1988), 'Fragmented firms, disorganised labour?', in Allen, J. and Massey, D. (eds.) ,*The Economy in Question*, Sage Publications, London, p.207.

[59] White, M. (1983), *The Long Term Unemployed and Labour Markets*, Policy Studies Institute, London.

McLauglin argues about the efforts of the UK government:[60]
> So, although there have been policy efforts directed at moving
> unemployed people into work, it has been moving people into full time
> low paid work that measures such as low wage supplements (Family
> Credit and Jobstart) and 'motivation' programmes (for example, Restart)
> are all about. Yet as the analysis of labour demand above has shown, it is
> other kinds of work which are increasingly available.

There may thus be a mismatch between the policies designed to deal with
unemployment and the economic forces which generate it. This is the crux
of the full employment problem. Is full employment no longer possible in the
market economies because they have been subject to a set of economic
changes which governments are powerless to resist? Alternatively, is there
an appropriate range of responses which allows economies to change and
remain competitive while retaining conditions of full employment? The
former suggests that unemployment is an inevitable consequence of current
economic developments; the latter that it reflects a failure of policy as it did
in the 1930s. This does not necessarily imply a return to simple demand
management, but may embrace a combination of supply-side and demand-
side policies. However, it does require that full employment retains a high
priority in economic policy. This is so if only because:[61]
> ....some two-thirds of all income in industrial countries consists of wages
> and salaries and fringe benefits. So understanding the working of the
> labour market is no minor or peripheral interest for economists.

Ashton[62] has drawn attention to this dilemma by demonstrating how
unemployment has been officially conceptualised at different times. He has
identified three distinct phases in the modern period: from 1910 to 1940
neoclassical theory emphasised the role of the business cycle in influencing
the 'natural' rate of joblessness; from 1940 to the late 1970s Keynesian
economics stressed the role of government in managing aggregate demand
at a level which would stimulate sufficient output to ensure full employment;
and from the late 1970s monetarism and supply-side economics have
decreed that fiscal and monetary rectitude by government, combined with
deregulation of markets, would be the optimal guarantee of the lowest levels
of unemployment in the long term. But importantly, he has analysed not just
what the shifts in official perception have been but also why they succeeded
in legitimising their definition.

Two distinct, though connected, sets of relationships have been crucial in

---

[60] McLauglin, E. (1991), *op.cit.*, October, p.489.

[61] Solow, R. (1991), 'Unemployment As a social and economic problem', in Cornwall, J.
(ed.), *The Capitalist Economies: Prospects for the 1990s*, Edward Elgar, Aldershot, p. 92.

[62] Ashton, D.N. (1986), *Unemployment under Capitalism: The sociology of British and
American labour markets*, Wheatsheaf Books, Brighton.

this regard: at a global level, changes in trade and labour, and at a national level, changes in the power balance amongst the social classes. As some countries suffered from global trading competition and lost market share, they were more likely to suffer unemployment. However, the actual degree of unemployment experienced within particular countries depended on the balance of power between capital and labour. The elaboration of these relationships is discussed in subsequent chapters.

2. Unemployment and Poverty

In the market economies, being unemployed is usually associated with poverty. Some of the income lost through the interruption of earnings may be replaced by the benefits system, although the application of various conditions of eligibility and exclusion ensures that this is by no means automatic. In economies with a large proportion of the labour force in agriculture in the form of smallholdings, unemployment may be substantially under-recorded and individuals may have no recourse to the protection of benefits. In any case, this 'replacement ratio' between benefits and earnings is invariably less than 100 per cent. A benefits system which replaced the entire loss of earnings would contradict both the work ethic and the material work incentives, which are integral elements of these economies. Thus:[1]

....the majority of income received by individual households in Europe is still allocated through the labour market. It follows that persons who occupy relatively weak competitive positions within the labour market, or are excluded from it, are likely to run a considerably increased risk of poverty.

In this respect, Marxists have argued[2] that the unemployed constitute a reserve army of labour, which simultaneously acts to depress the wages of the employed and as a potent symbol of the consequences of being without work. The unemployed must therefore endure a lower standard of living than the employed.

Historically, market economies have wrestled with the problem of how to set the level of benefit for the unemployed. If the level is set too low, the consequence may be political instability. Even when this can be easily contained, the problem of the quality of the labour force persists. Since the demand for labour fluctuates, provision has to be made for the welfare of

---

[1] Walker, R. Lawson, R. and Townsend, P. (1984), *Responses to Poverty: Lessons from Europe*, Heinemann Educational Books, London, p.78.

[2] See for example, Braverman, H. (1974), *Labour and Monopoly Capitalism*, Monthly Review Press, London.

those out of work. Otherwise, their productivity will be adversely affected by periods of less than subsistence living while unemployed. Conversely, high levels of benefit are said to undermine the efficiency of the market economy, either through demotivating the unemployed or imposing a high fiscal burden on business and those in employment. Consequently, unemployment benefits are normally set below the level of income that can be obtained through working, but high enough to maintain very basic living standards. Even where the unemployed are no longer subject to mass starvation, they inevitably suffer a loss of income and, in most cases, a very high risk of poverty. Moreover, some of the unemployed may never have had a job. For young people entering the labour market, it is deemed even more important to restrict the level of benefit to coerce them to find employment. The fact that a majority have few domestic responsibilities, makes the imposition of a low benefits regime an easier task.

This relationship between worklessness and poverty is not causal, since unemployed individuals may belong to households where the income of other members sustains them. A study in France found that in households with one member unemployed, 60 per cent of household income consisted of wages earned by the partner and only 20 per cent of unemployment benefit.[3] However even in this case, the decline in aggregate household income may restrict household activities so that, in relative terms, it will be poor even if consumption remains above an absolute poverty threshold.

Nevertheless, benefit levels vary over time and among countries. They are not decided by their functional relationship to the economy, but are the product of specific political, and labour market, struggles. In general, the unemployed have a high poverty risk, but the actual risk is determined by the nature of the political regime. In the 1980s, the widespread governmental concern about inflation generated a preparedness to accept high levels of unemployment, while an equally high prioritisation of fiscal prudence reduced the real value of unemployment benefits. It was thus a period when there were many more unemployed with less command over resources. The unemployed then became the largest single group among the poor.

Despite this, it has often been claimed that if benefits replace a significant proportion of earnings, the end result is even greater unemployment. As Minford argues:[4]

A flat rate unemployment benefit entitlement which continues more or less indefinitely when unemployed, is an ideal candidate to generate an increase in the long run labour supply elasticity. For as long as the

---

[3] Foudi, R. and Stankiewicz, F. (1988), 'Very Long Term Unemployment: The French experience', in Junankar, P.N. (ed.), *Very Long Term Unemployment*, Commission of the European Communities, Brussels, p.3.14.

[4] Minford, P. (1990), 'Corporatism, the natural rate and productivity', in Philpott, J. (ed.), *Trade Unions and the Economy: Into the 1990s*, Employment Institute, London, p.95.

average real wage falls relative to this benefit, people will withdraw from labour supply - indefinitely, until the wage picks up again - substituting their time into better-rewarded leisure (or 'black-economy') activities.

According to this thesis, a rise in benefit levels, relative to wages, will have a disproportionate effect on the preparedness to seek employment, and will thus increase the 'natural rate of unemployment'. Conversely, a fall in benefits levels will reduce the level of unemployment by depressing the wage levels at which the unemployed are prepared to accept work. Consequently, in periods of economic downturn, benefits establish a floor below which wage levels cannot fall and, by imposing additional costs on industry, exacerbate the levels of unemployment. Benjamin and Kochin's analysis of unemployment in inter-war Britain concluded that its exceptionally high levels could be attributed more to excessive replacement ratios than to the demand deficiencies identified by Keynes.[5]

Minford suggests that, with few exceptions, increasing unemployment in European countries in the 1980s can be attributed to state intervention to subsidise unemployment. The exceptions, like Switzerland and Sweden, occurred where benefits were for short duration and there was extensive monitoring of the job search activities of the unemployed. In Sweden, the unemployed were automatically put on a state-funded community job after one year out of work. While this reduced unemployment, it merely transformed the problem into a public expenditure burden. The US, with weak trade unions and a limited benefits system, did not suffer similarly. Nor did Japan with even more restricted benefits and wage flexibility in both its primary and secondary labour markets.

The weakness of this argument is that other empirical studies have found little relationship between trends in unemployment and the replacement income provided by benefits. For example, Layard and Nickell discovered that replacement ratios in Britain were higher in 1966-70 than in 1971-80.[6] Yet unemployment dramatically increased in the latter period. A survey of the unemployed in the UK in 1987 found that 78 per cent of males and 69 per cent of females strongly disagreed with the statement: 'With the benefits you get now, it's not so bad being out of work.' Similarly high percentages declared that they would prefer to work, even if unemployment benefit was high.[7] Tipping estimated that the unemployed's sense of their own monetary value in the market-place was a better predictor of job acceptance than their

---

[5] Benjamin, D.K. and Kochin, L.A. (1979), 'Searching for an explanation of unemployment in interwar Britain', *Journal of Political Economy*, vol.82, no.3, June, pp.441-478.

[6] Quoted in Fallon, P. and Verry, D. (1988), *The Economics of Labour Markets*, Philip Allan, Oxford, p.270.

[7] Piachaud, D. (1991), *Unemployment and Poverty*, Campaign For Work, research report, London, vol.3, no.3, May, Table 14.

individual replacement ratios.[8] Moreover, replacement ratios vary substantially among different unemployed individuals, reflecting whether married or single, the number of dependents and the duration of unemployment. The diversity of replacement ratios among a group of the unemployed is illustrated in the table 2.1.

These figures demonstrate the degree to which different individuals have very different replacement ratios. Even with R1, which allows for other sources of income, one-third of the sample received less than 50 per cent of their in-work income while unemployed. With R2, the figure rose to nearly half. Those who see high replacement ratios as the cause of unemployment, have argued that no more than 70 per cent of in-work income should be available to the unemployed. The data suggest that only a small minority of unemployed males reached that share.

Table 2.1 Percentage Distribution of Average Replacement Ratios for Those in Weeks 5-13 of a Spell of Unemployment, UK Males, 1973-77

	<25	25-49	50-79	80-99	100+	All	<50	≥80
R 1	4	29	47	16	4	100	33	20
R 2	7	39	41	9	4	100	46	13

Note: Replacement Ratio 1 (R1) is the ratio of all, after tax incomes, out of work and in last job. R2 excludes income unrelated to employment status.

Source: Fallon and Verry (1988), *op.cit.*, p.270

Tightening up eligibility and careful monitoring of the unemployed's job search activities is expensive. In the UK, the cost of administering social security rose from 15.5 per cent of benefits expenditure to 24 per cent between 1988-89 and 1989-90. The reason for the increase was given as the imposition of a new framework for tighter monitoring of the unemployed. Further, a small study of the unemployed revealed that only a minority was aware of the new procedures. It concluded: 'The implication must be that a large proportion of the substantial administrative expenditure allocated to the New Framework is wasted.'[9]

In any case, even if it could be demonstrated that the reduction of unemployment benefits would lead to a fall in unemployment, the living standards of those who remain out of work cannot be ignored. Driving their living standards to meagre subsistence levels, should not be regarded as an acceptable price for the removal of labour market distortion.

A further issue is that the unemployed are not a mass of people

---

[8] Tipping, B. (1982), 'Scrounging in Northern Ireland: The beginnings of an investigation', *The Economic and Social Review*, vol.13, no. 3, Dublin.

[9] *Unemployment Unit & Youth Aid* (1991), 'Actively seeking work', London, November, p.6.

permanently outside the labour market. The actual unemployed are constantly changing as some find work and others become unemployed. The probability of finding employment is, however, not the same for all. Some experience substantial periods of unemployment. For example, in 1985 about one-third of the unemployed in the UK had been out of work for two years or more. In Belgium the proportion was more than half; in France it was around a quarter.[10] Individuals who are excluded from work for long periods have even greater difficulty in finding employment, are more frequently under-supported by benefits systems and are thus even more likely to be in poverty.

Unemployment as a Cause of Poverty

The difficulty of identifying the precise significance of unemployment as a cause of poverty is complicated not just by the differentiation of the unemployed in terms of duration, age, gender and domestic responsibilities, but also by the variety of causes and conditions attributed to the concept of poverty itself. For example, do the causes of poverty lie more in the labour market with conditions of low pay and instability of employment, or in the failure of social policy to adequately compensate for these necessary market structures? Alternatively, does poverty result from familial circumstance where large families put severe consumption pressure on earnings or benefits income? Is poverty a condition of individuals, households or families? When individuals become unemployed, the degree to which they experience poverty depends on the nature of their household: whether it includes others, whether they have access to alternative incomes and, crucially, whether household income is distributed among all, or some members hold a disproportionate share. One contribution to the debate on the feminisation of poverty points to the considerable volume of evidence that the incomes of poor households are frequently allocated so as to particularly benefit the male partner.[11] The experience of poverty for women may thus be significantly worse than for men.

In turn, these issues are complicated by the difficulties in drawing poverty lines. The most straightforward approach is to specify a basket of goods and services, whose consumption is regarded as necessary/desirable to eliminate poverty. A poverty line can then be defined as:

$$Y = (1+h)px$$

where Y is the income needed to avoid poverty, x represents the basket of goods and services required, p their prices and h makes allowance for

---

10 Eurostat (1988), *Long-term unemployment*, Brussels, table A3.1.

11 Millar, J. and Glendinning, C. (1989), 'Gender and Poverty', *Journal of Social Policy*, 18, 3, pp.363-381.

'inefficient' expenditure.[12] The difficulties of defining poverty as a particular consumption pattern, while overall consumption is rapidly changing, are well-known. An alternative approach regards poverty as a form of exclusion from 'normal' social activities.[13] For example, in July 1975, the European Council of Ministers defined the poor as: '....individuals or families whose resources are so small as to exclude them from the minimum acceptable way of life of the Member State in which they live.'[14]

Poverty may thus exist when sections of a population are unable to participate in activities determined by national normative standards. It has been argued, however, that divergences in lifestyles and tastes make difficult any assumption of a normal lifestyle: 'The combination of two factors - that there is a diversity in styles of living, and that poverty is relative - mean that you would not, in fact, expect to find any threshold between the poor and the rest of society.'[15]

Others have argued that the lifestyles of the poor are more driven by resource scarcities than divergent tastes and accordingly, a relative poverty threshold can be empirically established.[16] This may be represented as

$$Y = (1+h)px.A.z$$

where A is an input-output matrix relating the input of goods and services (px) to activity outputs (z). Essentially, this specifies the range of goods and services required to sustain 'normal activities'. In practice, much more simple measures are employed to establish a poverty threshold. The European Community, for example, currently employs a range of measures which compare individual and household incomes with fixed percentages (50% and 40%) of national and Community averages.[17] The problem with this approach, like all headcount procedures, is that it yields percentages below the poverty line, but says little about the intensity of poverty, i.e. how far below the line the poor are actually living. The US employs a budgetary measure specifying in dollars the sum required to purchase minimim goods and services. This approach is marred by largely ignoring the relativistic dimension of poverty. In Germany and Britain, poverty thresholds are determined by levels of social assistance. As a result, the poor are largely synonymous with those dependent on benefits.

An alternative approach to both is to discover what the public says should

[12] Atkinson, A.B. (1989), 'Poverty', in Eatwell, J. et al. (eds.), *Social Economics*, MacMillan, London.

[13] Townsend, P. (1979), *Poverty in the United Kingdom*, Penguin, Middlesex.

[14] Espoir Ltd. (1980), *Europe Against Poverty*, p.5.1.

[15] Piachaud, D. (10/10/1981), 'Peter Townsend and the Holy Grail', *New Society*, p.421.

[16] Desai, M. and Shah, A. (1988), 'An Econometric Approach to the Measurement of Poverty', *Oxford Economic Papers*, No.40.

[17] Commission of the European Communities (13/2/1991), *Final report of the second European poverty programme*, Brussels.

be provided as the minimal level of living. This has the advantage of offering a socially determined poverty threshold, although it might be argued that the threshold is determined, in fact, by those who frame the questions.[18] The largest regular exercise in this respect is the Eurobarometer Survey conducted in all EC member states, which records perceptions of poverty, the poor and the efficacy of national anti-poverty policies.[19]

If poverty is relative, it can be related to social inequality - the overall distribution of resources within society. The issue is not merely what proportion of the population falls below a poverty threshold, but how this is determined by sources and patterns of distribution. In order to understand the relationship between unemployment and poverty, it is necessary to examine all of these dimensions.

Table 2.2 Rankings for Poverty, Unemployment, GDP per head and Social Expenditure as a Percentage of GDP, Selected European Countries, 1985

	Poverty	Unemp.	GDP	Social Expenditure
Belgium	11	3	5	10
Denmark	10	11	11	7
W.Germany	8	10	10	8
Greece	3	9	2	1
Spain	2	1	4	3
France	5	6	9	9
Ireland	4	2	3	5
Italy	6	5	6	4
Netherlands	9	7	8	11
Portugal	1	8	1	2
UK	7	4	7	6

Source: Calculated from Commission of the European Communities (13/2/1991) *op.cit.* table A.8 and Eurostat (1991), 'Basic Statistics of the Community', tables 2.2, 3.22 and 3.31

Table 2.2 indicates the association between the aggregate levels of poverty, unemployment, GDP and social expenditure for 11 European countries. It does so by ranking each country according to the proportion of persons there living below 50 per cent of the Community average income, by their unemployment rate, by GDP per head and by expenditure on social protection as a percentage of GDP. The last two are ranked so that the country with the lowest output per head and lowest social expenditure is ranked first. Thus a ranking of 1:1:1:1 would indicate the highest percentage

---

[18] Piachaud, D. (1987), 'Problems in the definition and measurement of poverty, *Journal of Social Policy*, 16, 2.

[19] See for example, Commission of the European Communities, (1990), *Eurobarometer: The perception of poverty in Europe*, March, Brussels.

in poverty, the highest rate of unemployment, the lowest GDP per head and the lowest social expenditure as a proportion of GDP.

The association between the variables can be clearly seen in a number of countries. For example, Denmark has the second lowest percentage in poverty, the lowest rate of unemployment and the highest GDP per head. Nevertheless, four other countries spent a greater proportion of GDP on social protection. In other countries, such as West Germany, Spain, Ireland, Italy and the Netherlands, the rankings were reasonably consonant. There were, however, obvious exceptions where unemployment did not seem to figure as a major contributor to poverty. Portugal and Greece had high proportions of their populations in poverty and the lowest GDP rankings, but eight of the other countries had higher unemployment rates. In these cases, the very low rankings for social protection expenditure may be better indicators of poverty. The UK's unemployment rate was high, while its other indicators fell in the middle of the range. The results for Belgium also demonstrate very high unemployment and relatively low GDP, but the lowest proportion of population in poverty, and the second highest social expenditure ranking.

Table 2.2 thus provides examples both of countries with substantial levels of poverty but low unemployment, and those with high unemployment but low levels of poverty. Those in the former category tended to be countries with large proportions of their labour force in agricultural activity which provides low incomes. In such circumstances, unemployment would not be the single greatest contributor to poverty. Countries in the latter category offered sufficient income support to the unemployed to take substantial numbers out of poverty as defined by a European threshold. It should be emphasised that when the measure is taken as 50 per cent of national average household incomes, the proportion in poverty in the UK substantially increases. By this measure, the UK would have ranked second among the same 11 countries. Belgium would still retain the lowest percentage of those in poverty.[20]

Some indication of the measure of financial support for the unemployed is given in table 2.3. The table refers only to unemployment benefit and not to other programmes of social assistance which come into operation when entitlement to unemployment benefit has ended. Because of differential costs of living, the different amounts in each country cannot be compared in terms of their purchasing power. Countries which offered benefit in the form of percentages of previous earnings, even if of limited duration, offered the highest average levels of support. At the same time, those countries which provided most subsidy to their unemployed, were ranked lowest on the poverty measure while the country with the lowest financial support (Portugal) had the highest poverty ranking.

Nevertheless, there remained important exceptions. Spain paid

---

[20] Commission of the European Communities (13/2/1991), *op.cit.*, table A.3.

unemployment benefit at nearly twice the level of Italy, but suffered a higher proportion of poverty. The UK had a relatively low poverty ranking while providing a low level of benefit. In this case, unemployment benefit could be supplemented by other forms of social assistance to meet need and, to that extent, the figure is misleading. In other countries, significant proportions of the unemployed receive neither unemployment benefit nor social assistance. It has been calculated that this affects 96 per cent of the unemployed in Greece, 83 per cent in Italy and 60 and 42 per cent respectively in France and Germany.[21]   Because of these factors, official data cannot easily establish the actual link between aggregate unemployment and the overall level of poverty within different countries. However, a relationship of some kind is clearly suggested.

Table 2.3   Average Yearly Unemployment Payment Per Capita, 1987-88, Selected European Countries, (ECUs)

Belgium	9439
Denmark	12563
W.Germany	7997
Spain	2407
France	5158
Ireland	3636
Italy	1302
Luxembourg	3833
Netherlands	10170
Portugal	495
UK	3752

Source: Calculated from Eurostat (1990), *op.cit.*, tables 3.22 and 3.36

Other sources support this contention. In 1984, Brian Abel-Smith argued:'The present high level of unemployment....is directly and indirectly the largest single cause of poverty in the Community.'[22] This was echoed in the Commission's report on its own second poverty programme. Moreover, there would appear to be a general social consensus within the Community that poverty is primarily generated by unemployment. In the 1989 Eurobarometer Survey, unemployment was given as the most frequent cause of poverty in nine of the 12 member states. In two, it was advanced as the second most common cause and in the remaining state it was ranked third.[23] Certainly there was a close correlation between the growth of poverty and

---

[21] Commission of the European Communities (13/2/1991), *op.cit.* table 3.

[22] Abel-Smith, B. (1984), 'Anti-poverty policies and the European Community - powers and possibilities', in Brown,J.C. (ed.), *Anti-Poverty Policy in the European Community*, Policy Studies Institute, London, p. 259.

[23] Commission of the European Communities (1990), *op.cit.*, March, p.41.

unemployment within the EC. The average unemployment rate in Europe 12 increased more than threefold between 1973 and 1984. At the same time, the numbers in poverty grew by more than 5 million.[24]

Evidence from individual countries for income loss experienced as a result of unemployment tends to support the contention that it is a major causal factor in the production of poverty. An OECD survey in 1984 showed the unemployed suffered income loss in the United States according to domestic circumstances and the duration of unemployment. The income loss for a single unemployed person was greater than for a couple with two children with the sole earner unemployed. In the first six months of unemployment, their replacement ratios were about 48 per cent and 56 per cent respectively. After that period, replacement ratios fell to 24 per cent and 48 per cent.[25] In the same year, 14.4 per cent (nearly 30 million) of US citizens were judged to be in poverty using the official census money income threshold.[26] Merritt cites a case study in France in 1982 where total in-work income consisted of a net wage of 3,600 francs per month with an additional 520 francs in family allowances. After a year of unemployment, benefit fell to 750 francs per month, but rent and child allowances rose to 1,800 francs giving a replacement ratio of 62 per cent. However, since rent was 1,200 francs, the replacement ratio after accommodation costs had been met was 46 per cent.[27]

The unemployed themselves emphasise income loss as the primary cost of unemployment. Studies in West Germany and the UK found that in both countries, 45 per cent of the unemployed emphasised monetary problems as the major difficulty associated with unemployment. Respondents emphasised problems paying bills, the need to cut down on personal spending and getting into debt.[28] A study of benefits for the unemployed in the UK in 1988 revealed that 52.9 per cent of the unemployed had a net income of less than £56 per week compared to 14.3 per cent of the general population.[29] Another UK study showed that in 1987 42 per cent of households in the bottom decile of the income distribution (after housing costs had been met)

---

[24] Donnison, D. (ed.), (1991), *Urban Poverty: the economy and public policy*, Combat Poverty Agency, Dublin, p.12.

[25] OECD (1984), *Employment Outlook*, chart 19, Paris, p.95.

[26] Smeedling, T.M. (1988), 'Reagan, the recession, and poverty: What official estimates fail to show', in Danziger, S.H. and Portney, K.E. (eds.), *The Distributional Impacts of Public Policies*, MacMillan, London, p.61.

[27] Merritt, G. (1982), *World Out Of Work*, Collins, London, pp.75-6.

[28] Daniel, W., Honekopp, E. and Kind, V. (1981), 'Survey of the structure of unemployment', in Commission of the European Communities, *The European Labour Market*, Brussels, pp.69-70.

[29] Atkinson, T. and Micklewright, J. (1989), 'Turning the screw: benefits for the unemployed 1979-88', in Dilnot, A. and Walker, I. (eds.), *The Economics of Social Security*, Oxford University Press, Oxford, p.31.

had an unemployed head. Moreover, while unemployment grew two and a half times between 1979 and 1987, the number of individuals living in families with less than half the average income and headed by an unemployed person, grew threefold. Finally, the average expenditure in households with an unemployed head was only 60 per cent of that in households with an employed head.[30]

One of the key features associated with the poverty of the unemployed is debt. Because of the fall in income, the unemployed are frequently forced to incur debts to maintain standards of living. Moreover, creditworthiness is assessed mainly on employment status. The unemployed are often driven to accept high interest debt because of the assumed risk of repayment failure. Also, many of those who become unemployed have already accumulated large debts while in employment, particularly with regard to house purchase. In Britain in the late 1980s, very large numbers of the unemployed lost their homes as a result of their inability to service their mortgages. In December 1991, the British government negotiated to pay directly to banks and building societies the £750 million per year paid through income support to cover mortgage interest for home owners who had lost their jobs. Critics argued that while previously the unemployed had the choice of feeding their children or servicing their mortgage, the change left them with only the option of the latter.[31]

The significance of the duration of unemployment in affecting the income of the unemployed is emphasised in table 2.4. In two of the five countries, the level of social support was hardly affected by the length of unemployment. In West Germany, it eventually declined to just over half of former earnings. However, in France and the UK, the fall was more severe over time. The UK ratio went down after six months owing to the ending of earnings-related supplement to unemployment benefit, and declined further when eligibility for this insurance-related benefit ceased. In both, the unemployed received support of less than half former net earnings.

This suggests that one of the key relationships is between long-term unemployment and poverty. However, it should also be recognised that many short-term unemployed only find work in poorly paid or temporary jobs and are thus frequently unemployed at regular, short intervals.[32] Poverty is the general experience of those who inhabit this margin of the labour market. None the less, the long-term unemployed endure substantial exclusion from the labour market, experience the stigma of being unable to find work for very long periods, and suffer extensive income loss in the majority of the

---

[30] Piachaud, D. (1991), *op. cit.*, tables 3, 5 and 13.

[31] Travis, A. (13/12/1991), 'PM backs aid plan to stem home losses', *The Guardian*.

[32] See Sinfield, A. (1981), *What Unemployment Means*, Martin Robertson, Oxford, pp.49-57.

market economies.

Table 2.4	Net Unemployment Benefit, Selected European Countries, 1980, as a Percentage of Former (average) Net Earnings after Unemployment of:				
	1 Month	7 Months	13 Months	25 Months	31 Months
Denmark	87	87	87	87	87
N'lands	85	82	82	82	(82)
W.Germany	68	68	(58)	(58)	(58)
France	61	61	(36)	(36)	(36)
UK	68	49	(46)	(46)	(46)
Note:	Figures in brackets refer to social assistance payments excluding housing additions, rather than insurance related unemployment benefits.				
Source:	Walker *et al.* (1984) *op.cit.*, p.86				

Poverty and Long-term Unemployment

The overall increase in unemployment between the 1970s and 1980s brought with it a disproportionate jump in long-term unemployment (those who have been out of work for a year or more). This trend can be seen in table 2.5. The five countries which were members of the European Community saw substantial increases in long-term unemployment. In some cases, unemployment rates doubled but the proportions of long-term unemployed increased by a factor of three. The benefits systems of the North American economies offer very little support to the long-term unemployed and traditionally have had very low proportions of their unemployed in this category. Yet in Canada, the proportion of long-term unemployed increased eight times. In the US, the two indicators moved in different directions - unemployment fell, but long-term unemployment increased. Sweden's benefits system offers a community job to the unemployed after a year out of work, which explains its low increase in the proportion of the long-term unemployed.

A Eurostat report commented:[33]

> The current indications are that the modest improvements which have occurred in the labour markets over the last few years have not carried over into any significant alleviation of long-term unemployment.... While the challenges presented by the prior existence of a large residual group of hard-core long-term unemployed are, of themselves, serious enough, there is the additional likelihood that the problem has the capacity to keep reproducing itself.

---

[33] Eurostat (1988), *op. cit.*, p. 14.

Table 2.5 Unemployment Rates and Long-term Unemployment as a Proportion of Total Unemployment, Selected OECD Countries, 1975 and 1986

	1975		1986	
	Unemp. Rate	% Long- term	Unemp. Rate	% Long- term
Belgium	5.0	29.8	10.8	70.3
Denmark	4.9	9.4	6.3	31.5
W.Germany	3.6	11.8	6.9	48.9
France	4.6	16.3	10.3	47.8
Ireland	7.3	19.1	18.0	64.5
N'Lands	5.2	18.6	9.9	59.5
UK	4.3	14.8	11.1	45.0
Canada	6.9	1.3	9.5	10.9
US	8.3	5.3	6.9	8.7
Sweden	1.6	6.2	2.7	8.0

Source: Eurostat (1988), 'Long-term unemployment', Brussels, table 1.2

The distribution of the long-term unemployed varies by gender and duration of unemployment. In Belgium, Denmark, Greece, France and Italy in 1985, the majority of the long-term unemployed were women. This was to be expected, given that rates of unemployment were higher among women. However, in Greece and France, women were a minority of the short-term unemployed and, in the other countries, the gender balance of the short-term unemployed was more even. This suggests that women figure disproportionately among the unemployed in a number of European countries primarily because they tend to be unemployed longer than men. In West Germany, Ireland, the Netherlands and the UK, men made up the majority of the long-term unemployed. It is not immediately clear why such divergent patterns appear other than the possible exclusion by different benefits systems.

In some countries certain age groups figure prominently among the long-term unemployed. In Belgium, for example, 74.1 per cent of the long-term unemployed were aged 25 years or over compared to 50.2 per cent of the short-term group. Similar differences were observed in most of the countries of the European Community, with Italy being the only major exception.[34] The geographical distribution of long-term unemployment is also uneven. It tends to be more a feature of northern rather than southern Europe. In the latter, the economic significance of agriculture, and the role of tourism with its dependence on seasonal employment, tend to reduce concentrations of long-term unemployment.

Beyond the problem of long-term unemployment, lies that of the very

---

[34] *Ibid.*, tables 3.4 and 3.6.

long-term unemployed: those out of work for two years or more. Between 1983 and 1986, the long-term, as a proportion of all unemployed in the EC, increased from 35.6 per cent to 39.9 per cent. However, those out of work two years or more increased from 47.7 per cent to 62 per cent of all long term-unemployed.[35]

Income loss and associated problems are even more severe for those suffering long-term unemployment. Junakar comments:[36]

The long-term unemployed....are not only a wasted resource....they are also a wasting resource. The LTU (long-term unemployed) and VLTU (very long-term unemployed) lose their skills, they lose motivation, they fall ill: in crude economic terms human capital is being depreciated. In human terms there is a mass of misery and suffering; often they live in poverty, they have lost their self respect and dignity and they accept the verdict of the labour market with a mixture of resentment and resignation. The social implications of this are very serious: some people argue it leads to increased civil strife, riots, divorce, suicide, illness and death.

In terms of relative poverty, long-term unemployment and poverty are synonymous. Exclusion from the labour market involves a host of social costs, of which income loss is but one. As mentioned previously, some studies suggest that sections of the unemployed are cushioned from these effects by their inclusion in households with other wage earners. It has been argued that a substitution effect occurs: as men become unemployed, their partners seek work to maintain household income. Since the largest rate of job growth has been experienced by women in services, this theory has a superficial plausibility. However, the Eurostat study of the long-term unemployed revealed that many households have more than one unemployed member. (see table 2.6).

In Ireland, for example, in 1985 35.7 per cent of households which experienced unemployment, had two or more members unemployed. In Italy the figure was 26.7 per cent and in the UK, 22.9 per cent.[37] There was also evidence that lower proportions of the spouses of the long-term unemployed were actually working In each case, there were significantly higher percentages of spouses working where the head of household was also at work. In six of the eight countries, the proportion of working spouses was lower for the long-term compared to the short-term unemployed. The addition of extra earnings was enjoyed most where both partners were in work, least where the household head experienced long-term unemployment.

---

[35] Commission of the European Communities (1988), *op.cit.*, Brussels, table 1.1.

[36] *Ibid.*, p.1.14.

[37] Eurostat (1988), *op.cit.*, table 5.3.

Table 2.6   Percentages of Spouses Working with Heads of Households (HOH) At
Work (AW), Short-term Unemployed (STU) and Long-term Unemployed
(LTU), Selected European Countries, 1985

	HOH AW	HOH STU	HOH LTU
Belgium	46.3	33.3	19.9
W.Germany	48.0	38.8	29.0
Greece	42.4	23.5	31.1
France	59.0	44.8	40.3
Ireland	24.6	19.7	13.4
Italy	37.2	9.8	14.0
N'Lands	36.6	26.7	17.4
UK	60.9	33.6	18.4
Source:	Eurostat (1988), *op. cit.*, table 5.5		

Unemployment and Poverty: First World and Third World

Although the developed market economies experienced severe unemployment during the 1980s, conditions in the late developing economies of the Third World were substantially worse. Most were adversely affected by the oil shocks. Many suffered crippling burdens of debt. Some endured political instability and military conflict. Nearly all increased their dependence on the First World, canvassing for its investment and seeking its loans.

Todaro has argued that unemployment in the Third World is a different phenomenon from that in the First:[38]

> Unemployment and underemployment regularly and chronically affect much larger proportions of LDC labor forces than did unemployment in the industrialised countries, even during the worst years of the Great Depression.
> Third World employment problems have much more complex causes than employment problems in the developed countries. They therefore require a variety of policy approaches that go far beyond simple Keynesian-type policies to expand aggregate demand.
> Whatever the dimensions and causes of unemployment in Third World nations, it is associated with human circumstances of abject poverty and low levels of living such as has rarely been experienced in the now developed countries.

Few of the developed economies are currently prepared to implement 'simple Keynesian-style' solutions to their own unemployment problems.

---

[38] Todaro, M.P. (1985), *Economic Development in the Third World*, 3rd Edition, Longman, London, p.224.

Nevertheless, unemployment in the Third World is so different from that in the First, that the use of the same term promotes ambiguity. In many developing countries, the poor have little access to formal employment, and thus the term 'unemployed' has less meaning. As a recent report from the World Bank declares: 'Most of the destitute mix many different earnings activities. It is common for the poor to work as cultivators, hunters, gatherers, small artisans, petty traders, and wage labourers at various times of the year.'[39]

Access to land is frequently a key factor in determining poverty. Fields reports a study of six developing countries which discovered that poverty was concentrated in rural areas and small villages among self-employed farmers and farm workers.[40] In Bangladesh, 93 per cent of the landless and those who had access to less than half an acre of land were poor in 1978. These amounted to over two-fifths of all households in the country. Even for the urban poor, there is rarely a formal structure of employment. For example, in Brazil in 1985, it was estimated that 75 per cent of the heads of poor families worked in the informal sector compared to 35 per cent of the population as a whole. This informal sector embraced not only construction, small-scale manufacture and transport services, but full-time begging, garbage sifting and prostitution. Moreover, social compensation for unemployment is almost nonexistent. For most developing countries, employment and unemployment, as they are experienced in the developed market economies, relate only to a fragment of their populations and a small segment of their labour markets.

This must be qualified, however, since the range of development amongst these countries is so great that a number of their faster growing, higher income members had higher GDP levels than some of the developed states. Singapore's GNP per capita in 1988 was 17 per cent higher than Ireland's, while Venezuela's was 32 per cent higher than Hungary's.[41] (Nevertheless, the bottom quintile in Hungary's income distribution received 10.9 per cent of total income compared to 4.7 per cent in Venezuela.) If China had matched Korea's export performance per head in 1981, its exports would have had to increase 2,512 times.[42] The Third World consists of countries at widely different levels of development. The four 'Asian Tigers', Taiwan, Singapore, Hong Kong and Korea are among the most rapidly growing economies on the planet, although their GNPs per head may remain relatively low compared to the advanced market economies. At the other extreme are countries such as Mozambique and Ethiopia with GNPs per

---

[39] The World Bank (1991), *Poverty: World Development Report 1990*, published for the World Bank by Oxford University Press, Oxford, p.33.

[40] Fields, G.S. (1980), *Poverty. Inequality and Development*, Cambridge University Press, Cambridge, pp.160-1.

[41] World Bank (1991), *op. cit.*, p.179.

[42] Harris, N. (1986), *The End of the Third World*, Penguin Books, London, p.31.

head of around $125.[43]

Given the disparity in levels of development of Third World countries, it is difficult to establish a common poverty threshold. The World Bank applied two poverty lines in 1985 - $370 per person per year as an upper poverty level, and $270 as the lower poverty line. In the higher bracket, it was estimated that 1,115 million were poor in developing countries, accounting for over 30 per cent of their total population. Of these, 630 million experienced extreme poverty. The World Bank report lists 24 countries whose GNP per head was less than the upper poverty threshold.

At the same time, few of the developed market economies fulfilled the Brandt Report criterion of transferring 0.7 per cent of GNP as aid to developing countries. In fact, Brandt set desirable targets of 0.7 per cent by 1985 and 1.0 per cent by the end of the century.[44] In 1988, the US delivered 0.21 per cent, the UK and Japan 0.32 per cent and West Germany 0.39 per cent. Norway, Sweden, Denmark and the Netherlands were among the highest donors at between 0.9 per cent and 1.1 per cent of GNP.[45] Meanwhile the developing countries' net outflow of resources (the difference between debt repayment and new loans/new aid) amounted to $286 billion between 1982 and 1987.[46] In some cases debt servicing consumed up to 40 per cent of export earnings. Yet in the early 1990s, many First World financial institutions were forced to renegotiate or write-off very substantial funds which debtor nations were unable to pay.

The solutions to problems of this magnitude are difficult to conceive. The World Bank sees the generation of productive employment and the creation of basic social welfare systems as a necessary step. It should be recognised, however, that the emphasis placed on industrialisation, and particularly on the manufacturing sector, over the past two decades has not resolved unemployment in the developing countries. There is frequently a mismatch between the demand for labour from new capital-intensive industries and the labour supply of developing countries. This is exacerbated when development depends on investment from external companies. Further, the manufacturing sector in many of these countries employs between 10 per cent and 20 per cent of the labour force. If a labour force was growing at three per cent per year, manufacturing employment would have to increase by 15 per cent just to absorb new labour.[47]

With the conditional ending of the Cold War, there may be fewer low-intensity conflicts between the superpowers fought out with Third World surrogates, although Afghanistan has shown how, once these are set in

[43] World Bank (1991), op.cit., pp.178-9.

[44] Donaldson, P. (1986), Worlds Apart, 2nd edition, Penguin Books, Middlesex, p.157.

[45] World Bank (1991), op. cit., p.214.

[46] George, S. A. (1989), A Fate Worse than Debt, Penguin Books, Middlesex, p.236.

[47] Todaro, M.P. (1981), Economics for a Developing World, Longman, Harlow, p.206.

motion, they are practically impossible to stop. A cessation of these conflicts would dramatically increase the Third World's development potential.

Nevertheless, unless the Third World's debt burden is reduced, prevailing patterns of poverty and dependency will persist. Equally, some of the fastest growing developing countries are ruled by market committed, but highly authoritarian governments for whom the reduction of poverty has an extremely low priority. Brazil, Argentina and Chile have all been examples of this tendency. Progress requires a new relationship between developed and developing worlds and new, democratic relationships within the developing world. But, even in the medium term, the figure of one billion poor in the developing countries is unlikely to change.

Overview

The growth of unemployment in the 1980s, accompanied by a disproportionate increase in long-term unemployment, has been a significant factor determining the levels of poverty in the market economies. On present evidence, there is little prospect of a substantial change in this situation. These economies are once again characterised by recession in the early 1990s and in any case, the very rapid economic growth of the 1980s did not reduce unemployment to pre-oil shock levels. The recomposition of employment in that period created a demand for skills and forms of working which the registered unemployed could not supply.

In the US, the rest of the decade will see the costs of over-spending and over-borrowing in the 1980s. Unemployment had reached a 15-year low in 1989, but thereafter rose alarmingly. While budgetary and trade deficits remain excessive and reduced interest rates are slow to kick-start the US economy, unemployment growth is the probable outcome, despite the optimism of the 1992 State of the Union address. In the EC, unemployment has fallen since the mid-1980s but remains a worrying problem. The financial discipline of the proposed European central bank would generate an anti-inflationary policy bias as opposed to a full employment bias and this is likely to have a negative effect on employment in the weaker economies. Unemployment is thus likely to be a continuing feature of the market economies for most of the decade.

In the newly marketising economies of Eastern Europe and the Commonwealth of Independent States, the unemployment problem will probably be even more serious. Labour shedding has been regarded as an essential concomitant of economic restructuring as state enterprises are forced to operate under market conditions. In addition, the ending of food subsidies has generated considerable inflation, thus limiting further the consumption patterns of the new unemployed. In states where the transition has been accompanied by violence such as Romania, Georgia or Yugoslavia, conditions have been even worse.

Outside of the developed world, around one billion people are without any formal employment and, at best, are living at barely subsistence levels. For most Third World countries, the development potential is less promising than it was two decades ago while, in some, famine has become a regular occurence.

For all the unemployed, the risk of poverty is very high. The majority of studies demonstrate that the conjunction of unemployment and poverty remains, even within the welfare states. To seriously tackle the problem would require a redistribution of resources within the advanced economies and a further redistribution between these and the developing states. The challenge of the 1990s will be whether sufficient political will can be generated to tackle a problem of such massive proportions.

3. The Economy and Jobs in the US

This chapter looks across the Atlantic to examine the economic experience of the US in the 1980s and, in particular, the record on job creation and unemployment. At first glance, it appears to offer a remarkably positive contrast to the European achievement. But, a central purpose of the chapter is to question whether the official upbeat version of renaissance is sustainable. Divided into five main sections, it begins with an account of the Reagan project, and its proximity to that of Thatcher's; the economic performance of the Reagan years is then reviewed; following this, there is an outline of the changing structure of the US economy, providing a context for the examination of patterns of employment and unemployment, which distinguishes the 1980s from previous recent decades; and, finally, the impact of the Reagan legacy since the ascendancy of President Bush is assessed. Essentially, it will be argued that the claims for a new dynamism in the economy, with promising implications for job growth, are largely illusory.

Reaganomics and Thatcherism

In the 1980s, the administrations of Mrs. Thatcher and Mr. Reagan dominated the political economy of their respective countries. The contextual, ideological and policy symmetries between the two regimes at first glance appear remarkable, explaining the close affinity between the two leaders. Both assumed power at the end of a decade when an oil crisis and subsequent recession accentuated a crisis in confidence in orthodox instruments of demand management in the economy. The Wilson-Callaghan Labour government in Britain and the Carter presidency in the US were widely portrayed as the embodiment of a political malaise - a crisis in governability. There seemed a gaping disjuncture between the range and depth of economic difficulties and the capacity of government to deliver sustained regeneration. At least this was the scenario depicted by their conservative opponents, who by the late 1970s had embraced the doctrines of the New Right, and were intent on radical challenge to the post-war order, rather than its incremental modification.

The early objectives of this project in both countries included the reversal of fiscal laxities, identified as fuelling inflation; the retreat from the 'stop-go' malaise of Keynesianism; and the removal of welfare 'impediments', perceived to stunt incentives for work and profit. In developing their policies, both administrations were heavily dependent on right-wing think tanks, amongst whom there was some cross-national fertilisation of ideas. The Thatcher government was disposed to learn from the experience of the US; because of her own Atlanticist leanings, she was intent on 'Americanising' the British economy. She was prone to laud the US economy for its supposed deregulation, labour market flexibilities, low trade union density, more residualised welfarism, and general individualist ethos. There was as well some reverse exchange. For instance, the enterprise zone experiment, initiated in Britain, was subsequently adopted in the US.

Both governments contributed to a deflationary 'crash' of their economies in the early 1980s, but presided over respectable levels of growth for several years thereafter, only to be plunged again into deep recession within 10 years. Both responded to the 'melt-down' of share values in 1987 with reflationary stimulus intended to ensure a soft landing, which subsequently contributed to escalating debt for individuals and corporations. Financial deregulation was also a common feature. In Britain, this included the abolition of exchange controls in 1979, and consumer credit controls in 1982, culminating in the convergence of the once distinctive roles of banks and building societies by the late 1980s. In the US the new competition engendered by banking deregulation, did not contain interest rate levels; if anything, the opposite happened. As financial institutions such as insurance companies entered the 'banking' sector, there was greater competition to attract funds, inducing many to offer higher rates of interest to depositors. However this, in turn, compelled them to charge higher rates to their borrowers.

Attempts to reinvigorate the competitiveness of both economies met with mixed results. Productivity in both countries improved, but insufficently to boost exports to levels which would prevent trading deficits. The combination of their social and economic policies left legacies of greater social and spatial disparities, reversing post-war trends of narrower gaps in income and wealth, and regional convergence in development.

The politics of the project in both places also shared some interesting characteristics. There was scant evidence in regular opinion polls that neo-conservatism was creating a new hegemony. Failure to receive such vindication was partly reflected in frequent indications of public preference for social spending over tax cuts. Yet, conservative governments were repeatedly elected in the 1980s, despite their espousal of greater self-reliance. Admittedly, both governments were elected on a 'minority' of votes, in Britain due to a first-past-the-post electoral system, and in the US because a minority of the electorate choose to vote at all in presidential elections.

Potential for conflict at the different levels of government was another common feature. While Republicans claimed the White House, Democrats dominated Congress. Similarly, Labour in Britain, though locked out of Downing Street, was typically the leading party in town hall. This division allowed the administrations in both countries to attribute responsibility for budgetary deficits or public spending over-shoots to their respective 'extravagant' oppositions, prone to fiscal imprudence and waste.

However, these and other similarities tend to over-shadow important differences. In the US, the Reagan agenda was popularised around the theme of curbing 'big government'. As such, it resonated with the undercurrent in American political culture, which is uneasy about too powerful a central state dominating local and individual affairs. This was formally enshrined in the Reagan doctrine of the New Federalism which, under the guise of devolving more authority to state level, was in fact designed to facilitate the reduction of federal funding for public works and welfare spending. While decentralisation was the means adopted in the US to curb social spending, in Britain the responsibilities of local government were eroded in favour of central government.

Both governments were concerned to liberate stifled enterprise from its 'crowding out' by the public sector. This involved a realignment of the balance in the mixed economy between public and private sectors. The extent of nationalisation in the US was always more modest and, accordingly, the imperative for privatisation was considerably less. Although both administrations prioritised sound money and supply-side policies, in the US the latter was more important than the former. In Britain, on the other hand, in the early 1980s there was notable emphasis attached to restricting the growth of money, broadly measured, and to achieving balanced budgets. While Keynesianism was formally forsaken in both countries, a kind of 'military' Keynesianism remained significant in Reagan's America as the Cold War went into the deep freeze, and the Pentagon raised the stakes in the arms race with the Kremlin. Finally, though both leaders personified the new 'conviction' politics, and both were populist enough to be expediently pragmatic, the tenacity of Thatcherism was ultimately distinctive from the less robust Reaganomics.

The Reagan Economic Performance

There was a rationale behind Reagan's supply-side strategy. Tax cuts on personal income were designed not only to enhance work incentives, but also to promote savings, which could be made available for industrial investment. Reductions in corporate taxation were similarly intended to boost post-tax profits and ensure more scope for investment in new products and technology. Together with deregulation, these combined changes would improve productivity which, in turn, would upgrade competitiveness and thereby strengthen export performance. Success here would guarantee job and wage growth, which would augur an increased aggregate demand, relatively free from the inflationary impediments of previous growth strategies.

It has been estimated that the tax changes on personal income amounted to a real tax reduction for the 5 per cent of the population with the highest income, and a tax increase for most of the rest. Lekachman speculated that 'approximately 85 per cent of the benefits will accrue to taxpayers above annual incomes of $50,000'[1]; and in the case of tax changes related to company depreciation costs, he claimed that '....about 80 per cent of the tax savings will flow to the 1,700 largest corporations that during the last twenty years have generated only four per cent of all new employment opportunities.'[2] The changes confirmed Americans as the least taxed citizens in the industrial world, but it did nothing to improve the savings effort. Starting at 7 per cent of disposable income in 1980, the savings ratio rose briefly in 1981, after which it was generally on a downward spiral, reaching a low of 2.9 per cent by 1987.[3] By 1989-90 the ratio rose again to 4.5 per cent, although this remained below that of most industrial competitors, and indeed below the average 6.5 per cent in the US in the post-World War II period.[4]

Company profit rates did improve. By 1984 they reached an average of over 7 per cent, significantly above the average of 5.7 per cent in the 1970s. From the depths of recession in 1982 to the close of 1986, US firms experienced an average real pre-tax profit increase of 92 per cent and, given the bonus of corporate tax rate reductions, post-tax profits rose by an even greater 118 per cent on average.[5] However, the combined effects of the tax, savings, and profitability performance did not induce substantial increases in investment. In the first half of the 1980s, investment levels did not show any great buoyancy. Moreover, the composition of the investment was hardly geared to spur sustained productivity gains, with '....only about 7 per cent of the investment dollar [being] spent on new productive equipment to be placed in operation on factory floors.'[6] Not until 1985 did spending on capital rates surpass the 1978-79 levels, and a year later this modest improvement tapered off.[7] This hesitant investment pattern could well have been linked to the difficulty many firms had in absorbing their excess

---

[1] Lekachman, R. (1982), *Greed is not Enough: Reaganomics*, Pantheon Books, New York, p.67.

[2] *Ibid.*, p.71.

[3] Council of Economic Advisors (1988), *Economic Indicators*, Government Printing Office, Washington DC, March.

[4] *Economic Report to the President* (1991), US Printing Office, Washington DC.

[5] Harrison, B. and Bluestone, B. (1988),*The Great U-Turn: Corporate restructuring and the polarizing of America*. Basic Books, New York.

[6] *Ibid.*, p.144.

[7] *Ibid.*

productive capacity.

As table 3.1 indicates, productivity in manufacturing in the period 1979-86, showed considerable advance on the previous period, 1973-79. This is related both to the poor US performance in the early period, relative to the OECD average, and to a genuine improvement, largely achieved in the process of deindustrialisation by dispensing with a good deal of the less productive 'smoke-stack' component. During 1979-86, there was also a modest productivity growth rate in the services sector, comparable to that of the OECD average though, again, the US was starting from a weaker performance of nil growth in the previous period, compared to a 1 per cent rate in the OECD as a whole.

Despite the Reagan rhetoric of a 'new morning in America', with the inference of renewal through rediscovery of enterprise, evidence of reinvigorated entrepreneurship is difficult to detect. Rather, the predominant image of corporate America in the 1980s is one of merger mania, a push for expansion and profit growth more through acquisition than organic development:[8]

> The value of mergers and acquisitions affecting firms listed on the New York Stock Exchange rose from an annual average of about $2 billion in the first half of the 1970s to $20 billion in 1980 and $95 billion in 1985....Michael Milken, the 40 year old innovator of the junk bond as a takeover weapon, was reportedly worth a half a billion dollars by 1986.

Of course, Mr. Milken was not the only one to come to grief in this speculative pursuit of the quick buck. Many others mis-read the durability of the property and consumer booms, and borrowed heavily on the expectation of further bonanzas. As a result, debt-to-equity ratios of non-financial firms, which had risen in the period, 1970-83, from under 2 per cent to just under 4 per cent, nearly doubled again in the following three years. This corporate over-extension was mirrored by a major consumer indulgence. Between 1981 and 1986, total consumer borrowing almost doubled, from $394 billion to $739 billion. It may be said that such growth is typical of a return from recession, as consumers feel secure with the improved prospects. However, this particular boom well surpassed its predecessors:[9]

> The ratio of such new debt to the net growth in disposable income ranged from 24 to 29 per cent in the four economic recoveries previous to the one that began in 1983. In contrast, in this one the ratio grew to 44 per cent.

---

[8] Hagstrom, J. (1989), *Beyond Reagan: The new landscape of American politics*, Penguin Books, New York, p. 247.

[9] Harrison, B. and Bluestone, B. (1988),*op. cit.*, p. 150.

Table 3.1	Sectoral Productivity Growth Rates[1] (percentage) US and OECD Countries, Selected Years.		
Sector	Period	US	OECD
Agriculture	1960-68	3.6	4.9
	1968-73	4.5	5.5
	1973-79	1.1	2.4
	1979-86	4.8	4.4
Manufact.	1960-68	3.2	4.5
	1968-73	3.5	5.1
	1973-79	0.9	2.5
	1979-86	3.3	3.5
Services	1960-68	2.3	2.9
	1968-73	0.6	2.1
	1973-79	0.0	1.0
	1979-86	0.4	0.5
Per Capita GDP	1960-68	3.1	3.9
	1968-73	2.0	3.6
	1973-79	1.4	1.8
	1979-86	1.4	1.6
Note:	[1.] Average annual rates of change of real value added		
Source:	Abstracted from Cornwall (1991), *op.cit.*, table 3.4		

The third passenger on board the debt train was government itself. During the Reagan Presidency, federal government spent over $1 trillion above the revenue it generated in tax and other government receipts.[10] This national debt binds future generations to the Reagan years:[11]

In 1980, less than 20 per cent of personal income tax revenue was needed to service debt; by 1986, the proportion had nearly doubled, to 38 per cent. Hence, almost $2 of every $5 we pay in federal personal income tax now goes for nothing more than interest payments. At the present rate, our grandchildren will still be paying for the Reagan recovery we bought on credit in the mid-1980s.

To this budgetary deficit was added the problem of the trading deficit. The trade balance on current account went from a surplus of $6 billion in 1981 to a deficit thereafter. As in the UK, government officials and their advisers had blithely maintained that the relative decline in manufacturing trade was not a cause for great concern because it was balanced by a surplus in exports

---

[10] *Ibid.*

[11] *Ibid.*, p.152.

of services.[12] But, in fact, a substantial part of this 'surplus' was not due to exporting success, but rather to income from US investment abroad. Much of it is in the form of interest payments on loans to Third World countries, a vulnerable base in the light of the international debt crisis.

Ironically, to help finance its debts and its domestic investment, the US was itself compelled to borrow from overseas. As noted by the Trading Office, the country has become 'a net debtor to the world for the first time in 70 years. In fact, America has gone from being the world's largest creditor to its largest debtor in less than three years.'[13] For the US to continue to secure loans on this basis, it is faced with the options of high interest rates to attract foreign money, or devaluation to stimulate exports. The former policy will, amongst other things, dampen domestic demand, and the latter may itself in time require high interest rates to offset any run on the dollar. Neither promises an easy exit from the dilemma.

Some economists in the early 1980s predicted disaster for the Reagan experiment because they considered the monetarist and supply-side components to be mutually incompatible:[14]

Supply-side policies clash directly with monetarism. The success of the former requires easy credit, low interest rates, and a resulting boom in investment. Monetarism can slaughter the inflation dragon only by starving the economy of funds for new machines and factories, and keeping interest rates high enough for long enough to shove the economy into a good, old-fashioned recession.

But, concern with this apparent contradiction neglected another crucial feature of the Reagan strategy, namely, 'military Keynesianism'. The military-industrial complex was never so visible. The defence priority was reflected in the fact that by 1987 spending, at $282 billion, was absorbing some 60 cents out of every personal and corporate tax dollar, and was over twice the 1980 figure of $134 billion. This represented in real terms an average annual growth rate of over 7 per cent, nearly three and a half times real GNP growth. It accounted for at least 1.2 million new jobs in the first half of the decade.[15] This largesse in military spending was not geographically evenly distributed. Just 10 states absorbed nearly 60 per cent - including California, Texas and Florida - and such contracts were not insignificant to their differential growth rates.[16]

---

[12] Council of Economic Advisers (1984), *Economic Report to the President*, Washington DC.

[13] Office of the US Trade Representative (1984-85), *Annual Report of the President of the United States on the Trade Agreements Program*. Washington DC, p.2.

[14] Lekachman, R. (1982), *op. cit.*, p.17.

[15] Harrison, B. and Bluestone, B. (1988), *op. cit.*

[16] Hagstrom, J. (1988), *op. cit.*

It is interesting to compare the French attempt at reflation with that of the US. Mitterrand's expansionary efforts in the early 1980s, though modest, produced difficulties for the current account, put the franc under pressure, and subsequently led to reversal in fiscal policy. Reagan cut taxes and reflated domestic demand. The related deficit in the current balance which emerged in 1982 was considered containable. This shows an important distinction between the US economy and national economies in Europe. Explaining the greater latitude at the disposal of US governments relative to their British conterparts, Andrew Britton notes:[17]

The US monetary authorities are better able than our own to dictate the movement of capital by adjusting relative interest rates. Moreover essential ingredients of the US situation were low inflation, monetarist rhetoric and a booming stock market. The sheer size of the US economy, the wide and deep market for dollar assets and the absence of alternative currencies to hold may all have been important as well. It is not an example we can follow at all closely in this country.

As it was drawing to its close, the Reagan administration was able to boast the prospect of the longest peacetime expansion in the post war era, with the economy entering its fifth year of growth, employment expanding, and inflation contained at around 4 per cent over the previous five years.[18] But, there were at least four basic problems with these achievements. First, they were purchased partly by an increase in social and spatial polarities, which is the subject of the next chapter. Second, spending rates surpassed growth rates. This will be a drag on future economic development:[19]

The requirement to service the external debt will result in incomes that are lower than otherwise for future generations to the extent that the foreign funds are used for current expenditure rather than for productive investment, as has been the case in the USA during the 1980s.

Third, the capacity to secure growth with low inflation seemed to rely heavily on the restoration of managerial prerogative and the further taming of trade unions. The share of the private workforce unionised fell dramatically in the 1980s, from over 20 per cent in 1979 to about 14 per cent in 1988.[20] The combination of this with the shift from manufacturing to services has seen the continuation of the decline in the real weekly wage of the average worker, from its peak in 1973. By 1986, it purchased almost 14

---

[17] Britton, A. (1989), 'Full employment and the balance of payments' in Shields, J. (ed.), *Conquering Unemployment, The case for economic growth*, Macmillan in association with the Emploment Institute, London, p.202.

[18] *Economic Report to the President* (1987), Government Printing Office, Washington DC.

[19] Cooper, R. (1991), 'Prospects For removing imbalances in the world economy', in Cornwall, J. (ed.), *op. cit.*, p.167.

[20] Economic Report to the President (1990), *op. cit.*

per cent less than it had done 13 years previously. This obviously affects personal disposable income:[21]

> Wages alone (not counting the value of fringe benefits) are responsible for more than three-fifths of our total national income. When benefits are added, the labor share accounts for nearly three-fourths. Hence, underlying trends in individual wages strongly influence trends in household income.

Fourth, the Reagan years failed ultimately to redress the underlying malaise of manufacturing decline. This last issue becomes more apparent if consideration is given to the changing structure of the economy.

Changes in the Structure of the US Economy

Before proceeding to examine in detail the patterns of employment and unemployment over recent decades, it is instructive to outline some key features of the US economy, in particular its changing structure. The most notable shift in the immediate past is that from goods-producing to services-producing sectors. In this respect the US is following in the path of other industrialised countries. In the two decades 1966-88, in all OECD economies, the share of manufacturing employment in total employment fell from 37 per cent to 30 per cent. In the US, the current share is lower than the average for the OECD. Just after the war, the goods-producing sector accounted for 41 per cent of all non-farm employment. By 1980, this had fallen to 28 per cent, and by 1990 to 23 per cent. Some 70 per cent of all workers are now in the service sector.

A sizeable shake-out of manufacturing jobs occurred in the recession of the early 1980s. Between 1980 and 1982, nearly 3 million were lost and, even after the growth in the rest of the decade, only half were regained. Though manufacturing retained approximately the same share of real gross national product over the period 1982-90, the improvements in productivity - averaging annually 4.5 per cent - contributed to the need for less labour in this sector. A significant proportion of the service sector growth was concentrated in a few areas. For instance, business and health services accounted for over 5 million net new jobs, amounting to 27 per cent of net job gain in the decade. The sizeable expansion of health is scarcely surprising, given the high share of US GDP devoted to it in a very health-conscious society, and the demographic and economic trends, which put an extra premium on professional care for both the elderly and the dependent young.[22]

---

[21] Harrison, B. and Bluestone, B. (1988), *op. cit.* p.113.

[22] *Economic Report to the President* (1991), U.S. Government Printing Office, Washington DC..

Some economists cogently refute the real sectoral demarcations represented by the official figures. For instance, Cohen and Zysman estimate that instead of the 3 million jobs conventionally assigned to farm production, a total of 6 to 8 million jobs is more accurate if account is taken of agriculture-dependent employment. Similarly, they insist that if such linkages are heeded in the case of manufacturing, its significance for the economy is traditionally understated:[23]

Manufacturing employment would not be discussed...as something that was about one-third of all jobs in 1953 and is now down to one-fifth and doomed to continue down that trend line. Instead...manufacturing production in the United States...makes the employment of perhaps 40 or 50 or even 60 million Americans, half or two-thirds or even three quarters of whom are conventionally counted as service workers, depend directly upon manufacturing production.

This is not an academic point. Accurate estimations of the full multiplier impact of manufacturing might well determine greater policy priority for its resurgence. Nevertheless, the role of the service sector is important and expanding. Its capacity to absorb labour is critical to any strategy for unemployment. Table 3.2 is interesting in this respect. It charts the sectoral absorption of labour in the period from 1960-73 to 1974-86 for three categories of industrial country. Group A refers to those countries which had a low rate of unemployment prior to 1973 but which experienced a notable increase after that year; Group B countries had a relatively high level of unemployment before 1973 but had a more modest rise in the period thereafter; and Group C includes those which, in the first period, had a similar average rate to those in Group A, but did not experience such a sharp rise after 1973.

The US is in the Group B. In general, Group A countries lost more net jobs in the de-industrialisation process. Their absorption of labour in services was similar to that in Group B. Despite performing as poorly in terms of manufacturing job drain as some of those suffering the greatest increase in unemployment in Group A, countries like Sweden and Norway in Group C compensated by significant increases in services. The US emerges from this comparison distinctively. Compared with its Group's average, it shed considerably less labour in farm production, but underperformed both in terms of industry and services, yet came out with a lower rate of unemployment growth.

The growing share of employment in the service sector in the traditional industrial countries is mirrored in that sector's rising share of national output. The increased role of a sector, whose capacity for productivity improvement has been consistently less than that of manufacturing, does not augur well for a sustainable return of the growth levels once enjoyed by the

---

[23] Cohen, S. and Zysman (1987), *Manufacturing Matters : The myth of the post-industrial economy*, Basic Books, New York, p.19.

mature economies. It is, however, problematic to deduce any definite consequence of this for unemployment, partly because the probability of many face-to-face services becoming less labour-intensive is subject to much dispute, and partly because economic growth is no longer as closely related to job growth as was previously the case.

Table 3.2 Changes in the Sectoral Absorption of Labour (percentage), 1960-73 to 1974-86

Country	Agricult.	Industry	Services	Unemployment
Group A				
Australia	-2.9	-7.9	+6.3	4.5
Belgium	-3.1	-11.4	+8.1	6.4
Denmark	-6.7	-7.5	+8.1	6.1
France	-8.2	-4.9	+8.4	4.7
W.Germany	-4.6	-6.2	+6.4	4.4
N'lands	-2.5	-10.8	+6.6	6.7
UK	-1.2	-10.7	+6.4	5.5
Avg. A	-4.2	-8.5	+7.2	5.5
Group B				
Canada	-4.0	-5.0	+5.5	3.5
Finland	-13.5	-0.4	+11.1	2.8
Italy	-10.3	-1.6	+9.2	2.7
US	-2.3	-5.3	+5.1	2.5
Avg. B	-7.5	-3.1	+7.7	2.9
Group C				
Austria	-7.6	-2.7	+9.5	0.8
Japan	-11.1	+1.6	+8.6	0.9
Norway	-7.9	-6.1	+12.9	1.1
Sweden	-4.9	-7.6	+12.0	0.5
Avg. C	-7.9	-3.7	+10.8	0.8
Avg. A,B,C	-6.1	-5.7	+8.3	3.5

Source: Sundrum (1991), in Cornwall, *op.cit.*, table 2.11

Unemployment in the US

At the depth of the depression years in the 1930s, over one in four of the US workforce was unemployed. Even by 1938, it was close to one in five. It took the war effort to bring the rate down substantially, and in 1944 it stood at 1.2 per cent. Amid the general post-war determination to avoid a relapse into mass unemployment, an Employment Act was passed in 1946, obliging the Federal government to promote optimal production and purchasing power, and gainful employment for those capable, and in search of, work.[24] The period from the late 1940s to the late 1950s saw some volatility in unemployment rates, dipping to a low point of 2.9 per cent in 1953, helped by the demand stimulus of the Korean war, and rising to a peak of 6.8 per cent just five years later.[25] Between 1958 and 1964, the rates averaged close to 6 per cent, only declining in the latter part of the 1960s in response to factors including the Vietnam war.

This was a time when European economies achieved much greater success in containing unemployment than did their counterparts in North America. In the 1960s, the average unemployment rate was below 1 per cent in France and West Germany and just below 2 per cent in the UK. In the same period, it was 5.1 per cent in Canada and 4.7 per cent in the US. Even after the recessionary shocks of the first half of the 1970s, a similar, if less pronounced, disparity was apparent in the second half of the decade. While unemployment averaged 7.7 per cent in Canada and 6.7 per cent in the US, it stood at just over 5 per cent in the UK and France, and 3.7 per cent in West Germany.[26] The contrast seemed to validate the social democratic interventions typical in Europe, rather than the more liberal capitalism prevalent across the Atlantic. However, for most of the 1980s, this relationship of respective European and US economies to unemployment was reversed. On the face of it, this transformation is a recommendation of supply-side Reaganomics. In advance of such a verdict, however, more detailed inspection is necessary.

Table 3.3 illustrates the changing pattern of unemployment in the US over the four decades, 1950-90, broken down for gender and race. During the first two decades, the rate hovers mostly between 3 and 5 per cent, in stark contrast with the next two decades.

The declining rates from the mid-1960s, tied mainly to the impact of Vietnam, but also to domestic interventions such as the War on Poverty, went into reverse in the following decade. By the end of the 1970s, pressure mounted for government action. In 1978, a law with the cumbersome title, the Humphrey-Hawkins Full Employment and Balanced Growth Act, was passed, setting a 4 per cent unemployment rate as the goal of full

---

[24] Fishman, B. and Fishman, L. (1969), *Employment, Unemployment, and Economic Growth*, Thomas Crowell, New York.

[25] Bureau of Labor Statistics (1990), *Unemployment Rates*, Department of Labor, Washington DC.

[26] Solow, R. (1991), 'Unemployment as a Social and Economic Problem', in Cornwall, J. (ed.), *The Capitalist Economies: Prospects for the 1990s*. Edward Elgar, Aldershot.

employment, originally to be reached in 1983, later amended to 1985. The sharp increases in joblessness subsequent to the legislation were to cause Leon Keyserling, principal author of the 1946 Employment Act, to complain of the 'most flagrant, complete, unjustified, deliberate and explicit violation of law' in twentieth century US history.[27] The average unemployment rate rose from 5.4 per cent in the period 1970-74 to 6.5 per cent in 1975-79.[28]

Table 3.3	US Unemployment Rates (percentages), Selected Years, 1950-90				
Year	Civilian Workforce	Males	Females	Black 1	White
1950	5.3	5.1	5.7	9.0	4.9
1952	3.0	2.8	3.6	5.4	2.8
1954	5.5	5.3	6.0	9.9	5.0
1956	4.1	3.8	4.8	8.3	3.6
1958	6.8	6.8	6.8	12.6	6.1
1960	5.5	5.4	5.9	10.2	5.0
1962	5.5	5.2	6.2	10.9	4.9
1964	5.2	4.6	6.2	9.6	4.6
1966	3.8	3.2	4.8	7.3	3.4
1968	3.6	2.9	4.8	6.7	3.2
1970	4.9	4.4	5.9	8.2	4.5
1972	5.6	5.0	6.6	10.4	5.1
1974	5.6	4.9	6.7	10.5	5.0
1976	7.7	7.1	8.6	14.0	7.0
1978	6.1	5.3	7.2	12.8	5.2
1980	7.1	6.9	7.4	14.3	6.3
1982	9.7	9.9	9.4	18.9	8.6
1984	7.5	7.4	7.6	15.9	6.5
1986	7.0	6.9	7.1	14.5	6.0
1988	5.5	5.5	5.6	11.7	4.7
1990	5.5	5.6	5.4	11.3	4.7
Note:	1 Figures for blacks refer to blacks and other ethnic groups up until 1970.				
Source:	Bureau of Labor Statistics (1991), Department of Labor				

The reasons advanced for this failure during the Nixon and Ford administrations in the 1970s included the changing composition of the workforce, whereby teenagers, subject to above average unemployment rates, represented a higher share; the negative employment effect of the minimum

---

[27] Quoted in Hughes, J. and Perlman, R. (1984), *The Economics of Unemployment: A comparative analysis of Britain and the United States*, Harvester Press, Wheatsheaf Books, London, p.164.

[28] *Ibid.*

wage on low-productivity workers and teenagers; and the erosion of the work ethic due to previous unemployment benefit rises.

The teenage proportion of the total workforce grew from 7.3 per cent in 1960 to nine per cent by the early 1980s, representing a rise in their share of jobs by 23 per cent. For a variety of reasons, including lack of skills and experience, teengers represent the population sub-group with the highest incidence of unemployment. As one response to the growing problem of youth unemployment, there was an Amendment proposed to the Minimum Wage Act 1977, during the Carter administration, to set a more modest minimum level for this group, a move which failed narrowly. The concept of a minimum wage itself became subject to greater scepticism. Introduced in the Wage and Hours Law (Fair Labor Standards Act) 1938, the level was related to changing costs of living. During times of reasonable growth unaccompanied by high inflation, this would approximate to market levels, but once the phenomenon of stagflation emerged in the 1970s, the legislation was more problematic for low-productivity employment in a market economy.

In the early 1980s, the unemployment rate in the US reflected the severity of the economic downturn. It reached as much as 9.7 per cent in 1982, representing around 11 million people without work, and for a few months surpassed the 10 per cent mark, two and a half times that established in the Humphrey-Hawkins Act. As can be seen in table 3.3, there were higher unemployment rates for women in the 1960s and 1970s, linked to their higher rate of representation in the labour force. This increase in labour female market participation rates carried on into the 1980s, but the unemployment rate of women drew closer to that of men by the end of the decade.

Aggregate unemployment, after hovering around 7 per cent in the middle of the decade, fell sharply to 5.3 per cent by 1989. Lower jobless levels had not been experienced since the early 1970s - a much better recovery on the jobs front than had been achieved in Europe, where peak rates tended to be higher, high rates endured for longer, and decline proved less steady. The easy explanation, by which it is argued that the US job performance in the 1980s was a result of its more efficient and adaptable labour market, is a simplification. This would imply that these features must have emerged since their positive effects on jobless rates in previous periods are not perceivable. Similarly, it is scarcely credible to argue that the reversal in fortunes between Europe and the US, with regard to unemployment, demonstrate conclusively that Keynesianism had reached and surpassed its nadir with the onset of stagflation, and supply-side remedies as adopted in Reagan's America had proved a superior substitute. Such a proposition ignores the experience of the Nordic countries during this period. Norway, Sweden and Finland managed to contain unemployment rates within 2 to 5 per cent, while retaining most tenets of social democracy.

The argument that the superior jobs performance in the US can be understood in terms of the relative capacity of that country to reduce real wages is also difficult to corroborate. Certainly, in the inflationary aftermath of the oil crisis, real wages fell in the US in a way that they did not in many European countries. But, that movement alone is not necessarily decisive in creating favourable circumstances for job protection and growth. The critical factor is often most likely to be the level of wage rise relative to productivity gain. This issue of unit labour costs, which in turn is linked to the wider issue of competitiveness, presents a much more complex picture which does not permit straightforward comparisons between the two economic blocs. Nor can the relative generosity of benefits be the decisive factor. The US generally does have a more minimalist welfare system than that of Europe. As discussed in chapter five, no significant relationship can be drawn between levels of unemployment and benefits within Europe, despite wide variations in form and amount of benefit provision. As greater fiscal restraint in the 1980s operated to reduce the real value of such benefits in many countries, there is no clear evidence that this reduction, relative to average wages, helped to reduce unemployment relative to the cutback measures.[29]

Unquestionably, most European countries have higher levels of unionisation and regulation than does the US, and these, from a free market perspective, give rise to rigidities of various kinds. Classical economists argue that legislation designed to protect people at work in practice stifles job creation, particularly when employment is most at a premium. When employers are pessimistic about economic prospects, they will be all the more hesitant about hiring labour, fearing that if the market later demands redundancies, they will face tribunals and costs. This factor, however, is unlikely to account fully for the differential employment growth in Europe and the US during this period.

Solow, in an interesting article which addresses much of this ground, speculatively offers an alternative hypothesis.[30] He suggests that the different priority attached to curbing inflation on both sides of the Atlantic, at different times since the late 1970s, may provide some explanation. In the case of Europe, West Germany as the strongest economy was best placed, following the oil shock of 1973-74, to exploit its surplus capacity to go for growth, and, by doing so, spark a reflationary spiral for its neighbours. But, says Solow, West Germany has been so traditionally fearful of inflation, above all else, that it hesitated to make such use of its surplus, since that risked over-heating and the tightening of its markets. Politically, it has been able to pass up such opportunities to maximise its buoyancy because German governments can claim that they are constrained by a wary independent Bundesbank. Yet, if the most dynamic European economy behaves with such caution, it becomes even riskier for others to act unilaterally, as Mitterrand's France was to discover in the early 1980s, with its abortive reflation.

---

[29] OECD (1988), *Employment Outlook*, Paris, pp. 123-4.

[30] Solow, R. (1991), *op. cit.*

West Germany's circumspection may have been responsible for its relatively successful containment of inflation in the post-recession period of the 1980s. Between 1983 and 1989, consumer price inflation was 50 per cent in Italy, 35 per cent in the UK, 29 per cent in both France and Canada, and 24 per cent in the US. It was a mere 9 per cent in West Germany, though the cost of this was fairly stagnant employment growth for most of the period. The US did seem to get the best trade-off between unemployment and inflation because of its timing. In other words, instead of a mechanistic reading of the Phillips curve, the important consideration may be the point in both the inflation and unemployment spiral at which attempts are made to reduce the rate of either. As Solow illustrates in the case of the US:[31]

The monetary tightening that began in 1979 was intended to stop the inflation of the 1970s. It certainly did that: if we use the GNP deflator as a measure, the rate of inflation came down from nearly 10 per cent in 1981 to 4 per cent in 1983 and under 3 per cent in 1986. The price was a very sharp recession, the sharpest in 50 years....the turnaround came in the middle of 1982. There is no mystery about why. The Federal Reserve eased off when the recession began to look serious, and the Administration and the Congress weighed in with the massive tax reductions of 1981-83.

The administration made much of the fact that though jobless rates were successively higher at each business cycle peak in 1973, 1979 and 1981, the unemployment rate in 1989 was 2 percentage points down on its 1981 level. Nor was this decline in unemployment accompanied by accelerated inflation. Thus, the government claimed, '....the unemployment rate consistent with stable inflation, fell during the 1980s.'[32] The fact that wage inflation did not follow on the heels of the fall in unemployment was crucial. In this respect, the relative fragility of trade unions in the US cannot be discounted as a factor. During this time there was also publicity about the vulnerability of certain blue-collar jobs, given the increasing globalisation of production and the competitive edge being developed by alternative industrial locations such as the Far East. This may have had some impact on moderating wage expectation. But, such tentative conclusions beg other questions, not least the specific influence of Reaganomics on this outcome. The probe for a more comprehensive explanation may benefit from a brief excursion through relevant facets of recent US history.

Retracing the Recent US Experience of Unemployment

In comparing the US experience of unemployment with that of European

---

[31] *Ibid.*, p.101.

[32] Economic Report to the President (1990), *op. cit.* p.178.

countries, a number of interesting contrasts emerge. The sharp rise in joblessness in Europe from the late 1970s marked a significant departure, representing two decades of high unemployment after two decades of relatively full employment. The US post-war unemployment experience has been subject to much greater fluctuations. Up until the mid-1960s, successive governments pursued other economic priorities, such as the containment of inflation and the achievement of trading balances. The orthodox levels of intervention and subsidies in most of Europe would have been viewed in the US as meddling with the market, and offending against fiscal frugality.

By the 1960s, the economic debate about unemployment centred around the relative merits of structural and demand-deficient explanations. For the latter, the critical need was for government to stimulate more demand to absorb the unusually high surplus of labour supply. For the former, the key issues were the transformation from manufacturing to services, and the related substitution of capital for labour in the high technology production industries. These shifts had confiscated the traditional occupational opportunities from the blue-collar male worker in particular, while demanding higher skill and educational attainment for entry into the new, more technical industrial jobs. The failure of the labour market to adapt to this changed composition of demand had generated imbalances, including jobless growth. From this perspective, simply boosting aggregate demand would not address the supply-side deficiencies in general manpower training, and infrastructural capacity in the more depressed regions most vulnerable to these structural changes.

The government's Council of Economic Advisers at this time demurred about the mono-causal inferences of the structural view. It pointed out that demand for skill upgrading had been a feature of the labour market well before the job slump of the late 1950s, but had not prevented the attainment of low unemployment in the early years of that decade. In the Council's view, demand stimulation using fiscal instruments, was the critical pre-condition for a resurgency in the jobs market. But this need not preclude a complementary effort at targeting education and training to ensure reflationary activity would not encounter bottle-necks on the supply side.[33] It was this analysis which prevailed during Johnson's administration, and contributed to the decline in the jobless rate in the latter half of the 1960s; it stood at 3.5 per cent in 1969, compared to nearly twice that level in 1961, when it was 6.7 per cent.[34]

In the 1970s, the unemployment rate was successively higher at each business cycle peak. By the late 1980s, for nearly every main demographic group, unemployment levels were lower than they had been since the early

[33] Council of Economic Advisers (1965), 'Structural unemployment', in Bowen, W. (ed.), *Labor and the National Economy*. Wiley and Sons, New York.

[34] Bureau of Labor Statistics, *op. cit.*

1970s.[35] The Economic Report to the President was able to boast:[36]

Major industrialized countries such as the United Kingdom, West Germany, France, and Japan have all experienced slower employment growth than the United States throughout the 1980s. Indeed, the total increase in employment in the United States since 1982 is greater than the increases in Western Europe, Canada, and Japan combined.

In less than 3 years following the 1980-2 recession over 8 million jobs were created.[37] This success is attributed to the capacity of the private sector in the US to adjust to the challenges of dynamic economic change. This adjustment in turn allowed the US economy to combine high job turnover with employment growth, which absorbed the higher labour market participation rates of women and the effects of the post war baby boom without markedly high unemployment. Specifically, it meant that the increase in the supply of women did not result in higher jobless rates or lower pay rates for women:[38]

Instead, women have enjoyed substantial economic gains. Female and male unemployment rates converged in the 1980s for the first time since World War II. And women's wages increased substantially relative to men's, closing almost a quarter of the gap in pay rates between the sexes.

But this claim is deceptive. Part of the explanation for the convergence in male and female wages is that the average male wage has been performing so poorly. There has been a growth in jobs but many have been at wages lower than those in manufacturing they are supposed to replace. There are more family members at work, but this has not noticeably reversed the stagnation of household income.[39]

This job growth has been experienced very unevenly in social and spatial terms. The next chapter takes up these disparities in greater detail, but some of the implications may be usefully sign-posted here. Regions enjoying the most buoyant levels of expansion in the last decade include the southeast and selected areas on the eastern and western seaboards. Considerably more sluggish has been development in regions such as the midwest, still tied to many traditional industries subject to the most acute global competition, and the southwest, hit by the declining oil prices over the period 1981-86. This increased polarisation in the 1980s of so-called sunrise and sunset industries, in a labour market which prides itself on its adaptability, might reasonably

---

35 Economic Report of the President (1990), *op. cit.*

36 *Ibid.*, p. 144.

37 OECD (1985), *Quarterly labour force statistics*, no. 4, and *US Bureau of labor statistics*.

38 Economic Report to the President (1990), op.cit., p. 144.

39 Harrison, B. and Bluestone, B. (1988), *op. cit.*

have been expected to augur increased geographical mobility. The migration patterns over the period do not fully bear this out. Overall migration rates did not rise. Each year around 6 per cent of the population relocated to a new county and about 3 per cent moved to a new state, similar to the trends in the 1970s.[40] However, taking the last two decades together, the share of the country's population living in the northeast and the midwest fell from 51.9 per cent to 44.1 per cent, reflecting the pull of the relatively buoyant west and south.[41] The opportunity for labour mobility over an expansive terrain, sharing the same currency, language, and cultural boundary is a facility that will not be available to Europeans for the foreseeable future.

Data on occupational mobility indicate the considerable labour turnover in the US economy. In 1986, the most up-to-date statistics available, some 9 per cent of the employed workforce - around 10 million workers - left their jobs. While almost 90 per cent did so voluntarily, motivated by career or other considerations, the remainder - 1.3 million workers - were compelled to do so because of redundancy. Of those forcibly displaced, just over 25 per cent found alternative jobs immediately. Over 70 per cent of those so displaced between 1983 and 1987 had jobs in 1988. Another 15 per cent dropped out of the labour market for many reasons, including retirement, leaving nearly 15 per cent economically active but still workless.[42]

The theme of flexibility is again prominent in the 1991 Economic Report to the President, and is elevated to the virtue being eagerly pursued by former communist countries, which look to the American model for inspiration and guidance:[43]

> This dynamism has generated the high standard of living that the United States and other free-market economies enjoy and is one of the major reasons that people all over the globe are now moving to reform their economies to increase their reliance on free markets.

It is easy to be facetious about the hyped 'boosterism'[44] prevalent in much official US commentary about its economy. However, at least part of this is an optimistic 'can-do' disposition, culturally less pervasive in Europe. In so far as attitude can convert the economic shocks of the last few decades into a sense of challenge and opportunity, this American characteristic may contribute at least marginally to its need to make a fundamental shift in its economy. The trading and budgetary deficits, together with the enormous personal and corporate debt, pose major problems for the 1990s. Such deficiencies will not evaporate in the triumphalism of capitalism over

---

[40] *Ibid.*

[41] Economic Report to the President (1991), op. cit.

[42] *Ibid.*

[43] Economic Report to the President (1991), *op.cit.*, p. 111.

[44] 'Boosterism' refers to the aggressive marketing of cities in order to boost investment and development.

communism. The challenge of accommodating its changing workforce in the following decade in useful and competitive employment is quite daunting.

Changing Patterns of Employment into the 1990s

In the 1990s, the economy will have to adjust to demographic and household trends that include the ageing of the workforce, a reduction in new labour market entrants, accommodating further improvements in female participation rates and in the proportion of workers from ethnic and racial minorities. Between 1988 and the year 2000, it is estimated by the Department of Labor that over two-thirds of all new labour market entrants will be Hispanic, Asian, black or female.[45] This suggests that measures such as affirmative action to advance equal opportunity need to be secured, and indeed strengthened.

There will also be the challenge of whether the military-industrial complex can deliver on the 'peace dividend', and convert a high share of military spending to civilian research and development. The astronomic military expenditure of the 1980s resulted in many contradictions. At one level, it might be claimed that it stalled the free-fall in manufacturing decline. It could equally be contended that it distracted resources from much needed industrial diversification and modernisation, as well as contributing significantly to budgetary deficits. The consequent arms build-up played a vital role in compelling an economically stretched Soviet Union to call it quits in the arms race, a precursor to the ultimate collapse of that industrial-military complex. But its departure meant that it could no longer be presented as a threat which, in turn, demanded a halt to the ever escalating military capacity of the US. The impact on the economy and employment of President Bush's recent proposals for a $50 billion cutback in the military budget remains to be seen.

The US budget for 1993 highlights the continuing tensions in the relative priority attached to work and welfare. There are proposals for a $2 billion cut in relief for the needy, including the food stamp and family support programmes. It also makes the case for contraction in health spending, which otherwise it estimates will consume 30 per cent of GDP by the year 2020. But while $12 billion is being cut from health, tax concessions to the middle class are proposed. The hopes of reducing the budget deficit from the 1992 level of over $400 billion to $200 billion by 1994 are pinned on optimistic assessments of a rebounding economy. It is predicted that real GDP growth for the 3 years beginning in 1993 will be 3 per cent, that inflation will drop and steady at 3.2 per cent, and that interest rates will be maintained at around 5 per cent. For 1993 this still leaves a budgetary deficit running at almost $1 billion a day. This is an unwelcome addition to the federal debt which topped $3.6 trillion by the end of 1991 and which now

---

[45] Economic Report to the President (1990), *op. cit.*

consumes $294 billion in annual interest payments.[46]

As in the UK, the recession in the US in the early 1990s has involved the restructuring of the service sector, and consequently has had a wider social and spatial impact than the deindustrialisation of the early 1980s. The legacy of the Reagan years continues to impose restraints on recovery. In a recent review of such prospects, the *Economist* noted:[47]

> The real reason that a new New Deal will not take place in the 1990s is that the deficit spending that would have made it possible took place in the 1980s...True, Mr. Reagan preferred to spend the government's cash on bombers rather than welfare - but the deficits of the 1980s, like those of the 1930s, turned into a massive exercise in pump priming. New New Dealers, intent on expanding the welfare state and deficit-spending America out of recession, would swiftly discover that someone has already taken a hammer to America's piggy bank.

This then is the paradox faced by the US. Politically, it is apparently dominant in the 1990s compared to the 1930s, when the vulnerability of its capitalism held out the prospect that communism was better placed to survive. Yet despite its contemporary geopolitical pre-eminence, the economic options available to the US to enhance competitive efficiency and attain a sustained recovery are more circumscribed than in the era of the New Deal.

---

[46] Walker, M. (30\1\1992),'Pay-later US budget takes first steps towards reform' in *The Guardian*.

[47] *The Economist* (4/4/1992), 'New Deal Chic', p.50.

4. The Underclass in the US

This chapter addresses the contentious issue of poverty in the US. In a country where wealth and consumption are often taken as synonymous with 'the American way', poverty can be regarded as aberrant, inviting a punitive or palliative government response rather than resolution. The chapter comprises five main sections. Considered first are the key characteristics of the poor in terms of number, composition and location. Various theories about poverty are then considered and, in this context, the debate about the existence, not to say extension, of an 'underclass' is reviewed. An examination of the historical and contemporary public policy response follows, and the chapter concludes with an identification of some pertinent political considerations in redressing the problem.

Characteristics of the Poor

The impression created by the US popular media is that the poor are inexorably growing in number, that poverty is an almost exclusively black phenomenon, and that it is primarily black family life, fragmented by welfare dependencies, that lies at the root of the current problem. The official figures represented in table 4.1 invite a more circumspect interpretation. Both the total number of poor and the poverty rate peaked in the early 1980s, and were clearly linked to the growth in unemployment during those recessionary years of the decade. The entire decade witnessed a widening of the income gap. The top 1 per cent experienced an 85 per cent rise in their real incomes while the incomes of the bottom 20 per cent fell by 20 per cent.[1]

---

[1] Hutton, W. 'Taking the yellow brick road to ruin.' *The Guardian*, 4/5/1992.

Table 4.1	Poverty Status of Families and Persons in the US by Race, Selected Years							
Year	No (m)	Median Income $ 1988	Below Poverty Level				Persons Below Poverty Level	
			Total		Female HOH			
			No (m)	Rate	No (m)	Rate	No (m)	Rate
All RACES								
1970	52.2	30,084	5.3	10.1	2.0	32.5	25.4	12.6
1975	56.2	30,166	5.5	9.7	2.4	32.5	25.9	12.3
1979[1]	59.6	31,917	5.5	9.2	2.6	30.4	26.1	11.7
1983[2]	62.0	29,307	7.6	12.3	3.6	36.0	35.3	15.2
1988	65.8	32,191	6.9	10.4	3.6	33.5	31.9	13.1
WHITE								
1970	46.5	31,209	3.7	8.0	1.1	25.0	17.5	9.9
1975	49.9	31,374	3.8	7.7	1.4	25.9	17.8	9.7
1979[1]	52.2	33,305	3.6	6.9	1.4	22.3	17.2	9.0
1983[2]	53.9	30,688	5.2	9.7	1.9	28.3	24.0	12.1
1988	56.5	33,915	4.5	7.9	1.9	26.5	20.8	10.1
BLACK								
1970	4.9	19,144	1.5	29.5	0.8	54.3	7.5	33.5
1975	5.6	19,304	1.5	27.1	1.0	50.1	7.5	31.3
1979[1]	6.2	18,860	1.7	27.8	1.2	49.4	8.1	31.0
1983[2]	6.7	17,295	2.2	32.3	1.5	53.7	9.9	35.7
1988	7.4	19,329	2.1	28.2	1.6	49.0	9.4	31.6
Notes:	[1] Based on 1980 census population controls; comparable with succeeding years. [2] Based on revised methodology; comparable with succeeding years							
Source:	Department of Commerce, Bureau of the Census, various years							

Partly due to the reflationary response of the Reagan administration in the lead-up to the 1984 presidential election, both unemployment and poverty rates dipped by the late 1980s, though to a level higher than in the previous two decades. The disparities by race are striking. Though there has been a bigger increase in the number of white people pushed into poverty in the 1980s than of black people, in 1988 one out of every three black families was in poverty, compared to one out of every 10 in the case of white families. Even with general economic improvement in the late 1980s, the black family poverty rate was over three and a half times that of the white family. The median black family income in 1988 was 57 per cent of the median white family income. This itself disguises the widening income gap within the black community. Between 1978 and 1988, the average income of the bottom 20 per cent of black families dropped by 24 per cent, while that of the richest 20 per cent increased by almost as much.[2]

This is not explained by the complete exclusion of black people from new job opportunities in the decade, but it suggests that the quality of jobs secured did not offer good prospects for earnings growth. The Economic Report to the President in 1990 implicitly acknowledged this:[3]

Inflation-adjusted weekly earnings among full-time minority workers have not risen since 1980. After several decades of steady growth, relative weekly earnings of black men have remained flat throughout the 1980s, at about three-fourths of white men's weekly earnings.

The 1990 national poverty rate was 13.5 per cent, while for blacks it was 31.9 per cent. Over the whole of the previous decade, there was a 49 per cent rise in the number of blacks living below the poverty line. This disparity carries over into other areas of social life. Blacks are more likely to be the victims of violence than whites. Though representing 12.5 per cent of the US population, they make up 40 per cent of those on death row. The health profile and life expectancy of blacks also compare unfavourably with those of whites. Higher rates of coronary and lung disease, alcohol and drug dependency and Aids are particularly evident.[4]

Black poverty is often most visible in young males. The average black boy is more likely to be destined for a penal institution than for one of higher education. He is seven times more likely to be murdered as his white counterpart. The likelihood is nearly two to one that he will be reared in a female-headed household.[5]

While in 1970 female-headed families constituted one-third of all families in poverty, a decade later they represented 45 per cent. Because there was considerable growth in the total number of female-headed families, the proportion of such families who were poor actually fell from 33 per cent in 1970 to 30 per cent in 1980. This pattern provides an important reminder that not all female-headed households survive on low income. Perhaps the most telling and direct indicator of the changing significance of such poverty is the average annual growth rate in the number of poor families headed by women. In the 1970s, this was 3.43 per cent,[6] which as Jones and Kodras note '....translates into a doubling time of only 20 years for the 2.5 million

---

[2] Editorial in *The Independent on Sunday*, 3/5/1992.

[3] *Economic Report to the President* (1990), US Government Printing Office, Washington DC, p.146.

[4] Urban League (1992), State of Black America, referenced in Tisdall, S. (24/1/1992), 'Black America waits for a rallying call', *The Guardian*.

[5] *The Economist* (30/3/1991), 'America's wasted blacks'.

[6] US Bureau of the Census, 1982.

poor families headed by women in 1980.'[7] Considerable variation in this 'doubling time' calculus was evident, with the northeast registering the greatest annual growth rate (14 years 'doubling time') and the South, the slowest (31 years). By 1988, 53 per cent of poor families were headed by women, and 90 per cent of such families included children below the age of 18.[8]

This illustrates how the demographic and socio-economic determinants of the feminisation of poverty also pertain to child deprivation. In 1970, 10.7 per cent of all children were reared in female-headed households compared to 18 per cent in 1980, an increase strongly related to the growth rates in divorce and unwed motherhood. Since such families have disproportionately high poverty rates, these changes in family structure are related to the growth in child poverty. Again, racial differences are notable within these trends. In 1980 'the percentage of white births to unmarried women rose to 11 per cent (5.4% in 1970); for blacks the comparable figure is an astonishing 55.3 per cent (37.5% in 1970).'[9]

This correspondence between 'non-marital' fertility and family poverty has allowed some commentators to present an unproblematic causal relationship between 'irresponsible' parenthood, welfare dependence and poverty. The first problem with this assertion is that the relationship of demographic and economic factors in the feminisation of poverty is complex. The share of married-couple households has declined from 71 per cent of total households in 1970 to 57 per cent in 1988. Within most of these marriages, both partners work. Even in the case of married women with pre-school children, 53 per cent are employed at least part-time outside the home. This suggests that the absence of this common dual income is a major comparative disadvantage for single parents. By 1985 female earnings accounted for 28 per cent of all income among white households and 46 per cent of all income among black households.[10]

Second, analysis which emphasises concepts of wilful dependency underestimates the simple truth that poverty in the US is not confined to non-earners. In the late 1980s, nearly half of all poor families contained an employed member, with 16 per cent having a full-time worker.[11] In the 1970s, the total number of working poor was approximately 6 million. In the 1980s, it was over 9 million, 2 million of whom were in full-time work for

---

[7] Jones, J.P. and Kodras J.E. (1990), Restructured Regions and Families: The feminisation of poverty in the US, *Annals of the Association of American Geographers*, vol.80, no.2, pp.163-183, p.165.

[8] *Economic Report to the President* (1991), US Government Printing Office, Washington DC.

[9] Jones and Kodras (1990), *op. cit.*, p. 171.

[10] Economic Report to the President (1990), *op. cit.*

[11] Economic Report to the President (1991), *op. cit.*

the entire year. This rise in the number of working poor is related to the shift from manufacturing to services, and to the fact that for much of the 1980s the level of the minimum wage was unaltered. In real terms, this wage rate is at its lowest since 1955. Despite the impression given, the minimum wage is not the exclusive preserve of the young employed. Just under a third in this category are teenagers but 28 per cent of minimum wage earners are heads of household. While most of the full-time, year-round working poor are white, male and living in non-metropolitan areas, women constitute a disproportionate share of low earners in part-time work. Unsurprisingly, they represent 66 per cent of those on the minimum wage.[12]

There has been a notable shift in the location of poverty over the last 30 years, as the table 4.2 indicates. In 1960, the rate of household poverty in the rural areas was twice that in the central city. Two decades later, deprivation levels in the urban core had overtaken those in non-metropolitan areas. In the 1960s, rates nearly halved in suburban and rural areas, and the level in the urban core in 1970 was similar to that in the suburbs in 1960. Since 1970, the situation in all parts of urban areas has gone into reverse, particularly in the central city, where since 1980 the percentage of households with incomes below the poverty line has actually increased from its 1960 level.

Table 4.2 Households with Incomes Below the Poverty Line, the US, 1960-87			
Year	Central City	Suburb	Non- metropolitan
1960	13.7	9.6	28.2
1970	9.8	5.3	14.8
1980	14.0	6.5	12.1
1987	15.4	6.5	13.8
Source: Bureau of the Census, 1972,1982,and 1989			

The most obvious spatial concentration of poverty is found in the ghetto, defined as a metropolitan census tract in which the poverty rate is greater than 40 per cent. Between 1970-80, the number of poor living in ghettoes in the 50 largest cities increased, in some estimates, by 66 per cent.[13] If we take the national picture over the same period, the number of poor living in ghettoes in metropolitan areas rose by 29.5 per cent, from 1.9 million to 2.4 million. But the aggregate national figures obscure the fact that some metropolitan areas experienced a decrease, while 'the number of ghetto poor in those SMSAs [Standard Metropolitan Statistical Areas] with increases

---

[12] Levitan, S. and Shapiro, J. (1987), *Working But Poor: America's contradiction*, John Hopkin's University Press, Baltimore.

[13] Nathan, R. and Lego, J. (1986), 'The changing size and concentration of the poverty population of large cities, 1970-1980', *memorandum*, Princeton University.

more than doubled.'[14]

Ghettoes are characterised a concentration not only of space but also of race:[15]

....the 2.4 million ghetto poor were 65 per cent black, 22 per cent Hispanic, and 13 per cent non-Hispanic white and other races. Thus ghettoes are predominantly populated by blacks and Hispanics, and black and Hispanic poor are much more likely than white poor to live in a ghetto.

While in 1980, of the 27 million poor people in the US, fewer than 9 per cent lived in ghettoes, some urban areas had over the preceding decade witnessed a significant increase in their ghetto poor, whose racial composition continued to be overwhelmingly black and Hispanic. Whereas in 1970 the 10 metropolitan areas with the greatest concentrations of ghetto poverty accounted for one-third of the total ghetto poor, by 1980 the top 10 comprised nearly half. Because some of the biggest increases occurred in the most populated urban centres, the spread of the ghetto in these areas was highly visible, causing this image to be reproduced across the country at large to a degree unjustified by the actual data.

Explaining Poverty in the US

Three broad theories of poverty have dominated the social agenda in the US. Cultural explanations in the recent period can be traced back to Oscar Lewis.[16] As initially interpreted, his work seemed to confirm the disposition of those who saw the problem in terms of a maladjusted minority, outside the mainstream of the American opportunity system. Policies designed to correct their attitudinal and behavioural dysfunctionings offered, from this viewpoint, the best recourse. Lewis himself later disowned this interpretation, and aligned himself more with those who argued that the sub-culture identified with the poorest was often a natural and rational response to their predicament, rather than a cause of it. Nevertheless, the tradition of perceiving poverty in terms of social pathologies survived, became associated with the right, and was translated and extended in the 1980s by the New Right into the concept of 'dependency'.

A second strand, which can be designated as the Reformist school, asserted the need to incrementally modify the operation of the work and

---

[14] Jargowsky, P. and Bane, M. (1991), 'Ghetto poverty in the United States, 1970-1980', in Jencks, C. and Peterson, P. (eds.), *The Urban Underclass*, The Brookings Institute, Washington DC.

[15] *Ibid*, p. 252.

[16] Lewis, O. (1968), 'The culture of poverty', in Moynihan, P.(ed.), *On Understanding Poverty: perspectives from the social sciences*, Basic Books, New York.

welfare systems. For liberals, this entailed a retreat from residual welfarism to one which was more comprehensive in reach, more coherent in structure and more even in geographical distribution. For the right, it meant a reappraisal of the disincentives engendered by the existing welfare system in terms of family stability, work ethic, and motivation for enterprise. In the case of low-income related to work, conservatives would stress the problem of marginal productivity, which essentially ensured that poor efficiency gave rise to poor wages for the less productive. The solution largely lay in skill-enhancement for low paid workers. For the liberals, this issue could be best understood in terms of a dual labour market, whereby the economy was increasingly polarising labour into two main categories: at the core were high-tech jobs which were highly paid and secure; at the periphery were jobs which were more menial, transitory and poorly remunerated.

These divergent views within the reformist tradition can be elucidated when we examine the issue of the feminisation of poverty. For the right, this phenomenon is principally a function of extensive social benefits, which encourage family disorganisation. The consequent imposition on women of exclusive parental responsibility deprives them of career and income opportunities. To such proponents, the prevalence of female-headed poor families in the northeast is congruent with the profligate welfare regimes in those states. Viewed through the liberal lens, female poverty is an outcome of the lack of effective legislative protection for equal opportunities and pay; the supply-side deficits with regard to a gender-specific curriculum in education\training, which perpetuates patriarchal hierarchies in labour-market recruitment and promotion; and under-provision of child-care.

The third perspective, associated with radical economic theory, sees poverty as an inevitable twin of wealth in an economic system based on the promotion of competition and inequality. Specifically, in the recent period, it would emphasise the way the process of de-industrialisation has been determined by the need to rehabilitate the structure of capitalism in its mature form.[17] While agreeing with the liberal agenda for removing social and political impediments to sexual equity, this view sees the issue of female poverty more in terms of the consequences of an economic restructuring, which generates manufacturing unemployment and a high share of new service jobs which are part-time and low-paid.

Given the general conservative bias of American political culture, this latter school has minority membership. The central debate is between the conservatives and reformers. What has sharpened their confrontation on the issue in recent times is the attention devoted to a particular section of the poor, which has been labelled the 'underclass'.

---

[17] Bluestone, B. and Harrison, B. (1982), *The Deindustrialisation of America: Plant closings, community abandonment, and the dismantling of basic industry*, Basic Books, New York.

The Underclass Debate

Over a quarter a century ago, Myrdal raised in somewhat lurid terms the persistent paradox of poverty amidst plenty in the US, when he spoke of an ugly odour emanating from the basement of the 'stately mansion' that was America - an 'underclass' of unemployed and increasingly unemployable people.[18] While much literature has been generated in recent years under the rubric of 'the underclass', transcending its conceptual and spatial ambiguity has proved problematic. In general, it connotes a persistent and concentrated poverty, usually associated with long-term unemployment, and located in isolating segregated spaces. It is a condition which pushes its participants beneath the traditional class system. But the additional critical attribute associated with the label is that of maladjusted deviant behaviour.[19] An intriguing implication of this characterisation is that those ghetto inhabitants trapped in abject poverty, yet socially conformist, would be disqualified. So too would be the drug-pushers who, though deviant, ply a lucrative trade that keeps them at a safe distance from penury. By the same token, estimating the numbers of those with the combined traits is a forbidding empirical endeavour.

To neo-conservatives in the US, the persistence of an underclass derives from the debilitating effects of welfarism. Government intervention against deprivation merely serves to create demoralising dependencies, which sap ingenuity and resourcefulness. The benefit system, designed to alleviate hardship, actually operates to corrode the authority and integrity of the family structure among habitual claimants. This often produces not only a female-headed family, but also one lacking any model to counter the proclivity for low educational attainment, stunted ambition, an enfeebled work ethic, and possibly drug abuse. Such families tend to congregate in concentrated social spaces, which come to acquire a negative cultural distinctiveness. In other words, misguided state policies, accentuated since the paternalistic Kennedy/Johnson era in the 1960s, have induced a ready posture of self-absolution amongst a hard-core section of the poor. They interpret state assistance as evidence of state guilt for having created their problems. This denial of any responsibility for their predicament becomes so internalised as to reinforce their exclusion from available market opportunities.[20]

These criticisms are evident in President Bush's recent tirade against Lyndon Johnson's 'Great Society' anti-poverty programme: 'This crusade backfired .... Programs designed to insure racial harmony generated animosity. Programs intended to help people out of poverty invited

---

[18] Myrdal, G. (1965), *The Challenge of Affluence*, Basic Books, New York.

[19] Auletta, K. (1982), *The Underclass*, Random House, New York.

[20] Murray, C. (1984), *Losing Ground*, Basic Books, New York.

dependency.'[21] Such a view implies that social engineering is flawed both in conception and execution, and thus accords conveniently with the individualist ethos, still pre-eminent in American political culture. The potential for social mobility for those who strive and achieve, the inevitable 'trickle-down' benefits of growth strategies, the primacy of the private sector, and the general equilibrating tendencies of the market are all verities too rarely subject to rigorous challenge. Instead, the ready rejoinder of the liberal left to this conservative critique tends to be couched in dismissive or accusatory terms. Either the argument is treated as beneath systematic rebuttal or its advocates are rejected as irredeemably reactionary, not to say racist.

An example of a more considered response is Wilson's book, *The Truly Disadvantaged: The inner city, the underclass and public policy*, which has become a seminal contribution to this discourse.[22] For Wilson, the underclass can be designated in social and spatial categories. It is a heterogeneous group of people outside the orthodox labour market and residing in the inner city. Though Wilson concedes potential membership for Hispanics, in his conceptualisation the underclass is almost exclusively black.

Some studies have portrayed the underclass in cross-racial terms. Williams and Kornblum[23] present a profile of a white and black underclass in cities such as Cleveland and New York. Though some like Auletta[24] identified a rural underclass in the southern state of Mississippi, for Wilson the underclass is not only a distinctively urban experience but also to a large extent is regionally demarcated in the northeast and midwest, a spatial designation broadly supported by Ricketts and Sawhill,[25] and Jargowsky and Bane,[26] among others.

Wilson addresses how the combination of migration flows to the large northern metropolitan areas and historic discrimination produced a weak attachment to the labour market amongst the urban minority population. The reference to a 'weak labour market attachment' is not to imply a weak work ethic. It is rather to acknowledge the particular vulnerabilities to economic

---

[21] Speech made at the University of Michigan, 4 May, 1991, quoted in the *Plain Dealer* (5/5/1991).

[22] Wilson, W.J. (1987), *The Truly Disadvantaged: The inner city, the underclass, and public policy*, University of Chicago Press, Chicago.

[23] Williams, T. and Kornblum, W. (1985), *Growing Up Poor*, Heath, Lexington.

[24] Auletta, K. (1982), *op. cit.*

[25] Ricketts, E. and Sawhill, I. (1986), *Defining and Measuring the Underclass*, Urban Institute, Washington DC.

[26] Jargowsky, P. and Bane, M. (1990), 'Ghetto Poverty: basic questions', in Lynn L (Jr.). and Mc.Geary, M. (eds.), *Inner City Poverty in the United States*, National Academy Press, Washington DC.

restructuring endured by urban blacks. This restructuring in the 1980s comprised a continued relocation of manufacturing jobs from the central city to the suburbs, a sectoral switch from manufacturing to services, a related bifurcation of the labour market into hi-tech/high wage and low tech/low wage, and an exodus of jobs and investment from the northern 'frostbelt' to the southern 'sunbelt'.

This process, accentuated by recessionary pressures on labour demand, has further peripheralised the minority populations in the 'rustbelt' cities of the traditional industrial region. Stranded at the margins of the job market, they are in turn deprived of what we might call a 'labour market intelligence system'. As expressed in another publication, Wilson contends that:[27]

....the central predicament of inner-city ghetto residents is joblessness reinforced by a growing isolation in impoverished neighbourhoods, as reflected for example, in the rapidly decreasing access to job information network systems.

Moving from such general propositions to disentangle the specific influence of class, race, and space in this outcome is where the problem really starts. Accepting for the moment that the disproportionately high level of black and hispanic poverty is related to the racially differentiated opportunity structure of the labour market, three distinct interpretative frameworks have dominated the explanations.[28] The first emphasises the negative employment impact for minorities of their spatial segregation in the central city while old manufacturing jobs were being shaken out and new information-intensive jobs were locating in the suburbs and southern regions. This so-called 'spatial mismatch' hypothesis can be traced back to Kain.[29]

The second perspective argues that it is not primarily a function of space but of race. Blalock, Dowdall, Barton et al, and Tienda, amongst others, subscribe to this view.[30] Sometimes referred to as the 'White Gains' hypothesis, it posits that racial discrimination on the part of whites is the telling factor. It is suggested that this will occur most acutely to produce a

---

[27] Wilson, W.J. (1991), 'Studying inner city social dislocations: the challenge of public agenda research', *American Sociological Review*, vol. 56.

[28] Farley, J. (1987), 'Disproportionate black and hispanic unemployment in US metropolitan areas: the roles of racial inequality, segregation and discrimination in male joblessness', *American Journal of Economics and Sociology*, April, vol. 46, no.2.

[29] Kain. J. (1968), 'Housing segregation, negro employment, and metropolitan decentralisation', *Journal of Economics*, vol.82, pp. 175-97.

[30] Blalock, H. (1967), *Toward a Theory of Minority Group Relations*, John Wiley New York; Barton, M. et. al. (1985), 'White, black, and Hispanic male youths in central city labour markets', *Social Science Research*, 14, September, pp. 266-86; Dodall, G. (1974), 'White gains from black subordination in 1960 and 1970', *Social Problems*, 22, pp.162-83; and Tienda, M. and Lii, D (1988), 'Minority concentration and earnings inequality: Blacks, Hispanics, and Asians compared', *American Journal of Sociology*, vol.93, pp.141-65.

'split labour market' where the minority population is the largest and thus job competition greatest. In such circumstances, whites have most to gain from excluding blacks from job opportunities. According to this view, it is not residential proximity as much as access to job opportunity that really matters.[31]

The third view emphasises social class and the 'skills mismatch'. Here it is suggested that sectoral shifts in the urban labour market have produced demands for new and higher qualifications amongst entrants. The relatively low skill and educational attainment of urban minorities has meant that modern recompositions of employment demand have not merely perpetuated but have exacerbated their long-standing disadvantage.

Wilson[32] has argued in this respect that current black economic deprivation is attributable more to class determinations than to traditional overt racial discrimination. Expressed at its simplest, black people are disproportionately represented in that low-skilled section of the working class most adversely affected by deindustrialisation. From this viewpoint, even if blacks and other minority groups are residentially proximate and racially open to employment opportunities, they may still not be functionally accessible because of their relatively low skill qualifications.

Moore and Laramore[33] conducted a study to identify the causal relationship among labour market and demographic determinants of racial disparities in employment patterns, using the 1970 and 1980 workforce censuses of the 100 US cities with the largest central city populations in 1970. The variables they examined included composition of employment demand, city size, minority concentration, group educational achievement and age. Their analysis emphasises the demand-side dimensions of the problem. Minority populations are concentrated in those urban areas which not only have endured the heaviest manufacturing job losses but also have experienced the slowest growth in service-sector employment. Thus, it is not primarily an issue of employment composition and, consequently, supply-side factors such as skill level. It is rather a matter of overall employment demand, in the context of spatial segregation and racial discrimination:[34]

> There is little or no relationship between the percentage of high school graduates and the labour-force participation and unemployment rates of the black workforce.... educational advancement alone is not likely to improve the economic situation of that population as long as it remains concentrated in central cities with low and declining levels of

---

[31] Ellwood,D. (1988), *Poor Support : Poverty in the American family*, Basic Books, New York.

[32] Wilson, W. (1987), *op. cit.*

[33] Moore, T. and Laramore, (1990), 'Industrial change and urban joblessness: An assessment of the mismatch hypothesis', *Urban Affairs Quarterly*, vol.25, no. 4, June, pp. 640-58.

[34] *Ibid.* p.655.

employment growth.

One study which tends to query the arguments about the declining significance of race and the demand-side emphasis, both of which downplay the importance of educational outcomes, is that of Farley.[35] In his analysis of the extent of inequality in male unemployment between whites and blacks/Hispanics, Farley used four main predictors: employment suburbanisation, black/Hispanic population concentration in the central city, the ratio of black/Hispanic high school graduates to whites in the same category. Amongst the findings were the following:

• In large northern metropolitan areas, the average black male unemployment rate was almost two and a half times as high as the average rate for white males.

• Relatively high black unemployment was related significantly to all four predictors but regression analysis suggested that the most significant factors were those of racial inequalities in educational attainment and the concentration of blacks in the central city.

• There were interesting regional variations. For example, in large southern cities with high black populations, the 'white's gain' hypothesis had the most statistically significant regression coefficient.

Comparing the data of 1980 with that of 1970, Farley concluded that race, far from dwindling in relevance, might be increasingly pertinent in the circumstances of more stringent economic times. In general, he suggests:[36]

.... major improvement in black and hispanic male unemployment levels is unlikely to occur until something is done about factors which produce racial/ethnic inequality in the distribution of unemployment, regardless of whether the overall level of unemployment in the economy is low or high.

Therein lies a difficulty in Farley's critique. Stimulating aggregate employment demand might not be the most effective means of achieving greater racial convergence in labour market patterns. But, is such a convergence attainable *regardless* of total unemployment levels, when a key inference of the 'white gains' proposition is that an economic downturn accentuates racial competition for jobs and thereby heightens motivation for discrimination? Expressed in policy terms, it is arguably more problematic to implement a successful affirmative action programme in the context of decreasing aggregate labour demand.

---

[35] Farley, J. (1987), *op. cit.*

[36] *Ibid.*, p. 148.

Spatial Mismatch

'Residential preference' models are premised on individual options determined by the efficient operation of the market.[37] On this premise, the individual, in choosing whether to live in the central city or suburbs, balances considerations like the higher cost of housing in the city with the wider range of proximate amenities, compared with the lower cost of similar standard housing in the suburbs, tied to longer, more costly commuting distance for central city employment. Likewise, employers exercise locational decisions on the basis of their sectoral activity and costs. Those demanding a relatively high ratio of space to capital will select the suburbs where land is cheaper and the once detracting factor of distance is now mitigated by enhanced and less expensive transportation. In contrast, those enterprises needing a high capital ratio to land use will be more constrained when it comes to relocation out of the central city.

One basic flaw in this theoretical position is its implicit neglect of those social strata not free to choose. As Holzer points out in this regard,[38] zoning regulations in the suburbs can effectively prohibit multi-unit affordable housing; racial discrimination can exclude blacks from the suburban housing market even if their income puts them in that market bracket. Consequently, those people compelled by such devices to reside in the central city are disadvantaged in the more promising suburban labour market. Even should a job opportunity arise, the cost and time factors involved in distance, particularly for those without private means of transport, might prove prohibitive if it should reduce net wages to at or near the 'reservation wage'. In concluding his review of 20 years of empirical work on the spatial mismatch perspective, Holzer gives a qualified endorsement of its relevance.

But whatever its validity in some places, clearly this view cannot be universally sustained. There is evidence that blacks may be physically adjacent to a vibrant labour market and remain jobless. For example, Ellwood[39] demonstrated that blacks on the west side of Chigago, where employment was buoyant, did not register a lower unemployment rate than blacks living in the job-bereft south side.

In the face of these competing claims, Kasarda[40] emphasises the combination of demographic and economic factors, and public policy response, in explaining the particularly concentrated forms of deprivation in

---

[37] For example, Tiebout, C. (1956), 'A pure theory of local expenditures', *Journal of Political Economy*, 64, October, pp. 416-24.

[38] Holzer, H. (1990), *op. cit.*

[39] Ellwood, D. (1986), 'The spatial mismatch hypothesis: are there teenage jobs missing in the ghetto?' in Freeman, R. and Holzer, H. (eds.), *The Black Youth Unemployment Crisis*, University of Chicago Press, Chicago, pp. 147-85.

[40] Kasarda, J. (1990), 'Structural factors affecting the location and timing of urban underclass growth', *Urban Geography*, vol.11, no.3, pp. 234-64.

large Northern cities. For him, the significant component on the demand side is the process whereby manufacturing jobs, offering relatively good pay for low educational attainment have been largely displaced by information-intensive jobs, requiring higher educational entry qualifications. Such trends have been exacerbated by supply-side considerations resulting from earlier migration patterns.

The selective black exodus from the ghetto, prompted by civil rights gains, left behind an imbalanced community of the least skilled and mobile. Such communities were, as a consequence, deprived not only of positive role models, and traditional jobs, but also of the multiplier impact of middle-class income. The resulting depression of economic opportunity had a deleterious effect on stable family life. It should be said that the extent and composition of black out-migration from the ghetto is contested. Between 1970 and 1980, migration patterns certainly show that both the poor and non-poor were leaving the central core, but the non-poor were leaving faster. However, some like Massey and Eggers[41] insist that the capacity of relatively affluent blacks to physically distance themselves from their poorer fellow blacks is less than for the privileged in other racial groups.

Kasarda argues that the multiple nature of the problem demands that a series of impediments to the mobility of urban core labour be addressed simultaneously, including racial discrimination, dependence on public transport, under-supply of affordable housing in the suburbs, family responsibilities and the lure of the underground economy. In a similar vein, Sullivan contends that it is the varied interplay of a number of factors which causes the deprivation in any particular instance:[42]

Although the majority of jobs are now in the suburbs, the vast majority of blacks continue to live in central cities. Moreover, an increasing share of central city jobs requires a college education, so most blacks are unable to take advantage of new job opportunities in the central city. Racial discrimination [also] contributes to the black poverty problem.

Rejecting the Underclass Label

Despite a plethora of research and theoretical discourse about the underclass in the 1980s, there is still some hostility to the term. Gans[43] sees it as part of a political project of those inimical to welfare and the poor, who, by employing a term which is value-laden and pejorative, imputes negative

[41] Massey, D. and Eggers, M. (1990), 'The ecology of inequality: minorities and the concentration of poverty', 1970-1980, *American Journal of Sociology*, vol.95, March, 1153-88.

[42] Sullivan, A. (1990), *Urban Economics*, Irwin, Boston, p. 329.

[43] Gans, H. (1990), 'Deconstructing the underclass: the term's dangers as a planning concept', *American Planning Association Journal*, no. 271, Summer.

labels onto the victims of deprivation. For him, its conceptual ambiguity permits neither rigorous calculation of the numbers involved nor precise policy prescription for its redress:[44]

....the term has taken on so many connotations of undeservingness and blameworthiness that it has become hopelessly polluted in meaning, ideological overtone and implications, and should be dropped.

Voices nearer to the right echo some of these misgivings. Peterson, for example, remarks how the concept contains:[45]

....none of the sturdiness of 'working', the banality of 'middle', or the remoteness of 'upper'. Instead 'under' suggests the lowly, passive, and submissive, yet at the same time the disreputable, dangerous, disruptive, dark, evil, and even hellish.

Certainly, calculations of the numbers involved have varied considerably, from 1.8 million by Sawhill,[46] to 4.1 million by Nathan,[47] to 8 million by Ruggles and Marton.[48] This difficulty is indicative of the general problem. For some, like Tienda,[49] features such as welfare dependence and weak attachment to the labour market are common amongst the poor in general. What particularly distinguishes the underclass is the persistence of these traits. Accepting many of the reservations of critics like Gans, Wilson concludes that it remains important for research to focus on this group. He sees a danger that the controversy now attached to the issue will repeat the experience of the fall-out of the Moynihan Report on the black family in the 1960s:[50]

The vitriolic attacks and acrimonious debate that characterised that controversy proved to be too intimidating to scholars, especially to liberal scholars. Indeed, in the aftermath of this controversy and in an effort to protect their work from the charge of racism or of 'blaming the victim', liberal social scientists tended to avoid describing any behavior that could be construed as unflattering or stigmatizing to racial minorities.

---

[44] *Ibid.*, p.272.

[45] Peterson, P. (1991), *op. cit.* p. 3.

[46] Sawhill, I. (1988), 'Poverty and the underclass', in Sawhill, I. (ed.), *Challenge to Leadership*, Urban Institute, Washington DC.

[47] Nathan, R. (1987), 'Will the underclass always be us?' *Society*, March-April.

[48] Ruggles, P. and Marton, W. (1986), 'Measuring the size and characteristics of the underclass', *mimeo*.

[49] Tienda, M. (1990), 'Welfare and work in Chicago's inner city', *The American Economic Review*, pp. 372-7.

[50] Wilson, W. (1990), *op. cit.* p.5.

Public Policy

Thirty years after the New Deal, poverty continued to afflict some 36 million Americans in the 1960s. The optimism of Johnson's Great Society programme was severely dented by three factors. First, the Vietnam war consumed economic resources and political attention that might otherwise have been devoted to the domestic War on Poverty. Second, black protest at the limited and hesitant progress on civil rights erupted into a conflagration in many urban centres, at once undoing some of the modest environmental improvements achieved, while also making it harder to sell increased social intervention to frightened and angry whites, prone to perceive extra welfare spending as appeasement of recalcitrant blacks. Third, the programmes themselves were typically fragmented and under-resourced. Nevertheless, a shift in the composition of public expenditure is perceptible. Between 1965 and 1980, the share of GNP allocated to welfare assistance, medical services, social security and food stamps doubled from 5 to 10 per cent.[51]

Certainly, compared to the 1980s, the climate of prosperity and growth in the 1960s permitted government to sell social spending as fiscally prudent. Enthusiasts of this intervention recall:[52]

....economic growth averaged 4.1 per cent a year during the 1960s, and GNP rose over 50 per cent over the decade. This meant that for the average family, real spendable income increased by a third....It was this prosperity for most Americans, combined with a growing awareness of the plight of the poor, that created a favorable climate for President Johnson's sweeping agenda for the poor.

Conservative critics of the War on Poverty contend that its achievements were unremarkable. Murray,[53] for instance, points out that the reduction in the poverty rate from 18 per cent to 12.8 per cent over the period 1964 to 1968 is roughly in line with previous trends, such as the decline from 32.7 per cent in 1949 to 19.5 per cent in 1963. In other words, despite the very modest welfarist programmes in the 1950s, there was a drop in the poverty rate not significantly different from that also witnessed in the 1960s, when state intervention was considerably enhanced. However, in the 1970s, when social spending was at its most generous in many respects, the poverty rate did not correspondingly improve. His conclusion is that there is no positive relationship between the level and range of state welfare on the one hand and rates of poverty on the other.

---

[51] Peterson, P. and Rom, M. (1988), 'Lower taxes, more spending, and budget deficits', in Jones, C. (ed.), *The Reagan Legacy: promise and performance*, Chatham, New Jersey.

[52] Markovich, D. and Pynn, R. (1988), *American Political Economy*, Brooks\Cole Publishing Company, California, p. 129.

[53] Murray, C. (1984), *op. cit.*

Peterson broadly echoes this analysis:[54]

> Poverty in the United States had been declining between 1940 and 1960, two decades in which the welfare state expanded hardly at all. Yet when the welfare state expanded in the 1970s, progress toward eliminating poverty came to a halt. What is more, poverty increased among young families and inner city residents.

This seems to support the official government argument that the only real panacea for poverty lies with economic growth and productivity improvements. From 1950 through to 1970, real GNP rose at an average yearly rate of 3.5 per cent, and productivity improved at an average annual rate of 2.3 per cent. In constant 1989 dollars, average weekly earnings increased from $273 in 1950 to $383 in 1970. The average income of families in the bottom fifth of the income distribution increased 81 per cent in constant dollars. Their proportion of all family income rose from 4.5 per cent to 5.5 per cent. In the period 1970 to 1980, when GNP grew at only 2.8 per cent annually and non-agricultural productivity dropped to 1.1 per cent each year, the average income of families in the bottom fifth of the income bands fell 4 per cent in real terms. After the economic slowdown in the early 1980s, growth brought with it improvements in median income. As mentioned earlier, poverty rates dropped from a high of 15.2 per cent in 1983 to 12.8 per cent in 1989.[55]

The difficulty here lies in disaggregating the effects of welfare intervention and economic growth on the poor. One attempt at an estimation concludes:[56]

> Economic expansion between 1965 and 1972 lifted out of poverty perhaps only one-tenth of the 21.3 per cent of Americans who were below the poverty line in 1965; government programs lifted more than half of the rest above the poverty line.

Overall, what can be said about the 1960s is that the gap between want and wealth was reduced rather than closed. With the onset of stagflation in the 1970s, social need bulged while, by the end of the decade, fiscal pressures mounted for the federal purse to tighten. Disillusionment among some sections of blue-collar workers with welfarism cannot be attributed exclusively to their conversion to unfettered liberal capitalism. As Skocpol

---

[54] Peterson, P. (1991), 'The urban underclass and the poverty paradox', in Jencks, C. and Peterson, P. (eds.), *op. cit.*, pp. 11-12.

[55] *Budget of the US Government, Fiscal Year 1992* (1992), US Government Printing Office, Washington DC.

[56] Brown, M. (1988), The segmented welfare system: distributive conflict and retrenchment in the United States, 1968-1984, in Brown, M. (ed.), *Remaking the Welfare State: retrenchment and social policy in America and Europe*, Temple University Press.

points out,[57] in the 1970s, real median family income dropped by 16 per cent while, at the same time, regressive taxes were increasing. The combination of a rising tax burden and falling living standards was a significant determination of the electoral desertion of blue-collar workers from the Democratic party in the 1980 election.

Between 1950 and 1979, government social spending rose from $23.5 billion to $430.6 billion, a factor of 19. In per capita terms, spending rose from $153 to $1,916 over this period, a 13-fold increase.[58] The relative continuity of welfarist policies, particularly from Johnson through Nixon to Carter, was challenged by the new presidency in 1980. Focus was shifted from welfare to work, ironically at a time when many more were being made workless by economic forces beyond their control. As mentioned in the previous chapter, this transition coincided with a more sceptical appraisal of the capacity of 'big government' to deliver people from their financial travails.

This criticism was partly founded on a concern that traditional, spatially targeted welfare programmes merely served to tie residents to those spaces. There was also a belief that affirmative action schemes which succeeded in moving some blacks to the suburbs, left behind a more concentrated and violent ghetto, which became a less desirable business location. The consequent business exodus further eroded the job opportunities for those residents remaining. In a similar vein, providing more employment opportunities for women could be seen as increasing competition for jobs, which had a negative impact on young black employment. In other words, each government intervention designed to achieve one effect, could readily produce a deterioration elsewhere for the poor.

The government has acknowledged the paradox, despite the achievement of creating 20 million jobs in the 1980s, that it has been most difficult to bring jobs to those who have most needed them. Again, the tendency has been to blame the underclass:[59]

> The need to increase employment is particularly acute among the minority populations in high poverty urban areas, a group that is sometimes referred to as the underclass....In areas of concentrated poverty and deprivation, however, there is evidence of high rates of drug use, low educational achievement, high rates of teenage pregnancy, and alienation from legitimate employment.

In the social policy component of Reaganomics, there have been continuities and departures. Aid to Families With Dependent Children (AFDC)

---

[57] Skocpol, T. (1991), 'Targeting within universalism: Politically viable policies to combat poverty in the United States', in Jencks, C. and Peterson, P. (eds.), *op. cit.*

[58] Stoesz, D. and Karger, H. (1991), The corporatisation of the United States welfare state, *Journal of Social Policy*, vol. 20, part 2, April, pp.157-71.

[59] Economic Report to the President (1990), *op. cit.*, p.174.

remained a central welfare benefit. Traceable back to the depression years of the 1930s, the programme is designed to supplement the income of poor families with children, and is funded by both federal and state governments. The rate of payment is set by individual states, giving rise to large variations. In some states families, receiving food stamps and AFDC, can obtain benefits below 50 per cent of the national poverty line, while in other states they are at 100 per cent.

In some states concern about long term reliance on these benefits led to the introduction of 'workfare' schemes, whereby recipients were required to participate in work search and placement programmes. Nominally designed to bolster the labour market prospects of those with irregular work histories, these schemes were intended to be especially advantageous to women. The 1988 Family Support Act universalised this principle across the US. All those in receipt of AFDC who are considered eligible, are now compelled to take part in JOBS (Job Opportunities and Basic Skills Training). This programme provides child-care support and, for a year after leaving AFDC, an individual is entitled to Medicaid and child-care assistance to reduce the likelihood of a 'poverty trap' in their employment. The government is opposed to bearing alone the financial costs of the new dependencies generated. In this respect, it has addressed the issue of parental irresponsibility, exemplified, it feels, in the underpayment of child support:[60]

> In 1987, only 44 per cent of poor female-headed families with children had child support awards, and only 72 per cent of these families (32 per cent of all poor female-headed families) received child support payments, many of which were less than the award.

Government's keenness to ensure that fathers are made to be financially responsible for their children can pose problems. For example, absentee fathers may, of course, themselves be out of work or on low earnings, and thereby incapable of paying child support. Moreover, the support payment is substracted from the AFDC benefit. Besides this, obliging fathers to pay child support threatens to put their wives into a 'dependent' relationship, and in cases where there is a history of domestic violence, this is unwelcome. Certainly in circumstances where the mother is in paid employment, such transfers could represent a genuine supplement to income and, accordingly, be helpful.

These measures cannot substitute for the fact that federal spending on social provision has been severely reduced in the 1980s. Between 1981 and 1992 federal support for subsidised housing dropped by 82 per cent; for job training and employment aid by 63 per cent; and for community service and development programmes by approximately 40 per cent. In the 1980s the average urban budget doubled, yet the federal contribution declined from 17

---

[60] *Ibid.*, p.171.

to 6 per cent.[61] Despite the government's ability to reasonably combine economic and job growth for most of the last decade, the persistence of widespread poverty, contradicts the glib assumptions about an automatic trickle-down benefit of growth to the most disadvantaged. Growth can be beneficial to the poorest, if only because of the standard practice of them being the last to be hired and the first to be fired. But clearly growth in itself is insufficient. The continued existence of a large poor population suggests that in the absence of specific targeting of investment, training and support services to the most deprived communities, the benefits of growth can by-pass them. The dilemma is how to achieve a targeting which does not become a cover for residualisation. As Skocpol argues, universalist programmes remain essential:[62]

> If social policies targeted exclusively on the poor have not fared well politically, more universal policies that have spread costs and visibly delivered benefits across classes and races have recurrently flourished. Broad political coalitions have developed to protect and extend these policies.

Amongst the policies which he thinks both fit this bill and offer opportunities to the poor are: child support assurance for all single parents, parental leave and child-care assistance for all working families, job training and relocation assistance for redundant workers and new entrants to the labour market, and universal health care.

The Politics of the Underclass Debate

Because poverty is popularly perceived as typically a 'black' phenomenon, the politics of welfare can become conflated with those of race. Ironically, the association of the liberal tradition with programmes of affirmative action has enabled Republican ideologues to present their platform as the only one genuinely faithful to the American dream of equal opportunity.[63]

> Conservative populism has permitted the Republican party to replace in the minds of many voters the idea of an 'establishment' ruled by business interests with a hated new liberal establishment adversarial to the common man; an elite - of judges, bureaucrats, newspaper editors, ACLU lawyers, academics, Democratic politicians, civil rights and feminist leaders - determined to enact racially and socially redistributive policies demanding the largest sacrifices from the white working and lower middle classes.

---

[61] The Centre on Budget and Public Priorities, Washington DC (1992), quoted in Walker, M. 'Less welfare, more wafare', *The Guardian*, 6/5/1992.

[62] Skocpol, T. (1991), *op. cit.*, p.420.

[63] Edsall, T. and Edsall, M. (1991), 'Race', *The Atlantic Monthly*, vol.267, no.5, May, p.54.

The dilemma for Democrats is acute. They cannot generate electoral majorities in presidential elections by constructing 'rainbow coalitions' of the most politically marginalised and economically dispossessed. Appeal to a substantial section of the relatively secure middle class is essential to electoral success. Many people in this category are susceptible to an analysis of poverty and the underclass which focuses more on factors such as family 'disorganisation' and drug dependency than on the ramifications of structural economic change. Once issues of welfare, work and family become inseparable from race, it is tempting for Democrats to be silent. They can become trapped between their sensitivities to minority populations from which they traditionally draw their core base of support, and their fear that association with welfare promotion is an electoral liability.

Any failure to confront and engage with these disputes allows their Republican opponents to interpret their reticence as connivance in the 'irresponsible' lifestyles of sections of the poor. An alternative reaction has come from the revisionist wing of the Democratic party, which wants to signal a clear retreat from the association of the party with welfarism. This would be comparable to committing suicide to avoid being murdered. It also underestimates the potential for engendering support for social spending. The results of a nationwide poll, conducted by Hart and Teeter for the Wall St. Journal/NBC News in May 1991,[64] indicate the basis of such support, as well as highlighting the critical racial differences in social perceptions. On the consensus side, 78 per cent of all voters believed that poverty had worsened during the 1980s, and two thirds - with 61 per cent of whites and 88 per cent of blacks - felt that federal spending was inadequate to combat it. A less impressive majority - 57 per cent - including a majority of whites and over eight in 10 blacks, agreed with the need for affirmative action programmes for blacks and other minorities.

However, the white approval rating for such intervention may be quite volatile, since elsewhere in the survey there is a sharp divergence of views about the significance of racial disadvantage. While 70 per cent of blacks thought that blacks were victims of discrimination, only a quarter of whites concurred, with one out of five whites believing that blacks were recipients of 'too many special advantages'. Only 39 per cent of whites approve of government making special provision for blacks and other minorities to compensate for past discrimination, whereas black voters favour such treatment by 82 per cent to 11 per cent. Also illustrated in the findings is the degree of dissension amongst minorities themselves. For instance, while a majority of blacks believe that Hispanics also face discrimination, they do not accept that this is true for Asian-Americans. Thus, it is not a simple black and white issue. There is a general concern about poverty, and support for greater spending to achieve its eradication, but this consensus fragments

---

[64] The survey is reported in detail in 'Voters' responses to poll disclose huge chasm between social attitudes of blacks and whites', *The Wall Street Journal*, (5/17/1991).

when the relationship of deprivation to race is introduced.

The challenge for the Democratic party is to confront, rather than dismiss, the basic propositions of their political opponents, which find resonance with sections of their traditional blue-collar vote. This involves summoning convincing arguments to counter Murray's provocative assertion that a small, but significant, section of the poor are not so much deprived as degenerate. For him, and fellow adherents of the right, the liberal view of the homogeneity of the poor is empirically unsupportable. In their view, while the majority retain values of decency, diligence and discipline, a growing minority live a hedonistic lifestyle, preferring leisure over labour, consumption over thrift, and indulgence in intoxicating substances over sobriety. The problem with them is not so much a lack of money as of manners.

In this sense, the 'underclass' does not refer to the extent of poverty, but to a type of poverty. In particular the young males of this group, lured by the exhilarations of the street, are prone to casual violence, imitating the macho personalities they respect. This is said to be accentuated because they often lack alternative authoritative role-models such as fathers. Murray does not equate this only with female-headed families. The specific difficulty, to which he attributes much responsibility, is the growing rate of 'illegitimacy'. He argues that while lone parenthood can arise from all kinds of exigencies:[65]

".....illegitimacy bespeaks an attitude on the part of one or both parents that getting married is not an essential part of siring or giving birth to a child".

Typically, the liberal/left response to these contentions has been to classify them as 'cultural' and, accordingly, deficient. More recently, there has been a belated recognition that for a section of the poor, the problem is not just that they have become marginal to the system of production, but that they have also become marginal to the system of reproduction. In other words, parenting skills may be relevant to the improvement of their situation, and not merely a convenient means to distract blame from structural causes.

In this respect, there is a need to progress beyond the old division between a right, ever ready to offer cultural explanations, and a left, prone to a reflexive retort about structural causes. The problem for the exclusive obsession of conservatives is that poverty, to say nothing of the underclass, did not diminish in the 1980s, despite the realisation of their objectives of market liberalisation and more limited welfare. Equally, the dilemma for those who espouse only structural theories is that they are not always able convincingly to demonstrate that improvements in structural factors produce some correspondence in the position or reaction of the disadvantaged.

---

[65] Murray, C.(1990), *The Emerging British Underclass,* Welfare Series no.2, Health and Welfare unit, IEA, London, p. 5.

Conclusion

Because of an unease in the US about discourse on class, the attention given to the underclass has been predominantly in terms of symptoms - rising levels of crime and violence, drug abuse, high numbers of public school drop-outs and teenage pregnancy. These features, though subject to sensational media coverage, engender real fears in many people that their spread may 'contaminate' the wider society. Such a context provides great opportunity for rash solutions to supersede rational ones.

Conservatives, opposed to state regulation of market inequities, present an up-beat message of opportunity, which resonates with American mythology about the early frontier. The inference is that 'bleeding heart' welfare campaigners not only carp and moan but ultimately sell America short. For example, the president of the US Chamber of Commerce, Mr. Lesher, refuses to acknowledge the existence of widespread racial discrimination. Speaking against the 1990 Civil Rights Bill, which at first Mr. Bush vetoed, he noted: 'If people are persuaded our society is permeated with bias, they are tempted to lose heart and quit trying. Such defeatism is truly tragic, for in reality our society is remarkably free of discrimination, and anyone with gumption and ability can make it.'[66]

The debate about the 1990 Civil Rights Bill reflected much of the dilemma about positive discrimination. It has been suggested that affirmative action, at best, reaches those middle class blacks who could likely succeed anyway, and absolves white middle class guilt while, at the same time, raising the wrath of working class whites, particularly at a time of economic dislocation. As the events in Los Angeles have demonstrated, the polarisation that President Johnson predicted in an address to Congress in 1965 still threatens US society; 'if we stand passively by while the centre of each city becomes a hive of deprivation, crime, and hopelessness...if we become two people, the suburban affluent and the urban poor, each filled with mistrust and fear for the other...then we shall effectively cripple each generation to come.'[67]

---

[66] Quoted in *Business and Society Review*, no.77, Spring 1991, p.5.

[67] Quoted in *The Economist* (1991),op. cit., p. 12.

5. Unemployment in the EC: The Limits to Corporatism

In the 30 years following the signing of the Treaties of Rome, the membership of the European Economic Community doubled, making it the world's largest trading bloc. It accounted for 22 per cent of world imports and 21 per cent of the world's exports in 1984, if trade within the Community itself is excluded from the calculation.[1] This was marginally greater than the share of world trade held by the US and substantially more than that of Japan. At this level, the Community has been a major success story - the biggest trading bloc, the biggest concentration of high income consumers and, in aggregate terms, the second largest GDP on the planet. It has been the dominant economic fact of European history since the Second World War, overshadowing and eventually dismembering its only rivals, the European Free Trade Association and Comecon.

At the same time, the Community has experienced substantial inequalities in its distribution of wealth, income and jobs. For example, in 1958 the per capita income in Southern Italy was only 65 per cent of its national average. Indeed, it was calculated that the per capita income of the most favoured region (Hamburg) was about seven times that of the least favoured (Calabria).[2] Although the income figure for southern Italy had risen to 68.7 per cent of the Italian average by 1978, GDP per head in that year was no more than 54 per cent of the Community average.[3] Thus, there remained significant imbalances in the economic performance of its different regions. The enlargement of the Community in 1973 brought in the UK with its own serious regional problems, exemplified by Northern Ireland, and the late developing economy of the Irish Republic. Three more newly industrialising economies, Greece, Spain and Portugal, joined in the 1980s. This latest expansion 'increased Community GDP by 10 per cent, population by 22 per

---

[1] Palmer, J. (1988), *Trading Places*. Radius, London, p.14.

[2] Swann, D. (1984), *The Economics of the Common Market*, Pelican, Middlesex, p.264.

[3] Nevin, E.T. (1982), 'Regional policy', in El-Agrad, A.M. (ed.), *The Economics of the European Community*, Philip Allan, Oxford, p.345.

cent and employment in agriculture by 57 per cent.'[4] By the mid-1980s, the Community had become a conglomerate of extreme diversity. GDP, income and employment grew rapidly in the core regions. However, areas in the northern periphery, particularly in the UK, France and Belgium, saw sharp declines in their manufacturing bases accompanied by serious unemployment. The southern periphery of Spain, Portugal, Greece and southern Italy remained substantially underdeveloped even though some areas saw rapid economic growth.

For over 30 years the Community has sustained a combination of rapid development with underdevelopment. In the 1980s, a 'golden triangle', located in the area bounded by southern England, Milan and Copenhagan, defined the centre and, surrounding this, were areas suffering varying degrees of marginalisation. Development differences survived periods of overall Community growth and became exacerbated during recession. Thus, any analysis of unemployment within the Community must focus not merely on overall trends, but also on the differential unemployment within and between member states. Accordingly, while the purpose of this chapter is to provide an overview of unemployment within the EC, it is also important to examine the relationship between the unemployment experiences of its constituent parts and to assess the possible impact of the Single Market on employment trends post-992.

Labour Markets in the Common Market

When the Treaty of Rome was signed in 1957, the stated objective was for balanced development:[5]

> The Community shall have as its task, by establishing a common market and progressively approximating the economic policies of the member states, to promote throughout the Community a harmonious development of economic activities, a continuous balanced expansion, an increase in stability, an accelerated standard of living and closer relations between the States belonging to it.

This goal was to be achieved by creating: a free trade area with neither tariffs nor quotas on the trade between the member states; a customs union with a standard level of tariffs on goods entering the Community; and a common market in which factors of production could freely move within it. The longer term goal was to create an economic union in which non-tariff barriers would also be removed, accompanied by a harmonisation of the monetary and fiscal policies of the member states.

---

[4] Hitiris, T. (1991), *European Community Economics*, Harvester Wheatsheaf, London, p.237.

[5] Rajan, A. (1990), *A Zero Sum Game*, The Industrial Society Press, London, p.8.

The core assumption was of economic liberalism whereby the spur of competition within a supra-national market would promote the rapid development of firms, facilitating overall economic growth. Article 92 of the Treaty of Rome expressly declared that state aid which destroyed competition would be incompatible with the Common Market. As the Community achieved growth, the gains were expected to 'trickle down' to all its parts, improving the welfare of all its citizens. The benefits were to be both static and dynamic. The former were to accrue from increased competition and expanded trade within an existing structure of production, the latter from improvements in the allocation and utilisation of resources within and among the member states, greater specialisation associated with comparative advantage and the achievement of economies of scale in production.[6] For both kinds of benefit, the driving force was to be largely deregulated markets in which obstacles to competition had been removed.

However, economic liberalism was the main, but not the exclusive, influence in the construction of the Common Market. The political complexion of the member states was Christian democratic or social democratic. Although the former's approach to social intervention was based on the principle of subsidiarity - the state only has a role when other societal institutions have failed - Christian democratic governments, for example in Italy, had already created large state-owned economic agencies to facilitate post-war reconstruction. Moreover, until the stagflation crises of the 1970s, social democrats were firmly rooted in Keynesian economic management. Both these types of government operated a conditional corporatism in which business and trade unions were involved in economic management. In some states, like West Germany, trade unions were represented on the boards of corporations. Accordingly, the Treaty of Rome embraced not just economic liberalism, but also declared a set of social objectives including equal pay for men and women, the development of vocational training and the maintenance of high levels of employment. Since most of the member states were experiencing substantial growth, little attention was given to the possible contradiction between economic liberalism, expressed in the provisions designed to maximise competition, and the corporatism manifested in the treaty's social objectives. Equally, since patterns of underdevelopment within the Community were less pronounced in its early years (Ireland, Greece, Portugal and Spain were not yet members), the difficulties in harmonising social provision were less apparent.

Thus, the principles of deregulation and competition were compromised in three ways.
• The most obvious was the Common Agricultural Policy (CAP) which established intervention prices and a commitment to buy up surpluses for agricultural produce. While the intention was to promote stability in agricultural production, it also appeased the politically significant

---

[6] See Hitiris, L. T. (1991), *op.cit.*, pp.1-33.

agricultural lobbies, particularly in France and West Germany. Since the CAP subsidised production, the highest levels of support went to the largest producers with only marginal benefits to smallholdings. As a production incentive it was highly successful, but generated huge surpluses which either had to be stored at high cost or resold below the intervention price. Indeed, in the early 1990s, one of the most pressing problems facing the Community has been the reform of the CAP, not merely because of its drain on the Community budget, but also because it has become a major obstacle to the completion of the Uruguay round of the GATT talks. The CAP has provided an impulse towards economies of scale, but cannot be said to have induced the most efficient allocation of resources.

• Second, the continuing regional imbalances within the Community, which were underlined by its expansion in 1973, created the need for regional development policies. These have been tentative and far from comprehensive. In the first instance, they consisted of no more than attempts to harmonise the regional policies of the member states. Later they took the form of the European Regional Development Fund, the resources of which were predominantly allocated to underdeveloped regions. The Social Fund, already in existence, was designed to provide resources for training and to promote labour mobility.

Moreover, following the Paris summit of 1972, a declaration was issued stressing the need for social as well as economic development. This was followed by an action programme, which the Commission submitted to the Council of Ministers covering such issues as workers' rights, sex discrimination and minimum wage thresholds. The response by the Council of Ministers was a declared commitment to '....full and better employment at Community, national and regional levels, which is an essential condition for an effective social policy.' Despite the apparent rediscovery of the principles of the UK's Beveridge Report, the statement refused to endorse the notion of common standards or the assumption by the Community of responsibilities better carried out by the member states.[7]

The Community also developed anti-poverty programmes of which there have been three so far. All have been criticised for the small level of resources involved, inadequate targeting and bureaucratic administration. Nevertheless, they clearly represent a departure from market-based solutions to social and economic problems.

• Finally, some of those most seriously committed to the development of the Community have argued that the pressures of economic development point to the necessity for a political union, at least in the form of a federal Europe. This would be accompanied by a single central bank, a single currency and significantly greater direction from the centre. Their opponents have

---

[7] Roberts, B. (1989), 'The social dimension of European labour markets', in Dahrendorf, R. (ed.), *Competing Visions for 1992*, IEA, London, pp.41-2.

countered with a vision of a free association of sovereign member states committed to trade liberalisation and the free movement of labour and capital. The archetypical representatives of these positions in the 1980s were Jacques DeLors and Margaret Thatcher, though Charles de Gaulle in 1962 first described the latter concept of the Community: '....there is and can be no Europe other than a Europe of the States - except, of course, for myths, fictions and pageants.'[8]

Post-Thatcher Britain has been essentially ambivalent about these two positions. At the Maastricht summit in December 1991, the new British prime minister secured an 'opt out' clause on the development of a single currency and forced an exclusion of the 'social chapter' from the agreement. It was not clear whether this was a principled action, designed to reinforce sovereignty, or a form of procrastination to appease the anti-Europeans within the Conservative party. Moreover since the Maastricht agreement, doubts have been raised in Germany about the costs of economic integration. The experience of German reunification, with its necessary fiscal transfers, raised taxes and the slowing down of German economic growth, has pointed to the probable costs should Germany be required to similarly subsidise the economic and social integration of the Community.

It remains to be seen whether the Community post-Maastricht, and indeed the Commission post-DeLors, can sustain the dynamic for full political and economic union with appropriate social provision. Given the example of Britain's opt-out at Maastricht, some of the less developed members may regard EC social provision as adding to their production costs and undermining competitiveness in an integrated market. Alternatively, Britain may feel sufficiently marginalised to make a new commitment to monetary union and the social chapter. The result of the UK general election, with the re-election of the Conservatives in 1992, may have been decisive in this respect. The UK prime minister may feel sufficiently confident to jettison opposition to full European integration with many 'European sceptics' having left parliament. At the same time however, the Maastricht agreement looks less secure on a range of other issues. The Irish government was refused permission to amend the protocol that supported its constitutional ban on abortion. Denmark, which requires a referendum to ratify Maastricht, has been facing increasing internal opposition which may secure a 'no' vote. Germany is concerned with giving up the Deutschmark for a single European currency.[9]

So far, the Community has been guided by a qualified economic liberalism. Certainly, this has generated an impressive record of growth, but its labour markets have not been insulated from the pressures which produce

---

[8] Pinder, J. (1991), *European Community: The building of a union*, Opus, Oxford University Press, Oxford, p.11.

[9] Marshall, A. (12/4/1992), 'Maastricht begins to split at the seams', *The Independent on Sunday*.

unemployment. The entire Community has been subject to the cyclical and structural changes evidenced in all the advanced economies. Moreover, a certain set of member states showed only sluggish recovery in employment following the 1979-81 recession while, at the same time, it was evident that the Community as a whole could not match the recovery rates of the US or Japan.[10] A document released by the Commission in February 1992 revealed that between 1985 and 1990 the Community's balance of manufactured goods declined by 66 billion ECUs. In the latter year only 17 per cent of the Community's exports were high technology goods compared to 31 per cent of US manufacturing exports and 27 per cent those of Japan.[11] The weakness of the EC economy, relative to its major rivals, was most visible in the 1980s when the possibility, rather than the desirability, of full employment was seriously doubted.

Table 5.1 indicates the increase both in unemployment rates and long-term unemployment in the decade after 1975. It refers only to those countries which were members of the Community then. Not only were there substantial increases in unemployment in each member state, but the rates of long-term unemployment rose alarmingly. Even Denmark, where the growth of unemployment was lowest, saw a three-fold rise in long-term unemployment.

By 1985, almost half of all the unemployed in Europe 9 had been out of work for a year or more. There were also substantial differences between the member states. The difference between the lowest rates (Luxembourg) and the highest (Ireland) was 15 percentage points. Of the four biggest member states, the UK had consistently the highest rates of unemployment although Italy had the greatest concentration of long-term unemployment. By the mid-1980s, it appeared that the era of full employment in the Community had decisively ended.

In contrast, the unemployment rate in the US actually fell between 1975 and 1985, from 8.5 to 7.2 per cent. Moreover, throughout the 1980s, there was a negative correlation between changes in unemployment and GDP in the US. In other words, as GDP grew, unemployment fell, and *vice versa*. The opposite was true for Europe. Unemployment and GDP had a correlation coefficient of .53.[12] Thus, economic growth in the Community was not associated with decreases in overall unemployment.

---

[10] The Northern Ireland Economic Council and the National Economic and Social Council (1988), *Economic Implications for Northern Ireland and the Republic of Ireland of Recent Developments in the European Community*, Belfast & Dublin, p.2.2.

[11] Commission of the European Communities (1992), *From the single act to Maastricht and beyond*, Brussels, p.24.

[12] Pearsons correlation matrix calculated from tables 3 and 5, Commission of the European Communities (1990), *European Economy*, Brussels, December.

Table 5.1   Unemployment and Long-term Unemployment within the Community, 1975-85.

	1975		1985	
	Unemployed %	Long-term %	Unemployed %	Long-term %
Belgium	3.2	29.7	11.3	68.2
Denmark	6.8	9.4	7.8	32.0
W.Germany	2.9	11.8	6.9	46.9
France	3.3	16.3	10.3	43.8
Ireland	9.6	19.1	18.0	62.2
Italy	3.3	33.8	9.2	63.6
L'bourg	0.6	-	3.0	36.8
N'lands	3.2	18.6	10.5	56.4
UK	4.6	14.8	11.5	48.7
EUR 9	3.7	18.4	9.6	48.5

Note: The unemployment percentages are standardised rates taken from Labour Force Surveys. The long-term unemployment percentages represent the proportion of all the unemployed out of work for one year or more.

Source: *Final Report on the Second European Poverty Programme*, European Commission, 1991, tables A15 and A16

Curiously the Community's GDP/employment threshold was lower in the 1980s than during the previous decade. This threshold represents the minimum level of growth of real GDP that must be reached before employment begins to increase. In the period 1961-73 the average for Europe 12 was 4.4 per cent of GDP growth falling to 1.9 per cent for 1979-85.[13] The downward trend is explained by the growth of part-time employment, the reduction in average working time and the continuing movement of production away from manufacturing towards services. Since unemployment was relatively unaffected by the improvement in the GDP/employment ratio, it is likely that new labour market entrants took a high proportion of new jobs. This corresponded with the increasing labour market participation rates for women over the period. In fact between 1985 and 1990 a 6.7 per cent increase in total employment resulted only in a 2.4 per cent decrease in unemployment.

Unemployment did rise in Japan, but the rate in 1985 was 2.6 per cent, substantially lower than that of any member of the Community other than Luxembourg.[14] The very small size of Luxembourg, relative to Japan, reduces the validity of any comparison. The Community as a whole had a rate of unemployment three and a half times greater than that of Japan.

---

[13] Commission of the European Communities (1991), *European Economy, no.50*, December, Brussels, pp.134-9.

[14] *Ibid.*, table 3.

Certain groups within the Community experienced higher than average unemployment. This was true generally for young people and women. In some states (Belgium, Spain, West Germany, Greece, Italy and the Netherlands), the unemployment rate for women was around twice that for men. In all other states with the exception of the UK, it was visibly greater. Since the data represented harmonised unemployment rates, the fact that the UK unemployment count under-represents women does not account for all of this difference. In fact, the UK government unemployment rates for 1990 were 7.5 per cent for men and 3.5 per cent for women - the divergence is even more marked.[15] The more likely explanation is the very high participation in part-time employment by women in the UK, which having increased during the economic boom of the mid-1980s, reduced their unemployment rates relative to other women in the Community. Table 5.2 describes unemployment rates for men, women and young people for each member state in April 1990.

Apart from West Germany, the unemployment rate for young people in every member state was higher than the average unemployment rate. West Germany's education system and advanced training programmes for young people may explain its exceptional status. In some cases, the levels of youth unemployment are extremely high: nearly a third of young people in Spain and Italy, a quarter in Greece and a fifth in Ireland. This is clearly the group most generally vulnerable to unemployment within the Community.

Table 5.2	Unemployment Rates in the Community, April 1990			
	Total	Men	Women	Age< 25
Belgium	7.6	6.5	11.1	13.1
Denmark	7.9	7.2	8.8	11.1
W.Germany	5.2	3.9	7.2	4.7
France	8.7	6.5	11.5	16.9
Spain	16.4	12.1	24.3	32.1
Greece	7.8	4.9	12.7	26.1
Ireland	15.3	14.8	16.3	20.6
Italy	8.9	6.5	15.9	29.1
L'bourg	1.5	1.0	2.3	2.9
N'lands	8.0	5.8	11.4	11.0
Portugal	4.9	3.4	6.9	10.7
UK	6.3	6.7	5.7	8.9
Source:	Eurostat, (1991), 'Basic Statistics of the Community, Brussels', tables 3.23-3.30			

Thus, the 1980s saw substantial increases in unemployment within all of the Community's labour markets. This was accompanied by dramatic

---

[15] *Employment Gazette* (1991), August, table 2.1, pp. s22-s23.

increases in the percentage of the unemployed out of work for a year or more and, with few exceptions, women and young people were the most vulnerable groups.

Explanations for Unemployment

There have been a variety of explanations for the slower growth and higher unemployment of the Community relative to its major competitors during the 1980s. The Community's own explanation focused on the persistence of non-tariff barriers to the free movement of goods, capital and labour, coupled with the pursuit of individualistic policies by the member states. The solution was therefore to be found in the elimination of this 'non-Europe' factor through the creation of a wholly integrated, and openly competitive, market, hence the Single European Act.[16] Thus in an important sense the most recent impulse to Community integration represents a restatement of the economic liberalism which influenced the provisions of the Treaty of Rome in 1957.

Other explanations point to the more general failures of market systems. Economic liberals argue not only that markets are necessary to the functioning of an economy, but also that markets are sufficient for balanced economic development. This position may underestimate both the extent of market failure and the necessity for compensatory mechanisms. Market failure occurs in a number of situations.

• Markets are rarely characterised by perfect information available to buyers and sellers. While the price mechanism does transmit considerable information though a single signal - the actual price of the good in question - individuals are not usually aware of all the different prices that occur across the market place. Without perfect information, transactions frequently occur which represent less than the optimum allocation of resources. This information deficiency is accentuated in the capital goods market since long-term investment is based on estimates of future information. A tendency towards caution in this respect can result in under-investment for the economy as a whole.

• There may also be a conflict between general market needs and the capacity of individuals to supply them. For example, employers may be reluctant to invest in training if competitors can attract the trained labour with marginally higher wage rates. Yet, without training, there will be few gains in labour productivity.

• Markets are not efficient in dealing with 'spill-over' effects where the benefits to those trading in a particular market are offset by adverse consequences for those outside the market. The continued use of production processes which damage the environment is the most obvious example of

---

[16] The Cecchini Report (1988), *1992: The benefits of a Single Market*, Wildwood House Ltd., Aldershot.

this tendency: 'As a general rule, markets tend to allocate too few resources to goods in which the spillover effects from traders to other parties are positive, like health care or education, and too much to products with negative external effects'.[17]

• With the dominance of transnational companies, oligopolistic conditions abound and these raise real barriers to market entry by new firms.

As Estrin and Winter comment: 'The general point is that, while markets may be excellent for fine-tuning responses to changing demand and technology, they may not be good at stimulating large, non-marginal changes in the structure of the economy.'[18] Markets can only work effectively if there is an adequate infrastructure to compensate/regulate for conditions of market failure. When they are not working effectively, high unemployment is the most likely consequence.

While the EC has made substantial efforts to create conditions of maximum competition, it has remained institutionally undeveloped - the Commission has about the same number of staff as a large local authority in England - and has hence failed to develop an appropriate market supporting/restraining infrastructure.[19] Its belated attempts to do so in the 1980s were hindered by members like Britain, which had themselves embraced market liberalism and were reluctant to see social regulation reimposed from Brussels. Without such institutions, the Community's recovery has tended to be sluggish in conditions of market crisis, such as in the period following the oil shocks when unemployment rose. A counter-argument would claim that the US has an even less developed infrastructure to compensate for market failure but, in that case, the role of military Keynesianism, particularly under Reagan, was crucial in accelerating economic growth.

It should be said, however, that the 1980s was dominated by theories about the efficacy of marketised relations. As indicated in Chapter one, Keynesian solutions appeared to be decisively discredited by 1970s stagflation. Even a French socialist government's initial commitment to a demand-led economic recovery resulted in fiscal deficits and inflationary growth. Subsequent fiscal prudence on the part the French government reduced inflation to 2.9 per cent but unemployment rose to 3 million.[20] It was thus unlikely that the Community would adopt policies running counter to deregulated markets while nearly every member state was pushing market

---

[17] Estrin, S. and Winter, D. (1989), 'Planning in a market socialist economy', in Le grand, J. and Estrin, S. (eds.), *Market Socialism*, Clarendon Press, Oxford, p.108.

[18] *Ibid.*, p.112.

[19] For a fuller discussion of this issue see Grahl,J. and Teague, P. (1990), *1992: The big market*, Lawrence & Wishart, London, pp.17-60.

[20] Brummer, A. 'Problems remain no matter what the political flavour', *The Guardian*, (21/3/1992).

deregulation. Moreover, between 1958 and 1972, the necessity for a market-regulating infrastructure was less obvious. The period was one of constant economic growth, full employment and national economies managed mainly on Keynesian principles.

At a different level, it may be argued that the very existence of the Community is responsible for unemployment in most of the member states. The operation of a customs union created a situation whereby the dominant economy, West Germany, was able to distribute its output throughout the other members in the form of exports. For example in 1987, West Germany had a trade surplus amounting to 4 per cent of GDP. Belgium, Luxembourg, Denmark, France, Italy, the Netherlands and the UK had a combined trading deficit with West Germany in manufactures amounting to nearly 35 billion ECUs.[21] If that figure is divided by the average real wage in Germany, an estimate can be made of the additional jobs created by this export performance. In turn, the broadening of the tax base associated with the extra employment helped finance an advanced social welfare infrastructure and underpinned corporatism among the major economic actors.

In contrast, the members with trading deficits suffered a loss of employment proportionate to the ratio between their deficit and their real wage. In a complementary fashion, their tax base was weakened by the gap in employee tax contributions and the benefits' costs of unemployment. Thus, the price of the German economic miracle has been paid essentially by the other states of the Community.

This argument, advanced by Tony Cutler and his associates, implies that any customs union which has an economically dominant, successfully exporting member, will experience severe imbalances in unemployment. However, even without the existence of the EC, other European countries might have developed a large appetite for German manufactured goods. The real employment effect could only be calculated by subtracting the hypothetical effect - had the EC not been created but where West German exports would still be penetrating other countries' markets - from the actual effect on current trading balances. Although this exercise would be impractical, the concept of net trading effect suggests that the function of the EC, in permitting trading imbalances to develop, might be substantially less than postulated.

The differential rates of unemployment among countries have been extensively analysed by Goran Therborn who looked at the experience of 16 advanced industrial economies between 1974 and 1984.[22] Seven of these were members of the European Community. Therborn's argument was that 1974 represented not just a watershed between full employment and mass

[21] Cutler, T. Haslam, C. Williams, J. and Williams, K. (1989), *1992: The struggle for Europe*, Berg, New York, p.26.

[22] Therborn, G. (1986), *Why some peoples are more unemployed than others*, Verso, London.

unemployment within the market economies, but also a divergence in the unemployment rates of different countries. Countries could be divided into mass unemployment (more than 10%), medium high unemployment (5-10%) and low unemployment categories (less than 5%). This categorisation was more than just a distribution of unemployment rates at a particular point in time. Without radical policy changes, such differences were expected to persist until the end of the decade. EEC members in the first group included Belgium, the Netherlands, Britain and Denmark. Italy, France and West Germany were located in the second group. No EEC member was to be found in the low unemployment group.

Neither the general increase in unemployment nor the different rates in different countries were the result of impersonal global economic forces. Using multiple regression, Therborn tested for the relationship between unemployment and a variety of economic variables. Factors like economic growth, demographic growth, world market dependence, inflation, labour costs, social expenditure and unemployment compensation accounted only for a very small part of unemployment growth and unemployment difference. Unemployment was the result of specific decisions made by the governments of member states.

These findings confronted head-on three of the key explanations of unemployment in the 1970s and 1980s: that unemployment growth was a result of exogenous economic shocks in the form of oil price rises; that there was a trade-off between inflation and unemployment so that anti-inflationary policies required an acceptance of unemployment growth; and that unemployment compensation could push up unemployment by creating an unnecessarily high 'reserve wage' - the wage level at which the unemployed would accept work. Thus, in his view, much of the analysis of the causes of unemployment and the bulk of policy responses were entirely misplaced. For example, policies of wage restraint neither facilitated full employment nor increased international competitiveness.

Rather, different rates of unemployment depended on the 'existence or non existence of an institutionalised commitment to full employment.'[23] This involved: a clear commitment to maintaining/achieving full employment; the use of counter-cyclical mechanisms and policies; the conscious application of mechanisms to adjust demand and supply in the labour market with a view to attaining full employment; and a deliberate decision not to use unemployment as a means of achieving other policy objectives. Unemployment was thus a function of the lack of a political will to prevent it. Historically, that political will could be generated either via corporatism - the incorporation of some worker interests within the state - or through a conservative concern with order and stability. The latter circumstance explains the relative success of Switzerland and Japan and their permanent inclusion in the low-unemployment category.

---

[23] *Ibid.*, p. 23.

Moreover, states may positively respond to unemployment in two ways. They may either offer high benefits to the unemployed to compensate for the social costs of joblessness, or engage in extensive job creation to provide the unemployed with work. Some of the low unemployment countries score high on job creation but low on unemployment compensation (Japan). Other countries may score high on compensation, but low on job creation (Belgium). However, this relationship is not systematic because of the existence of some countries scoring high on both (Sweden) and others scoring low on both (Britain). The double nature of the response means that even countries which have similar rates of unemployment, for example Britain and Belgium, may be performing very differently with respect to their unemployed.

One obvious test of the Therborn thesis is to look at unemployment rates since 1984 to see whether the categories remain valid. Table 5.3 presents this information for the seven Community members which were included in his analysis.

Table 5.3	Unemployment Rates, Selected EC Members, 1985-90					
	1985	1986	1987	1988	1989	1990
Belgium	12.3	11.6	11.3	10.3	9.3	8.8
Denmark	9.0	7.8	7.8	8.6	9.3	9.6
W.Germany	7.2	6.4	6.2	6.2	5.6	5.1
France	10.2	10.4	10.5	10.0	9.4	9.0
Italy	10.2	11.2	12.1	12.2	12.1	11.0
N'lands	10.0	9.2	8.7	8.3	7.4	6.5
UK	11.6	11.8	10.4	8.2	6.2	5.5
Note:	Because Therborn's original analysis was based on OECD statistics, these, rather than EUROSTAT data, have been used for this table.					
Source:	*OECD, Economic Outlook*, 49, July 1991, table R.19					

Only one of the mass unemployment countries, Belgium, retained an average rate of over 10 per cent for half of the period. Italy, previously in the medium high group had moved into the mass group, while France was within a percentage point of the threshold. Both the Netherlands and the UK had dramatic falls in their unemployment averages and became medium high unemployment countries. West Germany remained clearly in the medium high group throughout the period, but Denmark remained close to its original classification.

On first sight, it would appear that the longer term validity of the Therborn classification is flawed. Nevertheless, the 1980s did see significant policy shifts in both the UK and France. Therborn's thesis was based on the assumption that economic policy would remain constant. In the UK, the Thatcher government quietly abandoned monetarism and, through the abolition of credit controls and tax cuts, initiated a boom based on consumer spending. The mid-1980s thus saw considerable GDP growth and substantial job creation, particularly in the services sector. Ironically, unemployment never fell to pre-1979 levels, despite considerable adjustments in its measurement. Conversely, the socialist government in France abandoned its Keynesian experiment and unemployment rose. In both countries, the changing unemployment rates can be related to policy change.

According to Therborn's analysis, the existence of a supranational institution like the Community is of little relevance to the levels of unemployment and the policy responses within the member states. Rather, unemployment is a product of very specific economic and political histories. In such terms, the growth and employment aspirations expressed in the Treaty of Rome and Community documents could never be more than rhetoric.

Whatever the explanation, the Community's record in minimising unemployment during the 1980s did not match that of its competitors, while some member states - Spain, Greece, Ireland, the UK and Belgium - consistently suffered unemployment rates greater than the Community average.

Labour Mobility

One traditional approach to the problem of unemployment is to encourage labour mobility. Indeed, neoclassical economic theory sees mobility as an important balancing mechanism within any economy. As a local economy grows, it generates greater demands for labour. If new local entrants to the labour market are inadequate to meet this demand, wage rates are pushed beyond the limits of marginal productivity and the system becomes overheated. In turn, this can cause inflation. Labour mobility permits the supply of labour to match its demand, reduces unemployment in depressed areas and prevents overheating in growth areas. The greater the mobility within the economy of all the factors of production, the greater the likelihood of their efficient allocation.

This theory however has been frequently criticised for its failure to take into account externalities. In the case of labour mobility, migration may substantially reduce the stock of skills in a depressed community engendering a cycle of decline, may prove difficult in the face of high accommodation costs in the more affluent areas and, even if successful, may cause congestion by increasing population density. In theory, these effects should eventually balance out but, since they occur with different time lags, they rarely do.

The establishment of the Common Market in 1957 was designed to enhance the degree of labour mobility between the member states. Until the mid-1980s, the majority of migrants came from underdeveloped areas to growth areas, many in search of low skilled or agricultural employment. In 1985 France had 400,000 workers from Spain, 94,000 from Italy and 98,000 from Portugal. West Germany had 103,000 from Greece and 199,000 from

Italy. These were distinct from a further 1,000,000 'guest workers' from outside the Community, particularly Yugoslavia and Turkey. The largest single number of EEC migrant workers were the 268,000 from the Irish Republic in the UK. However, the tradition of migrant workers from Ireland to Britain predates the 20th century. In the Community generally, nearly 2 million wage earners and 5 million nationals lived outside their own country. Nevertheless, migrants represented very small proportions of all employees in the member states other than Luxembourg (35.7%), where very specific circumstances prevailed. The average proportion of migrants in national labour forces was less than 2 per cent.[24]

It has been recognised within the Community that many migrant workers suffer discrimination and unequal treatment. The 1974 Programme of Social Action established as one of its priorities the protection of the rights of migrant workers, but many obstacles remained. Individual states were reluctant to fully implement Community regulations while migrant workers themselves were unaware of their rights and, in any case, faced opposition from other workers and forms of discrimination embedded in specific cultures.

It is not anticipated that the large flows from underdeveloped regions will continue in the future. The slow-down of economic growth in the 1980s reduced the demand for this kind of labour. Economic restructuring has wiped out many of the low-skilled jobs which traditionally went to migrants. Rather, it is expected that there will be greater movement of the employees of transnational companies and other workers as the result of inter-company cooperation agreements and programmes. Such migrants will exhibit greater skills profiles and their length of stay in other countries may be relatively short.[25] This changing pattern of worker migration suggests that unless the underdeveloped areas of the Community are able to sustain a more rapid development, their unemployment problems will increase.

A further migration problem in the 1990s arises out of the economic decline and growing political instability of parts of Eastern Europe and the Commonwealth of Independent States. The possibility of large-scale worker migration from the east adding to that from the south has not yet appeared on the Community agenda but has implications for the politics of some of the member states. Hostility to foreigners has become a common political theme of the far right in Europe. In Germany, hundreds of attacks have taken place on the hostels of foreign workers. The process has been exacerbated by reunification, which has generated a substantial unemployment problem in the former East Germany. In France, Jean Marie Le Pen's National Front has been gathering political support. A key element of its policies has been forced repatriation. In some states, including Britain,

---

24 Commission of the European Communities (1988), *Social Europe*, Brussels, p.19.

25 Commission of the European Communities (1988), *1992: The European social dimension*, Brussels, p.35.

legislation to limit asylum and immigration has been hotly debated. The EC only began to define its position at the Maastricht summit. If the EC is unable to resolve its internal unemployment problem, it will probably become much more restrictive to migrant workers from outside its borders.[26]

The Regional Problem in the Community

Mention has already been made of regional imbalances within the Community. These have persisted since its foundation and in the 1990s remain a serious problem of underdevelopment. The Third Periodic Report on the social and economic situation and development of the regions of the Community described regional disparities in the mid-1980s as follows.[27]

• About half of the Community's population lived in regions whose incomes per head lay within +15 or -15 per cent of the average.

• Around a further 12 regions, some of which were on the northern periphery of the Community, had an income gap of 15-25 per cent. These accounted for 6 per cent of its population.

• Another group of regions with about 20 per cent of the Community population, which were entirely located on the southern periphery, had an income gap of greater than 25 per cent. Most of these had young, fast-growing populations and were heavily dependent on agriculture.

• There was a final group of affluent regions whose per capita incomes were above 15 per cent of the Community average.

It was estimated that in 1985 there were just over 51 million individuals within the Community with an income of below 50 per cent of the average. This amounted to nearly 16 per cent of the total population.[28] The average income per head of the 10 strongest regions was about three times higher than that of the 10 weakest.

In order to rank regions within the Community, the Commission developed a synthetic index. This took four variables: GDP per head (25%); GDP per person employed (25%); unemployment adjusted for underemployment (40%); and prospective labour force change until 1990 (10%). The percentages in brackets represent the weights given to each of the variables in calculating the index. This was done for 1981, 1983 and 1985 and an average taken for the three years.

Essentially, the index was used as a measure of the intensity of regional problems. Since the variable given most weight was unemployment, it revealed those regions where the problem was most severe. With GDP per head an additional variable within the index, it also reflected the conjunction

---

26 *The Guardian* (19/11/1991), 'Fear of fortress Europe'.

27 NIEC/NESC (1988), *op.cit.*, p.3.8.

28 Commission of the European Communities (1991), *op.cit.*, February, table A8.

of high unemployment and low GDP.

On this basis, the most intense regional problems were clearly located on the southern periphery. Of the 36 regions which had an index value more than one standard deviation (32.9 points) below the Community average (100 points), only two (Ireland and Northern Ireland) were in the North. By far the largest group (17 regions) was in Spain, followed by nine in Greece, seven in Southern Italy and the whole of Portugal. Above these was a further group of regions located mostly in the UK and Belgium with moderately intense problems.

The index confirmed the nature of regional imbalance. Late developing economies with high proportions of their labour forces in agriculture suffered the worst unemployment and lowest GDP. Notwithstanding the fact that GDP growth in such economies was moderately high as they pursued modernisation, they had begun from a low base and suffered transitional costs in the form of high unemployment. The inclusion of both states of Ireland in the group of weakest regions reflected, on one hand, the Irish Republic's late start in industrialisation and, on the other, the very rapid decay of the traditional economic base in Northern Ireland. While declining regions in the north were marginally stronger, the impact of deindustrialisation could be clearly seen in these also. Northern Ireland was more like a weak northern region in terms of the processes it was experiencing, but being the most extreme example, had a ranking comparable to the weak southern regions.

The Fourth Periodic Report confirmed that regional disparities had changed little over the 1980s. In 1988, the average GDP per inhabitant of the 10 strongest regions was three and a half times that of the 10 weakest. In 1990, the difference in the average unemployment rates of the 25 highest and lowest regions was 14.7 percentage points. This compared with 13 percentage points in 1983.[29] Regional disparities, particularly in the form of unemployment, were sustained by the recessions of the early 1980s when the unemployment rates diverged both between, and within, countries. However, such disparities are not only generated by cyclical fluctuations in the European economy but, are also embedded in specific sets of economic relations at national and Community level.

At the level of particular countries, the development process will tend to favour some regions over others by a 'cumulative gravitation mechanism'. New industry will be attracted to areas where trade and industry are already developed. This process is exaggerated by the transition from manufacturing to services which need to be located close to consumers (the development of information technology has recently created something of a counter trend). In any case, manufacturing no longer needs to be adjacent to raw materials since transport costs have fallen, relative to production costs, and there are advantages in being closer to the final market. Gravitation is also fed

---

[29] Commission of the European Communities (1991), *The Regions in the 1990s*, Brussels, tables A6 and A7.

through economies of localisation where plants in the same industry geographically concentrate to take advantage of linkages and specialisation. Together, these developments create agglomeration economies in which disparate economic activities are served by facilities such as transport, financial institutions, a pool of skilled labour and a large final market.[30]

Underdevelopment is thus not just a question of 'lagging behind' or of finding the right combination of factors for growth. The development of faster growing regions underdevelops those which are weaker by absorbing the lion's share of new investment. The traditional function of regional policy has been to place curbs on fast-growing regions to inhibit congestion, inflation and environmental damage while, at the same time, offering incentives for economic development in depressed regions.

The existence of a common market enables gravitation processes to develop more easily at an international level. Even without a common market, the operation of transnational companies would tend to generate similar effects but, since the market is designed to encourage a free flow of the factors of production, the mechanisms of development and underdevelopment are enhanced. Thus, new industry and the relocation of existing industry may be concentrated in areas which internationally provide superior infrastructure, lower transport costs and the most skilled labour. In addition, the more efficient firms will expand to gain economies of scale in servicing a larger market while less efficient firms may go to the wall. Firms at the periphery tend to be less efficient than those at the centre and within a larger market may substantially lose out.

In the Community, however, the process is more complicated, since it encompasses a set of states at very different levels of development, each of which has their own underdeveloped areas. The Community core can expect to benefit from the location and expansion of existing companies. However, some parts of the periphery, particularly if labour costs are extremely low, may still benefit from new investment in low value-added, high-volume products where wage costs represent a significant proportion of total costs.[31] In turn, this can create dual, dependent economies, characterised, on one hand, by a high proportion of the labour force still in agriculture and, on the other, by a growing, new manufacturing sector heavily dependent on external investment. This form of development is most likely to occur in the Community's southern periphery. The northern periphery faces a different set of problems associated with the decline of traditional industry, inefficiencies in existing industries and difficulties in attracting new investment.[32]

---

[30] For a fuller discussion see Hitiris, L.T. (1991), *op.cit.*, pp.232-6.

[31] Commission of the European Communities (1989), *Employment in Europe*, Brussels, chapter 5.

[32] See Cambridge Econometrics (1991), *Regional Economic Prospects*, Cambridge, January.

There are thus two kinds of regional problems within the Community, both associated with high unemployment. This has been recognised for some time and a range of measures has been developed to tackle them. For example, the ERGO Programme launched in 1989, is designed to provide counselling, retraining and further education for the long-term unemployed. However, the scale of such measures is small relative to the severity of regional unemployment. Indeed, there is some concern that in post-1992 Europe, despite the claims made for the completion of the internal market, that regional underdevelopment will increase.

Unemployment and 1992

The Community's response to the sluggish recovery from the oil shocks was to amend the Treaty of Rome via the Single European Act. The Non-Europe factor had been identified as the source of the problem, and so the solution lay in the higher integration of the European economies. This was to be accomplished, on one hand, by the elimination of non-tariff barriers to the free movement of the factors of production and, on the other, by the greater harmonisation of monetary policy.

Non-tariff barriers were said to consist of fiscal, physical and technical obstacles to the expansion of trade. Before the end of 1992, nearly 300 measures are to be passed limiting the variations in VAT rates, ensuring that common technical standards prevail and ultimately removing physical barriers such as customs posts within the Community.

However, a major obstacle to trade continues to be volatile exchange rates between the currencies of the member states. These may cause sudden shifts in prices which create difficulties in export planning. Thus, a key concern has been to create a system of currency stability. The European Exchange Rate Mechanism was designed to achieve this task by establishing limits of variation for each member's currency and ensuring collective intervention to adjust currencies which move outside the limits. It remains a largely *ad hoc* measure since it contains two bands of variation and the UK was only persuaded to join in 1990. The ideal mechanism would be a single currency managed by a single central bank. The latter could also harmonise interest rates. This is important because, with integrated financial markets, there would be a temptation to save in countries with high interest rates and borrow in those with lower rates. Unless, interest rates were quickly harmonised, this would generate financial difficulties.

Some member states, particularly the UK, have been opposed to what they see as an unnecessarily high degree of centralisation of functions. The difficulty is that the Single Market can hardly work without such centralisation. The Maastricht solution was to set a timetable for the establishment of a common currency. If sufficient economic convergence occurs by 1996, it will be implemented then. Otherwise, the target date is 1999. Since there remains substantial variation in debt ratios, interest rates, trade deficits and rates of growth amongst the EC members, much will need to be done if a common currency is to be implemented. The UK obtained an 'opt out' clause so that only its parliament could decide to join the common currency somewhere along the way.

Nevertheless, from the perspective of the Commission, there will be substantial benefits arising out of economic integration. It will generate greater specialisation and efficiency leading to greater output. As indicated earlier, it is expected that firms will grow to achieve economies of scale and serve the larger market from fewer locations. Greater competition will also have a longer term effect on prices which, in real terms, should fall. These benefits are summarised in the Cecchini Report:[33]

• trigger a major relaunch of economic activity, adding on average 4.5% to EC GDP

• simultaneously cool the economy, deflating consumer prices by an average of 6.1%;

• relax budgetary and external constraints, improving the balance of public finances by an average equivalent to 2.2% of GDP and boosting the EC's external position by around 1% of GDP;

• boost employment, creating 1.8 million jobs; although unable of itself to make big inroads into the present stock of unemployment, the effect would nonetheless be to reduce the jobless rate by around 1.5 percentage points.

These calculations were made on the assumption that macroeconomic policies within the Community would remain relatively unchanged. If policies were adopted to take advantage of the new opportunities presented by the Single Market, the gains were expected to be even greater - a 7 per cent gain in GDP, and an increase in employment amounting to 5 million jobs, although with a smaller reduction in aggregate prices.

These predictions assume that the member states will fully implement the provisions of the Single Market. The examples of British resistance to monetary union and French opposition to food imports suggest that compliance may well be less than total. Even this optimistic scenario projects the closure of inefficient firms and whole industries (perhaps shipbuilding), thus increasing unemployment in the short term. The earlier discussion of regional imbalances suggests that many of the transitional costs will be experienced on the peripheries where, without a substantial increase in labour mobility, the unemployment increase will be long term.

Not everyone has been convinced by the postulated advantages of the Single Market. For example, John Grahl and Paul Teague argue:[34]

....these advantages can only be realised when and if the resources which are saved in one economic activity are redeployed in another. In a Community with some sixteen million unemployed workers, considerable

---

33 The Cecchini Report (1988), *op.cit.*, p.97.

34 Grahl, J. and Teague, P. (1990), *op.cit.*, p.40.

unused industrial capacity, and increasing areas of abandoned farmland, such redeployment cannot be taken for granted.

Although the conditions for sharper competition will exist after 1992, a European-wide infrastructure to compensate for instances of market failure will not. The redirection and efficient allocation of surplus resources will be left to market forces and, despite the current popularity of social markets, much of the evidence suggests they will not do so. The major surplus resource will be labour and the consequence of market failure will be unemployment.

Cutler and his associates regard the Commission calculations as hopelessly flawed.[35] In the first instance, they were mainly based on data from seven of the more industrially advanced member states and grossed up to provide estimates for Europe 12. They thus excluded information from the weaker peripheral members. Second, they did not allow for a partial implementation of the provisions by the member states which many regard as more likely. Finally, Cutler *et al* regard the assumptions about price convergence as 'arbitrary and optimistic'.

Rajan reckons that with greater competition, half the existing companies in Europe could go out of business by the end of the decade and that the economic gains will be extremely modest until the very long term. Even when output increases, this will not necessarily reduce unemployment since there will remain a series of labour market rigidities both on the supply and demand side. He describes these as 'time bombs' waiting to explode within European labour markets. They relate, on one hand, to demographic, gender and racial changes in the supply of labour and, on the other, to the effect of productivity changes on the demand for labour. Overall, in the absence of major new policy developments, the possible gains of European integration will not be realised.[36]

The EC requires a period of rapid growth and redistribution of output to weaker regions and groups if the backlog of unemployment problems from the 1980s is to be resolved. In the early 1990s, most EC countries are once again suffering slow growth, while Germany is preoccupied dealing with the economic and social costs of unification. While most predictions are for a recovery in the European economies, the average growth will be around 2 per cent, less than is required to produce employment for the very large numbers of unemployed or redress regional imbalances. If the more pessimistic predictions of the effects of economic integration in the EC are only half right, then unemployment will remain a key economic and social problem until the end of the century. This corresponds with an assessment made by Peter Townsend of the future prospects for the Community:[37]

---

[35] Cutler, T. et al (1989), *op.cit.*, pp. 57-67.

[36] Rajan, A. (1990), *op.cit.*, pp.1-5.

[37] Townsend, P. (1991-92), 'Hard Times', *European Labour Forum*, no.6, Winter, p.9.

To begin addressing 21st century social problems three major transformations are required: constitutional reform to enable democracy to operate coherently; constitutional reform to confer human and social rights; and legislation on social development and organisation, with a corresponding upwards surge in budgetary provision. None of these things have much hope of fulfilment. Our problem is that as the European Community grows in power - it is mainly a negative power to dismantle the national welfare states without much guarantee of what is to be put in its place.

6. Europe Against Poverty[1]

The previous chapter examined the substantial and persistent problem of unemployment throughout the European Community in the 1980s. Analysis of its changing composition highlighted uneven spatial, gender, and age distributions of the unemployed. It also pointed to the relationship between the growth, distribution and location of unemployment and the spread of poverty. This chapter takes up the latter issue and specifically reviews the response of the European Commission to a problem, which threatens to contradict in the most graphic way the more sanguine projections of the Single Market. In recent years, the leading architects of the Community have been keen to dispel the perception that it is merely an instrument for businessmen, intent on exploiting economies of scale and the prospect of more liberal trade. Partly for this reason, the appellation has changed from European Economic Community (EEC), to a more inclusive European Community (EC). Proclaimed in tandem with this change, is a stronger social dimension, nominally designed to engineer a greater convergence of economic well-being amongst social groups and regions. Combating poverty should be central to any serious endeavour to achieve such harmonisation.

Less vocal perhaps, but still influential, are those voices concerned about a longer-term project of federalising Europe. Again, this goal implicitly involves creating a sense of common citizenship, an identity which would prove more elusive should existing disparities in income and opportunity persist across the Community. In this context, the imperative to develop a viable anti-deprivation strategy is rooted strongly in both the modest and expansive ambitions for Europe. Eurocrats charged with policy formation have, of course, to balance the rhetoric of these grand designs with the relatively modest resources allocated for their fulfilment. How well they have managed to create and till such a 'narrow ground' can be tested in the three anti-poverty programmes they have so far initiated.

The chapter begins with a contextualisation of the scope of social policy in the EC. This is followed by a cursory retrospection on the first

[1] We appreciate the contribution made by Pat McGinn to this chapter in his provision of data and suggestions.

programme. Most attention is devoted to the second programme, which ended in 1989 and was compelled to engage with the fall-out of unemployment in the 1980s. Beginning with its objectives and project selection, there will be an attempt to penetrate its ideological assumptions. The form of its content, the structure of its implementation, the scale of its resources and the apparent impact of its delivery comprise the main issues subsequently addressed. Its influence on the current 'Poverty 3' will be assessed before concluding how far these interventions demonstrate a capacity for co-operation on this agenda by national governments, and the general efficacy of such efforts.

Social Europe

Social policy in the original EEC was addressed most explicitly in Part Three, Title 111 (Articles 117-28)[2] of the Treaty of Rome. These clauses included binding provisions such as equal pay for male and female workers, and the institution of a social fund, charged with the facilitation of employment opportunities and labour mobility. Among the non-binding declarations were the enhancement of working and living conditions, the establishment of uniform vocational training policy, and the provision of paid holiday schemes. Linked to the 'economic' commitment in Article 104 of the EEC treaty, to maintain high levels of employment as a key objective, such references apparently locate the treaty in the social democratic rather than liberal capitalist ends of the political spectrum.

Latterly there has been an acknowledgement that failure to harmonise on such issues threatened to give a competitive advantage to those countries with the least developed welfare states, whose social costs of production would be comparatively low. In the absence of greater standardisation to the best practice there was, in the light of this, a risk of 'social dumping' and a related prospect that the protections achieved by workers in the most socially advanced countries would be eroded. There have always been alternative voices proclaiming the efficient capacity of the market to achieve its own equilibrium in this matter. In their assessment, more ambitious social provision would escalate the marginal costs of labour and risk, amongst other repercussions, the substitution of capital for labour.[3]

The argument which has so far dominated this discourse is one that recognises that modern information-based economies demand an appropriately sophisticated social infrastructure. This said, it is the modesty of advances in this direction which is the most remarkable feature of the story so far. Evidence of this can be seen in the operation of the social fund. Despite undergoing a series of amendments in 1971, 1978, 1984 and 1985,

---

[2] EC (1973), *Treaties Establishing the European Communities*, Luxembourg.

[3] These issues are discussed in Hitiris, T. (1991), *European Community Economics, op. cit.*

it remains a deficient instrument to accomplish its central goal of improving the employability and mobility of European workers. It targets separate budgets for less favoured and high unemployment regions, resulting in about 40 per cent of the money available under its labour market heading being regularly destined for five candidates: the Republic of Ireland, Northern Ireland, Greece, the Mezzogiorno, and French overseas departments. In terms of age category, it focuses much of its resources on the under-25s, with nearly three quarters of its annual spending allocated to the young.

In the 1980s, the Commission was faced with recessionary pressures, which generated high levels of joblessness, while simultaneously constraining the fiscal capacity of government to respond. Thus it was keen to emphasise that the objective of lower unemployment, '....does not require new policies but it does require a much more effective co-ordination of existing policies.'[4] Clarity in policy response was not always helped by a somewhat confused analysis of the nature and causes of unemployment in the 1980s. For instance, on one hand, the Commission accepted that long-term unemployment was:[5]

....the result of the decline in the demand for labour and of structural changes that had occurred as new technology developed and as the international pattern of production changed under the influence of relative costs. The phenomenon was undoubtedly exacerbated by the fact that certain features of the labour market became factors of rigidity. The combined effect was to place the burden of adjustment on those in the weakest position, particularly low skilled workers, young people and women.

On the other hand, it referred to the jobless as formerly secure workers who had suddenly found themselves redundant because they happened to be in the wrong job, in the wrong place, at the wrong time. The suggestion here is that it was largely a matter of fortune and individual outcomes rather than wider structural forces. Clearly, a distinction is being drawn amongst the unemployed, imputing attitudinal and motivational short-comings to the long-term unemployed in particular. This perception is taken to be confirmed, 'by evidence that the probability of unemployed people leaving the unemployment register decreased the longer they remained on it.'[6] This simple deduction fails to question the extent to which this pattern is attributable to other determinants, for example, the prejudice harboured by some employers that those who remain workless for a considerable duration must be worthless or shiftless.

It is in such contexts that the Commission's intervention on poverty must be seen. An increasing number of studies were, by the 1970s, illuminating

---

[4] Commission of the European Communities (1989), Employment in Europe, *op. cit.*

[5] *Ibid.*, p.117.

[6] *Ibid.*, p.118.

the cross-national commonalities of industrial change and deprivation at the European level. While in some recognition of this, a Social Europe was accorded legitimacy, the resources allocated were modest. Alongside this constraint, was the nervousness about intruding into spheres considered best subject to national influence - a principle of subsidiarity, which offers any government devoted to a more minimalist state a rationale for marginal activity at the European level. Even prior to the extension of the Community to include members from the poorer southern region, there was a problem of divergences in development, with fundamental implications for social policy. A simple example was that no two states shared similar poverty lines. This inevitably complicated any attempt at a coherent, never mind uniform, solution to social problems across Europe.

The First European Combat Poverty Programme

In October 1972, following the Paris summit of EC member and candidate states, a communique was issued, giving expression to the social imperative. The national government leaders proclaimed that they:[7]

....attached as much importance to vigorous action in the social field as to the achievement of European and Monetary Union....They invited the Institutions of the Community, after consulting labour and management, to draw up...a programme of action providing for concrete measures and the corresponding resources.

An early draft of an anti-deprivation drive[8] spoke of the urgency of rehabilitating a neglected minority trapped in a cycle of chronic poverty, emphasising that the role of the Commission in any intervention was to complement rather than supplant the primary responsibilities of member states. In 1974 a consultative paper was sponsored by the Commission, suggesting a typology for pilot action programmes: area-based community action projects, schemes for specific categories of poor people, and ones for improving social services.

Three years later, the first combat poverty programme was initiated and ran until 1980. It comprised two cross-national studies, aimed at understanding the general features of poverty, and 29 action-research schemes distributed across member states. At least half the projects were 'process' rather than 'task' orientated, meaning that they were largely concerned with mobilising and supporting communities in their own determination of objectives, priorities and pursuits. Those addressing

---

[7] Quoted in ESPOIR, (1980), *Europe against Poverty: Evaluation report of the European Programme of Pilot Schemes and Studies to Combat Poverty*, vol. 1, The Programme as a Whole, p.1.

[8] Bulletin of the European Communities (1973), *Social Action Programme* , Supplement 4\73.

particular problems were extremely diverse in their focus - parents, children, battered women, vagrants, homeless, disabled, and elderly, amongst others. Most of the initiatives were small. In aggregate, the pilot schemes accounted for scarcely more than 2 per cent of the cost of the social fund, and comprised about 500 workers, about one third of whom were in one big Italian project at Padua.[9]

One of the cross-national studies was concerned with the perception of poverty in the populations of member states, the awareness levels and the extent of empathetic or censorious predispositions. While it did succeed in attracting publicity to the issue of poverty in Europe, there was some contention about its analysis. For instance, in highlighting the way in which public attitudes in particular member states can circumscribe the potential for government intervention, it underestimated the extent to which public policy itself can render the poor as victims of popular stereotype and stigma.

The evaluation report on the programme as a whole contextualised its influence in 1980, with a reminder that its launch coincided with a time of rising concern for the poor; when the requisite public resources still seemed relatively guaranteed from economic prosperity; and when the labour of the socially marginal was still anticipated to be potentially productive: 'Today all has changed. There are many more poor, but we seem more prepared to tolerate their existence as the price for stabilising the value of our currencies or for other over-riding social objectives.'[10] This note of despondency bodes ill for any substantive redress for the 11.4 per cent of households - approximately 30 million people - below the poverty line in the EC-9 at that time. In a summary verdict, the evaluation report accepted the additionality and relevance of the efforts for the poor in the particular activities, and the innovative and participatory character of the projects. But it lamented the fragility of cross-national contact and cooperation, which resulted more in a series of national projects than a European programme. Partly this can be blamed on the under-resourcing of the opportunity, but, it must also be an outcome of the diversity of ideological and administrative approaches.

An effective Commission response relied at least on substantive comparability, which itself demanded a greater homogeneity and coherence than materialised. Invoking the concepts of 'action-research' and 'pilot programming', inferred a pioneering role for such initiatives. But this metaphor of 'pioneer' itself pre-supposes that the 'settlers' are trailing not far behind, ready to occupy the territory secured. Yet, it is not at all apparent that national governments were so intent. Their relative opposition, commitment or agnosticism about the whole deliberation remained at best inscrutable.

While the first programme failed to commit the Commission to significant change, such as the 'bending' of all Community policies in favour

---

[9] *Ibid.*, p. 56.

[10] *Ibid.*, p.219.

of the most impoverished, it did raise the purpose and capacity of poverty research at a European level. It also helped to link action against want with the need to tackle unemployment by creating new jobs and sharing existing ones. A second combat poverty programme was endorsed for the period 1985-89. Taking a poverty line as 50 per cent below average earnings in the countries concerned, by the mid-1980s four member states - France, Belgium, Greece and Spain - had achieved a reduction in poverty over the first half of that decade. However, the absolute rise in the number of poor in many European countries was also apparent. For instance, comparing 1980 with 1985, the percentage of the population categorised as poor had increased in the UK from 9.2 per cent to 12.0 per cent; in the Republic of Ireland from 16.9 per cent to 22 per cent; and in Denmark from 13.0 per cent to 14.7 per cent. In order of ranking, the highest rates were to be found in Portugal, Greece, Ireland and Spain.[11] Thus, the accession of the southern European periphery to the Community had accorded an even greater urgency to the issue. In terms of numbers, the poor totalled almost 40 million in 1980 and around 44 million in 1985.[12]

The Second European Combat Poverty Programme

A relative concept of poverty was adopted in the second programme, representing an achievement of Poverty 1 in locating poverty in relation to the prevailing conditions at a particular point in history for a particular society. The Council of Ministers defined poverty as the condition of: '....persons whose resources (material cultural and social) are so limited as to exclude them from the minimum acceptable way of life in the Member State in which they live.'[13] The term 'exclude' was to become very significant in the appreciation of how poverty operated both to remove those languishing under it from mainstream channels of discourse and influence, and the non-poor from contact with its victims. The Commission also acknowledged two significant changes in the way poverty was socially distributed across the Community. The growth of both unemployment and the incidence of lone parenting had created a 'new poor', distinctive in many respects from the traditional poor population.

Many redundancies during the 1980s had resulted from an economic restructuring whose speed and scope had afflicted many workers previously immune to such processes. They were members of a primary labour market

---

[11] EC (1990), *Poverty in Europe: Estimates*, The Institute of Social Studies Advisory Service, Rotterdam University, Rotterdam.

[12] O'Higgins, M. and Jenkins, S. (1988), *Poverty in Europe*, Centre for Analysis of Social Policy, Bath University, Bath.

[13] Council of Ministers (1991), quoted in Final Report on the Second European Poverty Programme , *op. cit.*, p.2.

and their prior work histories were largely uninterrupted and, as such, they were likely to have been qualified workers.[14] Many would have been relatively well paid, and this income and assumed security would have induced them into financial commitments, which unemployment precipitatively transformed into debt over-extension. For such people, joblessness involved a traumatic adjustment not merely to inactivity and absence of long-standing routine, but also to major reappraisal of material lifestyle.

Social and legislative changes in many European countries in the 1960s and 1970s were both the cause and consequence of new fragmentations and reorganisation of family life. The rises in remarriage and single parenthood were part of this pattern, adversely affecting household incomes in many instances. Judged by dependence on social security, lone parenthood became for many synonymous with deprivation.

In the first 18 months of the second poverty programme, there were 65 action-research projects, with an additional 26, based in Spain and Portugal, joining in the Summer of 1987. The projects were selected by national governments and the Commission because their focus conformed to the eight major poverty themes identified. The distribution of projects across the eight themes is shown in table 6.1

Table 6.1   The Distribution of Anti-poverty Projects by Theme Groups

Theme	No. Of Projects
Long-term unemployed	11
Young unemployed	9
Elderly	12
Single-parent families	9
Second-generation migrants, refugees and returning migrants	12
'Marginal' and homeless people	11
Integrated action in urban areas	14
Integrated action in rural areas	13
Source: Commission of the European Community (1991), *op. cit.*	

Specifically, the most vulnerable groups were listed as the long-term unemployed, the young unemployed, the elderly, single-parent families, second-generation migrants, refugees and other marginal groups such as the homeless. There was also a spatial component. In addition to the acute problems of the new southern periphery, there were the persistent development shortcomings of a northern industrialising country like the Republic of Ireland; the depressed regions enduring accelerated decline of 'smokestack' industry; and rural areas accommodating to further de-

---

[14] *Ibid.*, p.8.

population and erosion of economic base. While it was clearly necessary to concentrate attention in this way, the cost of selection is always exclusion and some groups were by-passed in the process. For instance, the switch to the service sector had been accompanied by a more marked bifurcation of the labour market, whereby disparities in income and occupational welfare highlighted the contribution of low pay to poverty, particularly its feminisation. Yet, low pay, and poverty amongst women and children were not explicitly part of the Commission's priority list. Similarly, the issue of race was not addressed.

The goals of the programme included carrying out 'positive measures to help the underprivileged and identify the best means of attacking the causes of poverty and alleviating its effects.'[15] Emphasising the cross-national features of the exercise, there was reference to the need 'to promote the exchange of information, experience and models for action'.[16] Collaboration and exchange of ideas amongst the transnational theme groups was considered vital to the application of novel approaches and insights.[17] The experimental nature of the programme was again accorded central importance, and it was envisaged that materials produced from this cross-national co-operation should be disseminated to other practitioners outside the formal programme.

Implementation of Poverty 2

The diversity of the projects was reflected in the contrasting forms of implementation. Some involved themselves in traditional relief work - food, shelter, and organising rudimentary vocational training. Others saw themselves less in terms of ameliorating the symptoms and more in terms of tackling the structural roots. The practical composition of both approaches included permutations of a range of tasks: encouraging solidarity and networking; transmitting confidence and competence to help empower; confronting demoralisation; and establishing prefigurative forms of social provision. Some included research dimensions which offered the prospect of intensive locality studies complementing the macro-findings.

A system of self-evaluation was installed for each project, to complement that being undertaken at national and European levels. While this was designed to improve project management and team motivation by encouraging introspection, and interrogation of progress, it put them in, 'a situation of "pluralistic accountability", reporting on their activities to

---

[15] EC (1984), *Council of Ministers' Decision*. Brussels, article 1.1.

[16] Commission of the European Communities (1991), *op.cit.*, p.15.

[17] *Ibid.*, annex 2, p.2.

organisations with potentially competing expectations.'[18] In addition to having efficient evaluation systems, the effectiveness of the projects was said to depend on their adoption of the best practice in their respective countries; their being engaged with professional and policy debates in the anti-poverty field; and their having a requisite level of resources.[19]

On the issue of resources, the second programme mirrored its predecessor in sponsoring a multitude of activity on a shoestring. As Benington comments, 'Its budget was small (20 million ECU in total, which works out at less than 0.20 ECU per head of the European population in poverty).'[20]

Several drawbacks in the form of programme organisation were identified at an interim stage.[21] The primary linkage of projects with others in the same theme group in other countries restricted the capacity for co-ordination and mobilisation at national policy level. Moreover, motivation at the project level was at least partly contingent on signals from the Commission that this time, as an advance on Poverty 1, there was the political will to attempt to translate experimental success into policy. Yet the links which particular projects or theme groups were able to forge with the Commission were too tenuous for this process to be discussed and clarified.

A New Poverty?

As mentioned earlier, there is an argument that poverty in Europe during the 1980s not only became more widespread, but also changed in quality. This was in great measure attributable to the growth in long-term and recurrent unemployment and the complementary rise in underemployment. Disaggregating these patterns, certain distinctions can be drawn. In circumstances of relative economic buoyancy, a certain amount of frictional unemployment can be expected as a transient outcome of various rigidities and bottlenecks in the labour market. Unemployment in the 1980s was a different phenomenon.

Cyclical joblessness, resulting from the deflationary pressures of the period, affected many previously in stable and skilled employment. In former times they might have reasonably anticipated that the business downturn would be of short duration and, being equipped with experience and qualification, that they would be well-placed in the labour market when

---

[18] Room, G., Laczko, F. and Whitting, G. (1987), *Action to combat poverty: The experience of sixty five projects*, Working Papers Evaluation Section, no. 9, December, Centre for the Analysis of Social Policy, University of Bath, Bath, p.4.

[19] *Ibid.*

[20] Bennington, J. (1989), 'Poverty, unemployment, and the European Community: Lessons from experience', in Design, K. (ed.), *Combating Long-Term Unemployment: Local\EC Relations*, Routledge, London, p. 85.

[21] *Ibid.*

demand resumed. This time the cycle was both deeper and longer. The longer they remained jobless, the more de-skilled and demoralised they became, negatively affecting their employability.

For the under-employed, de-unionisation and casualisation eroded employment rights and remuneration. The greater incidence of such part-time and insecure employment was related to the demand for greater labour flexibilities to accommodate rapid and less predictable market shifts. The result was an increasingly close association between poverty and paid employment, and suggested that aggregate figures for job creation across the community misrepresented the degree to which they could be taken as compensation for the loss of full-time manufacturing jobs. As earlier mentioned, the specific issue of low pay did not command priority in the 'themes' selected for the programme. Yet, its importance to understanding modern day poverty is critical.

According to Britain's Low Pay Unit, in the UK in 1979, 38 per cent of workers earned below the Council of Europe's 'decency threshold', a share which had increased to 46 per cent by the early 1990s. By then, over 10 million adult workers fell below the calculation of the threshold for the U.K. of £193.60 per week. Earnings of the lowest paid manual employees relative to the average were less in 1991 than when records began in the Victorian era in 1886.[22] Those on low income may not always conform to the precise definitions of poverty in their particular countries. But many who elude the statistical calculation are poised precariously at or near the poverty line, so that its ominous prospect shadows their lives.

In addition, there were the hidden unemployed who were not on the official register because they lacked entitlements, or could not comply with the condition that they should be seeking work due to the under-provision of child care.

The issue which summoned great attention amongst the unemployment theme group was that of unemployment related to the structural changes in the economy. This has been a highly differentiated process. In some cases, it is a gloomy tale of deindustrialisation, with no alternative sectoral substitution. In others, job loss in the local economy due to work reorganisation such as intensification, or relocation such as the globalisation of production, was accompanied by employment alternatives, even if less plentiful and lucrative. Particular areas in Europe experienced this supposed rehabilitation from 'smokestack' to 'sunrise'. But many saw jobs drain from their 'rustbelt' regions, while significant job gain appeared in regions already characterised as 'sunbelt'. Their legacy in the 1980s was chronic and intense unemployment, sparking not only financial hardship, but also a sense of powerlessness. The new patterns of segmentation in the wider labour market were reflected on a smaller scale in the fragmented communities, once central to a previous industrial age dominated by coal, ship-building, textiles

---

[22] Low Pay Unit Study, referenced in *The Guardian*, (14/1/1992).

and metal-bashing.

The Europe of the 1980s witnessed a realignment of work and welfare. It was not simply that an ideology hostile to welfare had achieved prominence in a number of member states. The material basis of welfare had also changed. Partly this was a consequence of the fact that a system constructed on a fiscal base of tax and social insurance, dependent on full employment, inevitably frayed when that premise collapsed. But it was also linked to the new redistributions demanded by the economic exigencies. No longer was the mass of the working population contributing to a containable minority of dependents. There was every prospect that the share of dependents would grow, and their needs increase, implying a heavier tax burden particularly for the core workers on generous remuneration. Yet the new political credo enthroned in parts of Europe, keen to reward enterprise, succumbed to the tax-cutting lure of supply-side economics. In other words, the 'two thirds/one-third' societies being spawned in this upheaval were responsive to a different political economy to the one which validated the social democratic settlement of the post-war years.

Therborn has projected a scenario in which a trichotomous social division takes root in Western society:[23]

At the bottom, the permanently unemployed and the marginally employed, with certain welfare entitlements, almost certain to be reduced over time. Some of these will make a living in the black economy....In the middle there will be the stably employed, or with a stable likelihood of re-employment, probably increasingly divided according to enterprise, sector, and hierarchical rung, making a fairly decent living, no more...(and for the elite) the increasing wealth and incomes of capitalists and business managers.

For the 'one-third', there was no escape route out of the growing welfare and public service queues through occupational welfare or private insurance. Their apparent destiny as 'outsiders' was as mendicant clients of a deteriorating and residual public beneficence. For the 'two-thirds', particularly the most affluent of the 'insiders', there awaited the new democracy of consumer sovereignty. Accustomed to expect diversity of choice in a private sector refashioned to the designer age of post-Fordism, some were growing irritated with the uniformities of public service provision. For them, the solution lay in the privatisation of their own social needs. This desertion of the common fold need not be accompanied by personal guilt since a post-modernist social philosophy was now rationalising the illusory nature of collective social progress. In other words, even more significant than the 'new poverty' was the 'new inequality', validated as a necessary predicator and outcome of a new rigorous age of

---

[23] Therborn, G. (1989), 'The two-thirds, one third society' in Hall, S. and Jacques, M. (eds.), *New Times: The changing face of politics in the 1990s*. Lawrence & Wishart in association with Marxism Today, London.

enterprise. The political project of the New Right in the 1980s was about creating a new 'common sense,' in which those with moral or political reservations about the diminution of public space could be characterised as irredeemably unfit to be players in the new industrial game.

Bennington[24] applauded some of the distinctive aspects of Poverty 2. It facilitated a European-wide reach which, in turn, afforded a usefully 'textured' analysis of the poverty condition. Though each was small in scale, the combination of diverse projects added up to a substantial and authoritative body of action-research, which should have compelled the attention of the EC and its member states. He also felt that they drew further detail of how particular spaces and groups were the recipients of agricultural and industrial restructuring, a good deal of which emanated from a European process or, indeed, plan. By implication, their findings and recommendations demanded serious attention by the European Regional Development Fund and the Common Agricultural Policy. The programme also contributed to the debate about the links between impoverishment and joblessness, showing that the solution to both requires, 'an integrated programme which combines programmes of social development and skill training with economic development and job creation.'[25]

A detailed examination of the long-term unemployment theme group, however, hardly merits this assessment. For none of these projects was there a significant impact on long-term unemployment. One obvious explanation of the relative failure of the long-term unemployment projects to achieve the type of synergy which was at the core of this type of cross-national programme lay in the differences in cultures, histories, settings and origins of the projects themselves. Table 6.2 summarises some of the differences between projects, and shows where the long-term unemployment projects were based, their resources and orientation. The projects in the long-term unemployment theme group came from Britain (1), Northern Ireland (2), West Germany (2), Italy (1), and Spain (4). There were no projects from the Benelux countries nor from France or Greece. The Stuttgart and Milan projects were located in the economic core of the Community. For the most part, their origins lay in a variety of non-governmental organisations ranging from church agencies to unemployment centres and universities. One of the Spanish projects was part of the local government structure and was different from the rest in this respect. The national spread of the projects coincides to a large extent with the northern and southern peripheries of the Community.

Almost two-thirds of the projects' resources were made available to the three West German projects. Stuttgart, Bielefeld and Dortmund were allocated 60 per cent of the resources.

---

24 Bennington, J. (1989) ,*op. cit.*

25 *Ibid*, p.110.

Table 6.2 Staffing, Orientation and Resources of the Long-term Unemployment Projects in Poverty 2

Project & Staff	ECUs & Percentage of Total (1.28 MECUs)		Orientation
Stuttgart 8.5 staff	.347m	27.0%	Church based, social welfare organisation
Dublin 3.5 staff	.095m	7.0%	Unemployed action group
Bielefeld 5 staff	.193m	15.0%	Welfare work with the unemployed
Dortmund 9 staff	.227m	18.0%	Unemployed centre membership organisation
Milan 9.5 staff	.238m	19.0%	Lay church voluntary services
Wolverhampton 3 staff	.071	6.0%	Unemployed action groups with local polytechnic
Derry 3 staff	.055	4.0%	Trade union based unemployment centre
Belfast 5 staff	.233	18.5%	Trade union based unemployment centre
Girona	Unknown		Local government welfare service
Pamphlona	Unknown		University based training project
Other Spanish projects (2)	Unknown		Unknown
Source: Survey of Poverty 2 Long-term Unemployment Projects, Belfast, 1990			

Was this allocation based on need? At the beginning of the programme, 47 per cent of West Germany's unemployed were in the long-term category, compared to 69 per cent in Belgium, 65 per cent in Italy and 53 per cent in the Community generally.[26] Almost half of the projects' resources were used by church-based organisations; Milan and Stuttgart had 46 per cent between them. This is in contrast to the percentage used by trade union-related agencies (26 per cent taken by Dortmund, Belfast and Derry).

The goals which projects set for themselves differed according to the explanation of long-term unemployment which they accepted. There were two quite different approaches which may broadly be characterised as structural and individual. In the structural explanation economic factors, specifically de-industrialisation and government policy, accounted for the duration of unemployment. Existing policy responses to these economic forces were viewed as inadequate to the task. Individual explanations focused on 'supply-side' deficiencies in the unemployed themselves. Their training and educational levels were characterised as too low, their morale inadequate, and these factors were in turn related to the cultural milieux in which they lived their lives.

Different goals followed from these different explanations.   The

---

[26] Eurostat (1988), *Long-term Unemployment*, Brussels, April, table 1.2.

structuralist camp - Dublin, Stuttgart, Bielefeld, Dortmund, Wolverhampton, Derry/Belfast and Pamplona - was numerically stronger. The projects with individualist perspectives were Portugal, Girona, and Milan. Dublin emphasised the inadequacies of government welfare policy which was also the position of Pamplona. Wolverhampton, Belfast, Bielefeld and Dortmund looked to economic restructuring, and Derry to discrimination by the state against its area. Three of the four Spanish projects emphasised working with families to compensate for inadequate schooling.

In one sense, the goals which the projects acknowledged in the end-of-programme survey tell one little about their agendas. Perhaps fearing that they would have been setting themselves up to fail, the projects never set out specific objectives and measurable targets. This was certainly far from a 'management by objectives model', which is hardly surprising. Most projects had their origins in social work, as in the case of the southern European projects and Stuttgart, or community development, as in the case of the northern projects. Although much was made of the innovative nature of the programme by representatives of the Commission, the projects themselves could not publicly recognise their internal difficulties for fear of jeopardising their funding.

Transnational meetings among these projects were held periodically to encourage networking and information exchange, but they served no real purpose for the projects. Their contracts with the Commission required them to engage in such meetings, and so they did. There was little output other than abstract documents, which the Commission found unsatisfactory and of little practical use to policy makers in Brussels. However, it was unreasonable for the Commission to expect that detailed policy lessons could emerge from projects with diverse backgrounds and based on differing theories about the causes of poverty. This would have required careful preparation by the co-ordinating section of the Commission which was not the case.

Influence on the Third Poverty Programme

While all three combat poverty initiatives have been informed by certain similar principles, such as additionality, subsidiarity and participation, the Poverty 3 programme (1989-94), is different in significant respects from its predecessors. The general disposition of projects in the previous programmes was grassroots, which involved a community development strategy to organise target groups to both self-motivation and to lobby the statutory sector. A large number of small-scale projects was selected, and operated mostly as voluntary organisations exercising considerable autonomy. Evaluation, both internal and external, was often poorly serviced and developed. Success in goal-attainment was primarily related to effectiveness in working with target groups, and to establishing a funding and structural basis for continuity after the programme.

Poverty 3 involves a smaller number of larger projects. Each is meant to develop a management structure inclusive not only of relevant voluntary and community representation, but also of statutory, and possibly private agencies. Projects are encouraged to design and test actions on poverty, which offer prefigurative and prototype models, capable of being adopted across the whole Community. In this respect, networking both nationally and cross-nationally features prominently in order to maximise the 'transferability' of initiatives and insights. It is also more readily acknowledged that the multidimensional character of poverty demands greater integration of physical, social and economic planning.

The amount allocated by the European parliament to the third programme is 55 million ECUs over five years, a significant shortfall on the 70 million ECUs requested by the Commission. Compared to the budgets of the previous programmes - 29 million ECUs for the Second, over four years, and 20 million ECUs for the First, over five years - this allocation is not very much more generous. It is argued that because there is a smaller number of projects, each will be better endowed than before. Distribution of the budget is intended to concentrate 38.4 million ECUs on the 27 'model action' projects, with 2.3 million destined for the 12 'innovative projects', and the remainder on research, animation and evaluation.[27]

Perhaps the most significant departure is the emphasis attached to 'partnership', particularly between the statutory and voluntary/community organisations. A greater 'synergy' is claimed to be obtainable if the processes of conceptualisation, decision-making, and implementation involve negotiation and co-operation amongst the partners. There is also supposed to be a greater prospect of this permeating the agencies concerned, and influencing the agendas, priorities and practices of government.

Other interpretations of this concept are, of course, possible. It might be considered a device to incorporate community protest into a de-radicalising and sanitising structure which, through the attrition of frequent meetings 'educates' those making demands on statutory resources about the shortage of funds. It implies an equality amongst the partners, belied by the pre-eminence of those, mostly governments, whose professionalisation and budgetary largesse can be key determinants in decision-making. Moreover, a trade-off between partnership and participation is possible, whereby those suffering most from exclusion are the very ones excluded from this process. This may result from the limited life-span of the project. Since the main imperative is to achieve results in the time available, it may be thought that the involvement of the less experienced can only operate to impede progress.

Despite these reservations, Poverty 3, circumscribed by greater clarity and refinement of principles, subject to a more comprehensive evaluation procedure, and involving government and local government agencies, holds

---

[7] Much of the above information is derived from the UK Research and Development Unit of the Third European Programme for the Economic and Social Integration of the Least Privileged Groups, October 1991.

the prospect of a more substantial and coherent product. Whether the Community adopts, or even adapts, its conclusions remains speculative. It is a question which is inseparable from the issue of social cohesion in Europe.

Social Cohesion versus Economic Integration?

It might appear that demands to diminish social disparities within the Community are part of a commitment to greater social and regional cohesion which, in turn, is a requisite to economic convergence. Yet, there is a major problem with this assumption, as it is in the very vulnerable economies of countries like Greece and Portugal and regions like the south of Italy that the challenge of accelerated economic integration will be greatest. Achieving this will involve curbing inflationary impediments to growth and moderating social consumption in the interest of economic investment. Both imply monetary and fiscal policies at odds with redistributive policies.

Yet, it is in these countries which endure underdevelopment, where the burdens of deprivation are the greatest and the social infrastructure the weakest. In such circumstances, addressing rapidly and simultaneously, strategies for both wealth creation and redistribution is an awesome undertaking. To do so in some of the countries whose recent authoritarian political culture imposes the need for circumspection about any disturbance to a fragile social consensus, is an even greater task. But to do so within the disciplines of EC designs for monetary union beggars credibility.

European regional policy is effectively resourced from the 'structural funds' of the European Regional Development Fund (ERDF), the European Social Fund (ESF), and a section of the Agricultural Guarantee and Guidance Fund (EAGGF), together with lending facilities from the European Investment Bank. The Brussels summit decision in 1988 to double the structural funds to 14 billion ECUs per annum by 1993, means that these will then represent about one quarter of the EC's total budget. This will still only amount to 0.3 per cent of the Community's GDP. It is argued that because the funds are concentrated in the poorest regions, their effect is greater than the totals suggest; they are expected to amount to 3-4 per cent of GDP in Portugal, Greece and the Republic of Ireland.[28] Moreover in 1993 a new Social Cohesion fund will be launched. This will be targeted at the four least developed EC economies; Greece, Ireland, Portugal and Spain. A document from the Commission in February 1992 estimates that 'for these four countries together, the resources available for the regions in 1997 could rise by as much as 100%'.[29] Given the introduction of qualified majority

---

[28] Begg, I. and Mayes, D. (1991), 'Social and economic cohesion among the regions of Europe in the 1990s', *National Institute Economic Review*. November.

[29] Commission of the European Communities (1992), From the Single Act to Maastricht and beyond:, *op.cit,* p.21.

voting at the Council of Ministers, which shifts power towards the bigger economies, and the economic difficulties these countries are facing, it is problematic whether the resources will be made available to the Community budget to realise these ambitions.

The success of these funds must now be largely assessed in terms of their contribution to the attainment of the goals set out in Article 130A of the Single European Act:

> In order to promote its overall harmonious development, the Community shall develop and pursue its actions leading to the strengthening of its economic and social cohesion. In particular, the Community shall aim at reducing disparities between the various regions and the backwardness of the least favoured regions.

Such an objective implies a disavowal of the capacity of unfettered market forces to deliver harmony. Specifically, it largely discounts the theory that underdevelopment provides its own competitive advantages, such as lower costs of labour and land, which can induce the relocation of firms burdened by the costs and congestions of over-heated regions. The funds have tended to focus instead on the improvement of supply-side components such as physical infrastructure, telecommunications and training. While these might be necessary for economic development, it is increasingly recognised that they are not sufficient.

This suggests that additional criteria for sustained and balanced development are required, including, '....the encouragement of indigenous sources of growth rather than seeking an inflow of capital; identifying the region's native sources of strength; and, creating a local environment of innovation, linking education, training, research, business and finance in a network of private and public sector efforts.'[30]

But there remain at least two difficulties. First, the transfers required to make an impression on the scale of the multiple problems of depressed regions are not remotely commensurate with even the increased structural funds. Yet the Commission would likely encounter resistance to any attempt at substantial improvement from the dominant economies who fear extra budgetary demands imposing tax disincentives on their prosperity. Second, even should resources be considerably enhanced, arguably the existing forms of redistribution in regional policy are too broad-brush. They relatively neglect intra-regional differentiations such as urban decline, which is not always a phenomenon peculiar to poor regions. A different focus, which could be twinned with an anti-poverty drive, would be to:[31]

> ....target that poverty directly by transfers to households rather than concentrating purely on structural investment which may, because of the pattern of revenue raising and expenditure, result in a transfer from the

---

[30] *Ibid.*, p. 70.

[31] *Ibid.*, p. 71.

poor in rich regions to the rich in poor regions.

For the present, social policy at the European level remains very secondary to that at the national level. Given the current political and fiscal resources attached to it in the EC, it can scarcely be other than peripheral in its impact.[32] Whatever the worthiness of 'social charter' proclamations, their actual merit to the most disadvantaged citizenry must await the compliance of member states with more than just declarations of greater equity.

---

[32] Hitiris, L.T. (1990), *op.cit.*

7. The UK: Engineered Mass Unemployment ?

Brendan McDonnell
Belfast Centre for the Unemployed

This chapter sets out to examine whether measures adopted to arrest the relative decline of the British economy in the early 1980s required large scale unemployment as the condition of economic restructuring. The impact on the British labour market of the changing economic and social agenda and the uneven experience and social costs of unemployment will be the focus.

In the post-war period, the key priority for economic managers was the maintenance of full employment by ensuring appropriate demand, primarily via government spending. The period up to the 1970s is characterised as one of boom, continuous growth, low unemployment and low inflation, sustained by Keynesian demand management policy. However, although impressive, the performance was less so, when compared to Britain's major economic partners.

Figure 7.1 GDP Trends in Europe 1953-73 (% increase per year)

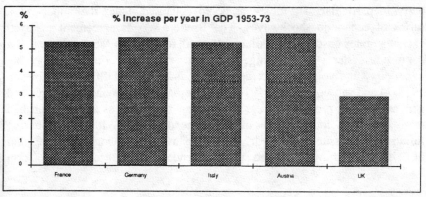

Source: Smith, K. (1986), op. cit., p. 81.

Underlying faults and weaknesses in the British system, particularly a failure to invest in research and development, meant that when the boom ended with the onset of the oil crises of the 1970s, Britain suffered more than others. As well as the crises being more acutely felt in Britain, the responses were also more radical. Stagflation, rising unemployment and industrial unrest led many to the conclusion that existing economic policies no longer worked, in fact they only made things worse. Therefore, what was needed was a radical alternative. The new or re-emergent economic doctrines of monetarism and supply-side economics became fashionable.

Monetary controls were first introduced by a Labour administration in 1976, basically as a tactical response to the deepening crisis brought about by the run on the pound and the intervention of the IMF. However the new right in the Tory party, which was now dominant under Margaret Thatcher, absorbed these notions completely and sought to implement a radical alternative economic strategy based on the doctrines of monetarism and neoclassical economics. Once elected in 1979, they implemented a major shift of economic policy, away from maintaining full employment to that of controlling inflation. The combined effects of world-wide recession, a strong pound and the ruthless implementation of a monetary squeeze on the domestic economy in the early 1980s produced a massive shake-out of British industry. The resulting huge rise in unemployment was seen as an acceptable, and indeed a necessary, part of the process to improve the efficiency and competitiveness of British industry.

The Conservative Agenda

The early 1970s were a traumatic time for Britain and the Conservative party in particular. The post-war boom collapsed under the impact of a series of economic shockwaves. The Bretton Woods agreement of fixed exchange rates based on the dollar collapsed, resulting in the emergence of a confused system of floating exchange rates injecting considerable uncertainty and volatility into the world economy. The OPEC price rises in 1973-74 and subsequently in 1978-79 exacerbated inflationary pressures and generated major problems in the world financial system as increases pushed many countries into balance of payments deficits.[1] With the mounting inflationary pressures of the early 1970s, many governments, including that of Britain, found that increased spending tended to feed through in the form

---

[1] Smith, K. (1986), *The British Economic Crisis*, Penguin, Middlesex, p.21.

of higher prices, rather than increased output.[2] The problem of unemployment had been swamped by that of inflation. By the mid-1970s, unemployment had risen to one million, but inflation was over 25 per cent.

The Conservative government under Heath, when it began its term of office in 1970, advocated a new commitment to free market ideas. However, the market-led approach was short-lived, as growing recessionary pressures forced the government into a 'u-turn' on the economy, by resorting to standard Keynesian reflation. This 'dash for growth' ended in a mounting trade deficit and rising inflation. In addition, Heath was forced into an accommodation with organised labour in attempting to promote an incomes policy. This eventually ended in humiliating defeat at the hands of the miners and rejection by the electorate at the polls. The Heath years had a profound effect on the Conservative party as it sought to re-group and re-organise following defeat. The dramatic failure of economic policy in these years led to a sharp change in their attitude towards economic management in general and unemployment in particular. A small but influential clique of far right thinkers emerged under the guidance of Keith Joseph. This new right sought a radically different approach to the management of the economy, advocating a return to basic free market philosophies and a limited role for government. This period saw the construction of the intellectual ground for Thatcherism and laid the foundations for the economic agenda of the 1980s.

The Joseph speeches of this time contained everything that is distinctive about the economic and political philosophy which later became known as Thatcherism.[3]

> He and she agreed on everything important about the most important issue of all, the economy. Government could not create jobs, Joseph kept saying. Government should not intervene on incomes. Government could not act in the public interest merely by increasing demand. The expansion of demand, as practised by successive governments, merely led to inflation, which itself soon put the stopper on expansion.

The basic message of the New Right was that government spending had to rise inexorably to sustain interventions in an ever increasing array of social, economic and welfare interventions. This, it was argued, had long-term detrimental effects. Increased taxation to pay for increased government

2 Dunn M. and Smith, S. (1990), 'Economic policy and privatisation', in Savage, S. P. and Robins L. (eds.) *Public Policy Under Thatcher*, Macmillan, London, p.25.
3 Young, H. (1990), *One of Us*, Pan Books London, p.103.

spending created a disincentive to work harder, particularly for lower paid workers caught in a poverty trap with incomes below the level of benefits.

Increased government spending was increasingly financed by increased government borrowing. This tended to force up interest rates, and to crowd-out investment by the private sector. Bacon and Eltis maintained that the non-marketable, mostly public, sector of the economy has grown too large in proportion to the wealth-creating marketable sector, thereby creating a 'structural imbalance'.[4] Such views were coupled with a perception that nationalised industries, and the public sector generally, were inefficient in terms of controlling costs, meeting public demand and in labour relations. Moreover, it was maintained that the growing militancy and power of the trade unions to command high wage settlements had distorted the labour market and restricted the scope for employers to deploy their workforces flexibly and profitably. In general, the rhetoric was one of less government, less welfare, lower taxation and curbed union power. [5]

What gave the New Right its ascendency was the marked deterioration in economic performance in the 1970s. Keynesian methods and techniques of demand management were increasingly undermined by rising inflation and unemployment. The doctrines of monetarism and supply-side economics were being widely espoused by the New Right as radical alternatives to Keynesian economic management.

The Monetarist Challenge

The doctrine of monetarism, which began to be advanced in the 1960s by Milton Friedman and others, was a restatement of the quantity theory of money and a major challenge, both as theory and policy, to Keynesianism.

Monetarism involves one central idea, which concerns the money supply. For monetarists, inflation was a purely monetary phenomenon. It could not occur if the growth of the money supply was kept under control. Milton Friedman argued that previous changes in the money supply could explain, after a time lag, subsequent changes in the inflation rate. Government's task, therefore, was to adopt a macro economic policy, aimed at controlling the money supply. [6]

---

4 Coates, D. and Hillard, J. (1978), *The Economic Decline of Modern Britain*, Wheatsheaf, Brighton, p. 88.
5 Morrissey M. Gaffikin F. (1990), *Northern Ireland: The Thatcher Years*, Zed Books, London, p. 72.
6 Smith, K. (1986), *op. cit.*, p.21.

The proposition that controlling inflation depended on controlling the money supply was complemented by the monetarist view of the effects of 'excessive' levels of government spending and taxation. Government could try to control the growth of the money supply in two ways: by reducing the demand for money via high interest rates; or by reducing the government's borrowing requirement by reducing government spending. For most monetarists, the optimal way to control the money supply was to reduce government borrowing.

The growth of inflation in the 1970s gave a new impetus to these ideas. Labour's approach to the International Monetary Fund in 1976 proved a major turning point in the appeal of monetarism. For the first time, spending limits or monetary targets were used as instruments of economic policy. The decisions to set monetary targets and allow the exchange rate to float up to protect those monetary targets were seen by many as milestones on the road to Thatcher's monetarism. [7]

Balance of payment problems, a sterling crisis and intervention of the International Monetary Fund were used as justification by Labour in 1976 to abandon the full-employment objective of post-war governments and to espouse a policy of deflation which came to be known as monetarism.

But, whereas Labour was forced into an accommodation with monetarisism in response to a particular crisis, the New Right adopted monetarism wholeheartedly in complete rejection of Keynes. [8]

The Thatcher government was different in that it set out determinedly to apply monetarism as a philosophy, relying heavily upon the evidence that the lax monetary policy introduced during the Heath government's term of office had been responsible for the inflationary boom of the early 1970s.

Supply-side Economics

The theoretical accompaniment to monetarism is that of supply-side economics, a central belief of which is that lowering taxes is the way to economic recovery. Lower income tax means a greater return on saving, working and investing. So, with lower taxes, people will work longer and harder and invest more. Output will rise and unemployment will decline. Despite the lower rates of taxation, rising income will, supply-side

---

7 Ball, M. *op. cit.*, p.67-68
8 Curwen, P. (1990), *Understanding the UK Economy*, MacMillan, London, p.12.

economists believe, increase the tax base to such an extent that total tax receipts will, paradoxically, rise.[9]

Supply-side economists also maintain that government spending should also be reduced, particularly on welfare benefits, as too high benefits reduce the incentive to work. Far from explaining unemployment by lack of demand - the cornerstone of Keynesian economics - supply-side economists assert that unemployment derives from the lack of incentive to invest. Supply must be created before demand if there is to be non-inflationary growth.[10]

While the two positions are compatible there was considerable debate as to the relative merits of monetarism and supply-side approaches. [11]

The supply-siders claimed that monetarists paid too much attention to the task of restoring financial stability and not enough to the problem of getting the economy moving again. They gave priority to reawakening enterprise and restoring incentives rather than to rebuilding the monetary circuits that underpin exchange. They urged major reductions in public expenditure and taxation as the priority for economic policy, because they believe that it is the high taxes social democracy requires to finance its programmes that are stifling enterprise, depressing productivity, and leading to high inflation and high unemployment....The task is to liberate energies by cutting taxes and deregulating economic activity. Then the budget will balance and prices will stabilise, if only production can be stimulated efficiently.

The first Thatcher administration had three basic economic objectives, which they perceived to be complementary: to reduce inflation, to curb the power of trade unions and to reduce the economic role of the government. They pursued a strict monetarist line on the economy and indeed were criticised by leading American supply-side economists for an over-reliance on monetary policy.[12] Later Thatcher administrations, however, moved away from monetarism and embraced supply-side policies more fully. The primary economic objective was (and remained throughout the 1980s) to bring inflation under control. Although Thatcherism did not cause the economic crisis which Britain undoubtedly faced at the end of the 1970s, its single-minded pursuit of inflationary goals did tip Britain into severe recession.

---

9 Armstrong, P. Glyn, A. and Harrison, J. (1984), *Capitalism Since World War II, op. cit.*, p.405.
10 Curwen, P. (1990), *op. cit.*, p.13.
11 Gamble, A. (1988), *The Free Economy and the Strong State*, MacMillan, London, p.46.
12 *Ibid.*

The Thatcherists targeted government as the biggest contributor to the expansion of money. The gap between government's income from taxation and what it spent was made up by borrowing. This gap, the budget deficit, is the basis of the Public Sector Borrowing Requirement (PSBR). So the policy decision was to attempt to restrict spending and thus cut borrowing. This approach gave rise to the Medium Term Financial Strategy (MTFS), which linked targets for the growth of the money supply to targets for government borrowing which were consistent with monetary targets. The government imposed 'cash limits' on the budgets of the main spending departments, and sought to impose tight controls on spending by local government and investment by nationalised industries, since borrowing by these were included in the borrowing requirement targets.[13]

Although control of the money supply was placed at the centre of the strategy, it proved impossible to achieve. In 1980-81, the MTFS set target growth at between 7 and 10 per cent. The actual growth was 18.8 per cent.[14] This was partly because the recessionary impact of the monetary policy had simultaneously increased the government's expenditure (on social security and unemployment benefit, for instance) and reduced its income from taxes. However, the squeeze did have a serious impact on cutting expenditure in a number of key areas (education, housing and health services) there was a sharp fall in capital expenditure by the government: programmes of construction and renewal of equipment and buildings were curtailed. This was an important aspect of the massive decline in the construction industry.[15]

The second strand of the policy of restricting money growth was to restrict the demand for money. Banks can increase the amount of money in circulation by lending. The way to restrict lending is to increase its cost. Thus a lowering of the quantity of money implied a rise in interest rates, which they did, rising steadily through the early eighties to rates of 16 to 17 per cent. The policy had a devastating effect on industry. Borrowing costs increased dramatically, while wage and salary costs continued to rise throughout the period. Because of increased foreign competition, firms were unable to increase prices. As interest rates rose, the foreign capital flowed into Britain. This raised the value of the pound, making exports more expensive and imports correspondingly cheaper. Unable to raise prices in line with increased costs meant profitability fell. In an attempt to restore profitability firms cut back on output and supplied goods not from production but by running down stocks. The lowering of current output led

13 Smith, K. (1986), *op. cit.*, p. 20.
14 Young, H. (1990), *op. cit.*, p. 201.
15 Dunn, M. and Smith, S. *op.cit.*, p. 25

inevitably to a reduction in the workforce: 'The object was to cut running costs and to reduce debt to the banks, the effect was to create a recession'[16]

The effect of implementing monetary policy between 1979 and 1981 was to accelerate the decline of British manufacturing and tip the economy into severe recession. The tight fiscal and monetary policy pursued during the first Thatcher administration, while failing to produce a reduction in spending, did however succeed in its main objective of reducing inflation, from 21.9 per cent in 1980 to 3.7 per cent in 1983, just before the general election. But this achievement was purchased at the cost of massive rises in unemployment and a much reduced manufacturing sector. By 1983, the economy was beginning to move out of the policy-accentuated recession and enter a period of growth.

Productivity, Output, and Growth

Since the failure of the British economy to match growth performance of other industrialised countries became apparent in the early 1960s, successive governments have tried a wide range of economic and social policies to seek to reverse the trend.[17] The Thatcher government claimed that as a result of its radical policy prescriptions they had succeeded in affecting a complete turnaround in performance of the UK economy. Certainly, between 1983 and 1988 the British economy experienced sustained and rapid growth. Over the period 1981-88 real output rose at an average rate of just over 3 per cent per annum.[18] The growth rate for GDP exceeded the OECD average, surpassing all the main industrial countries with the exception of Japan and the US.

These figures are less impressive though when viewed from a longer perspective. GDP growth in the peak Thatcher years, at under 2.5 per cent, in fact only surpasses the lean years of 1974-79 when the figure was 1.3 per cent. International comparisons show that between the second quarter of 1979 and the first quarter of 1988, the annual growth rate of total output was 1.9 per cent and that of manufacturing output 0.9 per cent, which puts the UK below the OECD average.[19] Moreover, the signs for long-term sustainable growth in the UK economy were not good. By 1988, clear signs

---

16 Smith, K., *op. cit.*, p.21.
17 Sayer, M. (1989), 'Industry' in Artis, M.J. (ed.), Prest and Coppock's *The UK Economy*, Weidenfeld and Nicholson, London, p.236.
18 Sedgewick, B. (1990), 'The Macroeconomy', in Peter Curwen (ed.), *Understanding the UK Economy*, Macmillan, London, p.13.

19 Morrissey M. and Gaffikin F. (1990), *op. cit.*, p.65.

of excess demand pressure had emerged, inflation was on the rise and the balance of payments showed the largest deficit ever recorded.[20] So, in 1989, the Chancellor had to take action to slow the economy down in order to counteract serious inflationary pressure. The result was plummeting growth and a slide into recession, with unemployment climbing back up to the levels of the early 1980s.

Productivity

Since 1981, there has been a sustained improvement in productivity in the UK economy. UK labour productivity in manufacturing has risen faster than that of any other principle competitor and, in the whole economy, at an annual average of 5.5 per cent, which is lower only than Japan.[21] This is in stark contrast to the 15 years prior to 1979, when growth in productivity in manufacturing, and in the economy as a whole, relative to other industrial countries, put the UK near the bottom. The rate of productivity increase since 1980 is, however, below the levels achieved prior to 1973. There has been a sharper decline in the rate of productivity increase in many other countries than in Britain (since 1973), thereby leading to an improvement in Britain's relative productivity growth record.[22] The UK still remains 25 per cent behind most other European countries in terms of productivity: of the 21 European countries it ranks only 16th.

Figure 7.2 Output per Person Employed (average annual percentage changes) for the whole UK economy

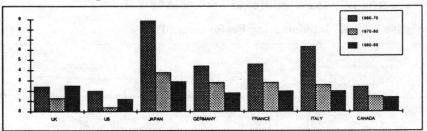

UK data from Central Statistical Office. Other countries data from OECD except 1988, which are calculated from national GNP or OECD employment estimates[23]

---

20 Sedgewick, B. (1990), *op. cit.*, p.48.
21 Morrissey M, Gaffikin F, (1990), *op. cit.*, p. 65.
22 Sayer, M. (1989), *op. cit.*, p.238.
23 Sedgewick, B. (1990), *op. cit.* ,p.52.

Figure 7.3 Output per Person Employed (average annual percentage changes) for Manufacturing Industry

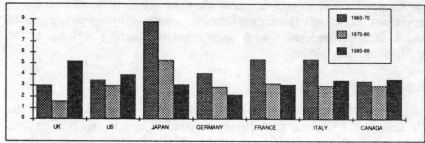

Source: UK data from Central Statistical Office. Other countries' data from OECD, except France and Italy which use IMF employment data. 1988 data for France   and Italy cover first three-quarters only[24]

Industry

The crux of the 1979-81 recession was a collapse in manufacturing. Britain's manufacturing industry has been in decline since the peak of the mid-1960s. Since then employment in manufacturing has steadily declined. This process is usually referred to as de-industrialisation. The trend is shared with most other advanced industrialised countries, except that in the case of the UK, the process has been much more pronounced. The proportion of the workforce in manufacturing in 1966 was 35 per cent; this had declined to 31 per cent by 1979 and dropped to 23 per cent in 1988 [25] .

Figure 7.4 UK Manufacturing Performance 1979-87.

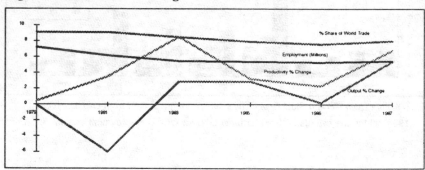

Source: Ball, M (1989), from Gaffikin and Morrissey (1990), p. 71.

---

24 *Ibid.*, p.52.
25 Sayer, M. (1989), *op. cit.*, p.230.

The main determinant of the rapid decline in British manufacturing after 1979 was the impact of a tight monetary policy on the exchange rate. High interest rates, together with the effect of North sea oil, prompted an increase in the value of sterling of over 20 per cent. The rising exchange rate increased the price competitiveness of foreign imports into Britain, and reduced the competitiveness of British-produced exports in overseas markets. The high exchange rate most directly affected those sectors of the economy exposed to foreign competition - primarily the manufacturing sector. Against this backgound the government tightened fiscal policy still further in the deflationary budget of 1981[26].

The effect on manufacturing industry was devastating, coming as it did on top of a deep-rooted neglect of investment requirements for innovation in many sectors: the number of manufacturing jobs fell by almost a quarter between 1979 and 1983, and 'de-industrialisation' became a political as well as an economic issue. The effect of this shake-out on less efficient firms, and of the heavy cuts in the labour force, was to produce a large rise in productivity, together with a notable weakening of trade union power, especially as the severest effects were felt in those sectors where union membership was traditionally high.

Of the nearly two million jobs lost during the period 1979-83 the majority were in full-time manufacturing. Output dropped by 14 per cent and about one-fifth of capacity was lost, representing the largest fall in output and biggest rise in unemployment since the war.

Figure 7.5 Manufacturing Output and Employment (1980 = 100)

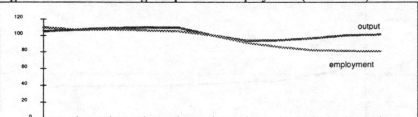

Source: *National Institute Economic Review*, p. 108; *Employment Gazette*, vol. 93, p. 12; *Monthly Digest of Statistics*, No 474, p. 42. from Smith (1986) p.242 [27].

---

26 Dunn, M. and Smith, S. (1990), *op. cit.*, p.30.

27 Smith, K., (1989), *op. cit.*, p.242.

Manufacturing did not recover its 1979 output levels until nearly seven years later in 1986. Although 30 per cent fewer were now employed in manufacturing, productivity had risen by 37 per cent in the period 1979 - 87.[28]

The 1979-81 recession hastened the process of industrial restructuring in Britain. There has been a significant shift in employment between the two main industrial sectors. While some 2 million jobs were lost in manufacturing between 1979 and 1988, 2.4 million were created in the service sector. There was continuous employment growth in service industries after 1983, while manufacturing did not begin to pick up until after 1988. However employment has been falling once again in both sectors as the current recession takes hold, as can be seen in figure 7.5.   Other aspects of the structural changes, which took place in the British labour market during the 1980s, has been the shift in employment in favour of females, the growth of self-employment, and the shifts in employment between the regions.

Figure 7.6 UK Employment in Manufacturing and Services Sectors 1980-91

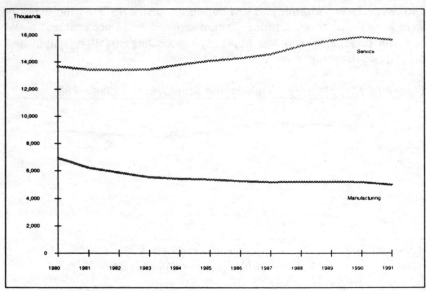

Source: *Employment Gazette 1991*

---

28 Morrissey M. and Gaffikin F. (1990), *op. cit.*, p. 65.

Figure 7.7 Distribution of the Workforce 1978 - 89 (at mid June each year)

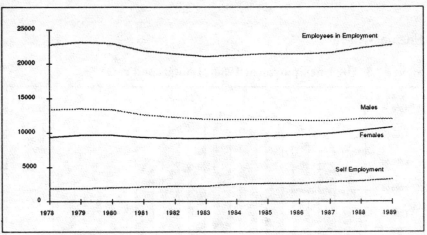

Source: Employment Gazette 1990

Between 1981 and 1988, the number of male employees in employment fell by 500,000, whereas the number of female employees in employment rose by over 900,000.[29] This reflects the fact that males were over-represented in the declining industries, while females have been dominating the expanding industries. However most of these new jobs dominated by females have been part-time. Around 60 per cent of jobs created since 1983 have been in part-time employment so that whereas in 1979 the workforce comprised 15 per cent part-time employees, by 1989 the figure was close to 22 per cent. [30]

The impacts of the recession and the recovery have also been unevenly distributed across Britain. The greatest numbers of jobs lost have been outside the south. During the period of the fastest job shake-out, 1979-83, 94 per cent of the job losses were outside the south. The traditional industries such as shipbuilding, textiles and heavy engineering, which suffered most from the shake-out, tended to be located in the northern regions. Meanwhile, jobs in the private services have been expanding more rapidly in the south. Since the 1960s there has been a reversal in the regional distribution of jobs. The southern regions have increased their share of employment from 47.6

29 Johnes, G. and Taylor, J. (1989), 'Labour', in Artis, M.J. (ed.), Prest and Coppock's *The UK Economy*, Weidenfeld and Nicholson, London, p.292.
30 Morrissey M. and Gaffikin F. (1990), *op. cit.*, p. 65.

per cent in 1965 to 52.9 per cent in 1987, while the northern regions' share has declined from 52.4 per cent to 47.1 per cent over the same period [31].

Unemployment

Figure 7.8   UK Unemployment 1980-91, totals and rates

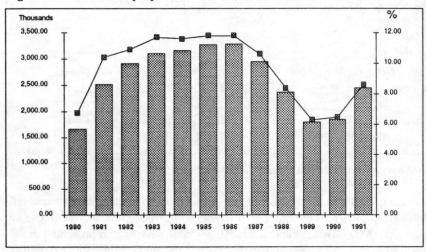

Source: DFP, *Monthly Economic Report,* October 1991.

Unemployment rose sharply as the recession struck between 1979-81, thereafter it continued to rise steadily until 1986, despite the fact that the recovery was well under-way by 1983. Having peaked at 3.3 million in 1986, unemployment fell steadily to 1.6 million in 1989, still well above its 1979 level. However, with the onset of the second major recession in a decade, in the latter half of 1990, unemployment is again on the rise and is forecast to continue to do so into the second half of 1993, when it is expected to rise once again to over 3 million.

With the Conservative party's continued emphasis on inflation as the number one economic priority, unemployment is set to remain at historically high levels. In recognition of the fact that the 'natural rate' of unemployment will have to remain high to achieve an acceptable level of inflation, part of the policy emphasis has been to redefine the way unemployment is calculated. Since 1979 there have been some 29 changes, making comparisons over the period difficult.

---

31 Johnes, G. and Taylor, J., (1989), *op. cit.*, p. 292.

Duration

As well as aggregate changes in unemployment there have been significant changes in the composition of the unemployed since 1979. The growth and persistence of the problem is most obvious in the figures for the long-term unemployed. In 1979 the percentage of the total unemployed who were jobless for more than one year was 25 per cent; by 1988 it had increased to 41 per cent.[32]

The duration of unemployment has always been a contentious political issue as the longer unemployment continues, the greater is the cost both to the individuals concerned and to the state. Indeed the Conservative government, as part of a process of redefining unemployment, sought to view the problem as being largely confined to long-term unemployment.[33]

Therefore, much debate has focused on the reasons for prolonged periods of unemployment. Writers like Minford have pointed to the level of benefits acting as a disincentive, arguing that unemployment support operates like a minimum out-of-work income available indefinitely. Those in the low-paid category, who have lost their jobs, could become long-term unemployed because it will not pay them to lower their wage expectations sufficiently to get a new job.[34] McCormick refers to the fact that a 'large fraction of the very long-term unemployed in Britain's depressed areas are former 'career successes', having previously held well-paid, long lasting skilled manual jobs, from which they were made redundant'.[35] The process of de-industrialisation and the restructuring of British industry, which accelerated in the 1980s, resulted in mismatches between skills and location of people without jobs and the requirements of employers who are seeking people to fill new jobs.[36] Those skilled manual workers from traditional industries, located mainly in the north, were therefore more prone to long bouts of unemployment.

Government responses have been based on notions of labour inflexibilities among the long-term unemployed, assuming the problem to be that of demotivation and lack of skills. Policy has focused on tightening eligibility for benefits and schemes to retrain and remotivate the long-term

---

32 *Social Trends*, (1989) HMSO, London.
33 Daniel, W.W. (1990), *The Unemployed Flow*, Policy Studies Institute, p.136.
34 Minford, P. (1984), *Journal of Economic Affairs*, July.
35 McCormick, B. (1991), *Unemployment Structure and the Unemployment Puzzle*, Employment Institute, p.6.
36 Daniel, W.W., (1990), *op. cit.*, p. 136.

unemployed. However, as Daniel notes, while the characteristics of the unemployed have a strong influence upon who among them are successful in being recruited for the jobs available, it is the general level of demand in the economy that determines the numbers of those jobs.[37]

Regions

As referred to earlier, the structural changes in employment over the eighties has meant that there have been regional differences in the distribution of unemployment. One of the most visible aspects of the 1979-81 recession has been the widening of the north-south divide. The severity of this disparity is best reflected by regional differences in unemployment rates, which have been greater during the 1980s than at any other time since the depression of the 1930s. The north lost over 1.4 million jobs between 1979 and 1986, a drop of employment of 12 per cent compared to a job loss of only 168,000 in the south, a fall of less than 2 per cent.[38] Even with ' the growth of employment since 1983 regional disparities have failed to narrow, with most of the growth occurring in the southern regions. Since 1979 the region with the highest rate of unemployment has continually suffered approximately twice as much unemployment as the region with the lowest rate. Regional policy had begun to close the regional gaps prior to 1979 but this has largely been reversed during the 1980s.[39]

The lack of growth in the north has been explained by the industrial and labour force composition of the region, rather than any disadvantages of the region as a location. McCormick comments that the widening differences between aggregate north-south unemployment rates are indicative of 'the worsening unemployment circumstances of both manual workers relative to non-manual and of former manufacturing employees relative to those in the service sector, together with the higher proportion of manuals and manufacturing that happen to be present in the North'.[40] While the north-south divide is a major economic problem, it is important to acknowledge that unemployment blackspots exist in all parts of the UK, even in regions of generally low unemployment. Inner city areas, in particular tend to have

---

37 *Ibid.*, p.137.
38 Johnes, G. and Taylor, J., (1989), *op. cit.*, p. 312.
39 McCormick, B. (1990), 'The Labour market', in Peter Curwen (ed), *Understanding the UK Economy*, MacMillan, London, p. 223.
40 Ibid. p.18.

highest unemployment whereas the surburbs and smaller towns tend to have lower rates.[41]

Age and Gender

Males have consistently been over-represented among the unemployed, this trend was accelerated after 1980, when male unemployment really took-off and continued to remain high relative to female unemployment throughout the 1980s. The slower rise among females can be explained by the way unemployment is counted and in the changing structure of the labour market. Following changes to the unemployment measure after 1982, many females seeking work, particularly married women, were excluded from the register as they were no longer entitled to benefit. The biggest shake-out of employment occurred in the male-dominated manufacturing industries, while the growth service industries tended to recruit females into part-time lower paid jobs.

Figure 7.9 Unemployment by Gender 1978-79

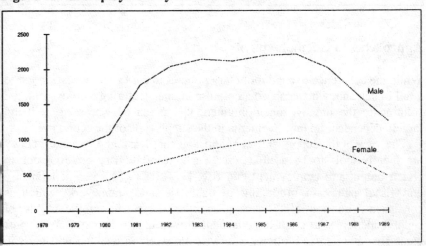

Source: Employment Gazette 1991

Age is a major factor in determining what happens to people after they become unemployed. Older workers have been consistently over-represented among the unemployed; it generally takes them longer to find jobs and these

---

41 Johnes, G. and Taylor, J. (1989), *op. cit.* p., 314.

are usually inferior to their previous employment.[42] In the 1980s this trend continued, but most striking was the increase in youth or young adult unemployment. Despite a range of special measures, prolonged unemployment among young people became considerably more prevalent in the early 1980s.[43]

Figure 7.10   Unemployment Rates by Age 1986-89.

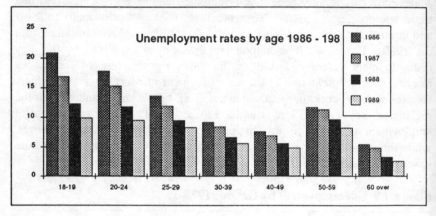

Approaches to Unemployment

While the adherence to rigid monetary policies in the face of recession led to a fall in demand, which caused a collapse in manufacturing employment, the solution to the massive unemployment this produced was seen as being largely dependent on improvements in the supply-side of the economy.

The view of the supply-side economists is that fiscal and monetary policy are merely tools to be used to create a non-inflationary environment in which output and employment can rise. However the success of monetary and fiscal policy in producing a stable demand framework, which is consistent with non-inflationary growth, is dependent on the ability of supply-side forces to produce consistent growth in real output. Supply must come first and demand follow, otherwise an excess in demand will outstrip supply and result in higher prices.[44] This is basically the opposite of the Keynesian position which advocated that the purpose of macroeconomic intervention was primarily to maintain demand during a recession in order

---

42 Daniel, W.W. (1990), *op. cit.*, p. 15.
43 Ibid., p. 16.

to boost output and employment. The supply-siders argue that this had a number of detrimental side effects. The focus on demand, they argue, meant the supply side was neglected which led to rigidities and inflexibilities in the economy. Expectations of full employment created inflexibilities in the labour market, whereby workers may not be prepared to accept lower wages, retrain or move to different locations to find work. Government spending could cause crowding-out of the private sector spending. Moreover, if aggregate supply is inflexible then a surge in aggregate demand will create excess demand and hence drive up prices.

The second Thatcher term saw a move away from monetarism to a greater concentration on supply-side policies. The administration continued the same counter inflationary zeal but, by 1985, the government's inflation policy was no longer based on targets for the rate of growth of the money supply, but on using interest rates to maintain a strong exchange rate. A strong pound made imports cheaper, so helping to control inflation. Cheaper imports also forced UK companies to become more competitive and reduce costs especially wage costs. The abandonment of monetary targets was coupled with an increasing emphasis on supply-side policies as the means to generate employment, mainly through the stimulation of enterprise.[45]

When, in the mid-1980s, unemployment showed little sign of falling despite increasing economic activity, the Thatcher government shifted the emphasis of its policy towards improving the supply-side of the economy.... As the government saw it, workers were 'pricing themselves out of jobs'. Their view was that the key to increasing output and employment was to change, by appropriate 'supply-side' policies, the response of individuals and firms to changing conditions in the market.

This focus on the supply-side of the economy also represented a fundamental shift in that it advocated the market as the main arbiter of demand as opposed to the state.[46]

unemployment, once considered a macro economic problem related to aggregate demand, was now deemed to be a micro-economic difficulty determined mostly by costs and rigidities in local labour markets. Those without work could best resolve their predicament by being prepared to 'price themselves' into a job.

In the same way firms could not be dependent on government to 'bail them out' when the economy was in decline.[47]

---

45 Dunn, M. and Smith, S. (1990), *op cit.*, p. 33.
46 Gaffikin, F. and Morrissey, M. (1990), *op. cit.* p. 64.
47 *Ibid.*

Government intervention in general, and industrial planning in particular, were predicated, in this view, on delusory assumptions about the capacity of politicians and bureaucrats to second guess the market. In Thatcherite rhetoric, the market could not be 'bucked'. Its regulatory and disciplinary power was an indispensable precursor to the 'real' jobs....The government would not bail out firms or industries which transgressed these nostrums.

The period after 1983 saw deregulation, in general, and privatisation, in particular, emerging as a key strategy. Government retreated further from providing direct support to industry, emphasising the market and the emergence of new service jobs to compensate for a lack of industrial policy. Labour-market policy concentrated on remotivating the unemployed back into employment through training schemes, increased policing and eligibility tests.

Industrial policy

Prior to 1979, governments, especially Labour, had sought to develop various forms of positive industrial strategy. Policy largely took the form of limited, selective intervention where potential growth areas were identified and firms were encouraged, sometimes with financial assistance. Thatcherism however, had no specific strategy except a trust in the efficacy of market forces.[48]

A new 'enterprise culture' had to be created in the country which would stimulate a more efficient and productive market. The government's role would be restricted to ensuring that the right external conditions for the self-revival of the market prevailed and that any constraints over its full and unrestricted operation - particularly on the 'supply' side - were effectively removed.

In June 1983, the Department of Industry was merged with the Department of Trade to form the Department of Trade and Industry (DTI). Policy was increasingly non-interventionist, to let market forces decide which firms survived and prospered. The DTI's role was not to support troubled

---

48 Atkinson, R. and Lupton, C. (1990), 'Towards an enterprise culture', in. Savage, S. P. and Robins, L. (eds.), *Public Policy Under Thatcher*, MacMillan, London , p.46.

industries but to promote free-market ideas and supply-side doctrines. In June 1987 Lord Young was quoted in the *Financial Times* as saying that he saw the DTI as the 'Department of Wealth Creation', which would represent the 'Power Station of the Economy', and create the conditions and confidence within which the economy could flourish.[49]

> These objectives were reflected in the title of the White Paper published in January 1988: DTI - The Department for Enterprise (Cm 278). Henceforth the DTI was to be at the cutting edge of Mrs Thatcher's revolution, championing the free-market cause and encouraging industry to adopt new attitudes and practices.

Despite the uneven impact of the 1979-81 recession, particularly on the regions outside the southeast, regional policy was also downgraded.[50]

> If there were regional imbalances (or a North-South divide) they would be rectified if the market were left to its own devices: high costs in the southeast would lead firms to rethink investment strategies causing them to look to regions where costs were low. 'Automatic' market adjustments were to be preferred to state intervention.

A series of reforms to regional policy during the 1980s resulted in the abolition of automatic investment grants in 1988, making all regional policy expenditure discretionary. The aim was to make expenditure more cost-effective, as well as allowing more centralised control over public expenditure. Another change has been to concentrate on setting up and developing small firms in areas of high unemployment, rather than inducing industry to move from other more prosperous areas to the assisted areas, as was the case with regional policy in the 1960s and 70s [51]. Indeed, in their eagerness to stimulate a wider enterprise culture, it seems that the Conservatives have been prepared to sacrifice both industry and the regions.

The main components of industrial growth were to be based on the promotion of the small firms sector and an expanding service sector. The long-term decline in the number of small firms was seen as a key cause of Britain's economic problems and a range of new incentives was introduced to encourage their formation. However, despite the considerable increase in formation, their high failure rate and low job creation record has meant that the impact on employment has been fairly insignificant: 'the socio-economic

---

49 *Ibid.*, p.48.
50 *Ibid.*, p 51.
51 Johnes, G. and Taylor, J., (1989), *op. cit.*, p. 317.

structures of regions which have been heavily dependent upon manufacturing industry for employment over the last hundred years are unlikely suddenly to change and develop a thriving small business sector'.[52]

The proposition that expansion in the service sector can compensate for any manufacturing decline is also debatable. Between 1985 and 1988, the surplus on trade in services dropped by about 40 per cent from almost £6 billion to £3.5 billion, a tiny figure compared to the £14.3 billion trade deficit in that year. Similarly, the notion that service sector employment can compensate for manufacturing job losses is invalid if the historic trend is examined. Private sector service employment rose by only 1 million over the two decades 1960-1980, compared with a loss of 3 million jobs in manufacturing, and there are many signs of substantial overmanning, which will tend to lead to stagnation or decline in service sector employment as productivity increases.[53]

Labour Market Policy

The main agency with responsibility for training and employment services, the Manpower Services Commission, was set up in 1973 in response to evidence of serious inadequacies in the nation's industrial skill-base and the need to intervene to ensure a better fit between the supply of, and demand for, labour. The first Thatcher administration, although committed to the removal of 'quangos' like the MSC, was forced to acknowledge its political usefulness in the face of still rising levels of unemployment. In an effort to counter rising unemployment, a range of different types of schemes was implemented, aimed particularly at the young unemployed and the long-term unemployed. In 1976, less than 100,000 people were on employment and training schemes; by 1988 the number had increased to over 500,000. Between 1983 and 1988, the main schemes in operation were the Youth Training Scheme (YTS), the Community Programme, the Enterprise Allowance Scheme and a number of smaller schemes.[54]

However, the Conservatives sought to align the operations of such schemes more closely with the government's wider political and economic strategies and use them as a vehicle to effect a central readjustment in the balance of responsibility between the state and the individual. The government argued that: [55]

---

52 Atkinson, R. and Lupton, C. (1990),op. cit. ,p. 51.
53 Gaffikin, F. and Morrissey, M., (1990), *op. cit.,*
54 Johnes, G. and Taylor, J., (1989), *op. cit.,* p. 318.
55 Atkinson, R. and Lupton, C. (1990), *op. cit.* p 51.

Those who remained without work... must accept some responsibility for their plight. The state should not support these individuals with benefits or employ them on schemes of 'make-work', but help them improve their employability. The role of the Commission was to encourage this process of self-responsibility: to refit and remotivate individuals for the world of work.

The problem facing the country was thus redefined from the economic problem of insufficient jobs to the social problem of poorly skilled or badly motivated unemployed people. The emphasis was on reducing the amount and cost of state responsibility for the unemployed while maximising their availability for work. This approach required that those without work be made to pay in some way for the benefits they received such as participation on training schemes. Increasingly training opportunities were to be more closely aligned with the operation of the benefits system. Programmes such as Restart were designed to direct the long-term unemployed into short-term work or training programmes. This introduced a greater degree of compulsion into the operation of such schemes, whereby refusal to participate could result in a loss of benefit.

The YTS has been by far the largest of the employment and training schemes. Although originally introduced to induce employers to take on unemployed youths, the operation of the benefits systems now ensures YTS is the norm for school-leavers. The Community Programme was directed specifically at those unemployed for six months or more. The main criticism was that it did not train people for real jobs, it merely reduced the unemployment rate by providing temporary employment which was of little value to those participating over the longer term.

Schemes such as the Community Programme, were seen as a response to the immediate crisis of recession, but by the mid-1980s the economy was supposed to be taking off again. So, the persistence of high unemployment, especially long-term unemployment, was seen as an aberration to be overcome through improving the supply and quality of labour. The long-term unemployed were seen as coming largely from low skilled production backgrounds, whereas the new jobs were in the expanding services sector of the economy. The problem was seen as one of a mismatch between the redundant skills of the unemployed and the skills demanded by the new industries. The solution required that the unemployed be matched to the jobs by retraining and remotivating them.

Therefore in September 1988, Employment Training (ET) was launched, replacing all previous schemes and programmes directed at the long-term unemployed. The aim was to overcome the skills shortage and inflexibilities which the government felt were undermining Britain's industrial performance. However, critics maintained that ET represented a considerable extension of the 'workfarist' approach: trainees were to be paid a benefit-related allowance and, attendance, while not compulsory, was to be encouraged for the 'more poorly motivated clients'.[56] Relating this to the changes under the 1989 Social Security Act, the offer of a place on a training scheme appeared to many to be an offer that unemployed people could not afford to refuse.[57]

However, ET ran into a series of problems. Trainees going through the scheme found they could not find suitable placements with employers after completing their training, despite the much vaunted claims of employer involvement. The high drop-out rate meant it was difficult to entice the unemployed onto the scheme, so undermining its financial viability. In addition, the trade unions withdrew their support from the scheme because of doubts about the quality of training. But the main problem with ET is the fact that its ultimate success depended on the underlying growth of the economy, since finding permanent jobs for those coming off the scheme was determined by the overall growth in employment. In the autumn of 1989 the rundown of ET began. The government announced cuts of £250 million to the ET budget, and a reduction in the places it provided of between 150,000 and 450,000.

The next phase was the abolition of the MSC and its replacement with the Training and Enterprise Councils (TECs). The TECs have taken over all the existing government schemes and the aim is to integrate these with various business enterprise schemes. The TECs are based at local level, and are led by business people and jointly funded from the public and private sector. As well as placing responsibility back onto the unemployed to find their way back into work, the TECs attempt to further delegate responsibility for organising and funding training programmes to the employers themselves [58].

The general aim of the TECs was to transfer the 'prime responsibility for investment in the skills and knowledge of our people' to employers (Norman Fowler, Introduction to the TEC Prospectus). Their central objective was to administer the YTS and ET programmes at a local level and ensure that enough places were made available to meet the government's guarantees to school-leavers and the long-term unemployed.

---

56 *Unemployment Unit* (1989), p.1.
57 Atkinson, R. and Lupton, C. (1990), *op. cit.* p. 56.
58 *Ibid.*, p. 56.

However, as stated in the White Paper Employment for the 1990s which set up the TECs, its starting point was 'sustained falls in unemployment'. The TECs were to emphasise new industries, new jobs and new ways of working. As the private sector took over the running of training and enterprise schemes, recession had just begun and unemployment started to rise again. The private sector managers of TECs saw their role in a wider context more as economic development agencies. Now they are forced into managing employment schemes. The result is that the TECs now run two major programmes which are principally designed to soak up unemployment; the typical TEC budget is 75 per cent dedicated to YT and ET.[59]

As well as trying to use training and enterprise schemes as a substitute for industrial policy and job creation, the Conservatives have also sought to reduce the headline unemployment figures by actively removing people from the register. Since 1979, there have been some 30 changes, which have been based on redefining eligibility or altering the way in which the unemployed were counted.

The 1980s have also seen a major restructuring of the social security system with a range of legislative changes. The changes in social security, instigated as part of the attack on public spending in general, also fitted in with the pursuit of the new enterprise culture. Basically government had to overcome the 'benefits culture' or 'dependency culture' which persisted among claimants of social security. This dependency on the state had been fostered by decades of welfarism and had acted as a disincentive to enterprise and work. The government believed that the payment of certain types of social security encourages people to become dependent on benefit, and lowers their desire to find work or behave in a responsible manner.[60]

The changes to the social security system were at first incremental. The first Thatcher administration, in the face of rising unemployment, was cautious. The initial measures included: not extending the increased rate of benefit to the long-term unemployed because of concern that this would interfere with work incentives; the abolition of earnings-related supplements on short-term National Insurance contributory benefits, such as unemployment, and sickness benefit; and the taxation of unemployment benefit and the restriction of benefit payments to strikers.

However in their second term of office, the Thatcher government announced its review of the social security system in a Green Paper in April 1984 which had four aims: to encourage self-reliance and independence; to be capable of meeting genuine need; to have ease of administration; and to be consistent

59 *Working Brief*, (1991) Unemployment Unit and Youth Aid, December.
60 McGlone, F. (1990), *op. cit.*, p.171.

with the government's overall policies for the economy .[61]   The   reforms published in a White Paper in 1985 were implemented in April 1988. Among the major changes was the introduction of income support and the replacement of single payments with a discretionary social fund. The work incentive elements were very much to the fore. From September 1988, most young people aged 16 and 17 have been unable to claim income support. Instead they are expected to take a place on a Youth Training Scheme (YTS) or go without benefit.[62]

On 9 October 1989 the government implemented new regulations to force the unemployed actively to seek work rather than simply be available for work. Now the unemployed must prove that they are looking for work or have their benefit stopped. The government's view is that the unemployed should either seek work or go on a training course. This is linked to the government's Employment Training programme (ET).... On top of these changes to the unemployed come an increase in the time limits for suspension from unemployment benefit for leaving a job 'voluntarily' from 6 weeks to 13 weeks and now 26 weeks. This is a method to penalise the unemployed for leaving a job without another job to go to, or for being sacked.

Despite the intentions of Government to create a more enterprising society, the number of people dependent on means-tested income support is now higher than ever. By May 1988 the number stood at 8.2m (claimant and family). Much of this increase has been directly related to government reforms in social security and the pursuit of economic policies in the early 1980s which led to a large rise in unemployment. Such facts do not fit easily with government talk of a 'benefits culture' or a 'dependency culture' among claimants of social security.[63]

Overview

In the 1980s, high unemployment not only became politically acceptable, but also came to be used as a deliberate instrument of economic policy. The stagflation and industrial unrest of the late 1970s produced a sea-change in economic thinking and in public perceptions about economic priorities. The pursuit of full employment objectives through demand-led growth were no longer considered viable or even desirable. The Tories successfully propagated an anti-inflationary, monetarist alternative. It was accepted that

---

61 *Ibid.*, p.163.
62 *Ibid.*, p. 169.
63 *Ibid.*, p. 171.

an all out attack on inflation was the key economic priority and that the price would have to be a temporary rise in unemployment. However, the implementation of a severe monetary policy on top of a deep recession in 1980-81 simply deflated the economy and caused unemployment to soar.

Unemployment was the inevitable and wholly predictable result of deliberate policy of deflation. The high levels of unemployment, which were sustained throughout the 1980s, also helped to fulfil other economic policy objectives, namely dampening wage inflation and weakening the power of trade unions. This, it was claimed, was essential to create the conditions for sustained non-inflationary growth.

Having successfully ditched full employment as a primary economic objective, the government then sought to off-load the responsibility for reducing unemployment onto the unemployed themselves - blaming the victim. As the economy began to recover in the second half of the 1980s, but unemployment continued to remain stubbornly high, the focus on supply-side policies intensified. The long-term unemployed in particular had to be coerced, remotivated and retrained back into employment.   Undoubtedly, while increasing the competitiveness of the unemployed will enhance their employment potential, it is only through sustained demand-led growth that the overall size of the unemployed pool can be reduced. The jobs that had been created in the consumer-led boom of the late 1980s were primarily in the service sector, were low-paid and part-time. These were concentrated not in areas of highest unemployment, but in the south and east of the country. Many were filled not by the registered unemployed, but by new entrants to the workforce such as women returners; thus overall employment increased but unemployment still remained high.

The effects of the past 12 years of market-led economy policy has been to create levels of unemployment far beyond anything envisaged or considered acceptable in the previous 30 years. At the same time, unemployment as an issue and the unemployed themselves have largely become marginalised, as the Tories successfully pursued an electoral strategy which concentrated on benefiting the better off two-thirds of the population .

The recovery and supposed economic miracle of the second half of the 1980s has been short-lived. Lack of investment and the 'hands off' approach of government, preferring to concentrate on enterprise rather than industry, has done little to restore the viability of Britain's manufacturing sector. Struggling to recover from the decimation of the early 1980s, British manufacturing is once again threatened by crippling interest rates and an overvalued exchange rate. Dis-investment and the abandonment of regional policy meant that regions outside the southeast benefited little from the late 1980s boom. In the midst of the second recession in a decade, unemployment is set to climb back to the levels of the mid-1980s.

Forecasters predict high unemployment is set to remain a permanent feature of the 1990s.

8. Unemployment in the Periphery: Ireland

In this chapter a comparison is made of the changing patterns of unemployment in the two Irish economies. It further examines other indicators such as employment, output and economic growth since these are the context within which unemployment occurs. However, the economy is not isolated from the rest of society. It is, therefore, appropriate to also examine features like demographic structure and public policy. Although Northern Ireland is part of the UK, it remains useful to analyse its unemployment together with that of the Irish Republic.

The Irish Republic had the second highest unemployment rate in the EC for much of the 1980s. Indeed, were it not for substantial emigration, its unemployment rates would have been even more serious. Northern Ireland consistently had the highest rates of unemployment within the UK, close to those in the Irish Republic. Moreover, Northern Ireland is the only UK region which has been given Objective I status by the European Community, giving it the highest priority in the allocation of EC structural funds. Admittedly, on the criterion of GDP per head at 75 per cent or lower of the Community average, Northern Ireland should not qualify for this designation. The determining factor is more the political-military conflict than its levels of GDP. Nevertheless, if British exchequer subsidy was removed from the region, its GDP would fall significantly below the Community average. The Irish Republic has the same Objective I status. The EC thus treats the two economies as having similar problems. Finally, recent debates about economic development in Ireland have focused on the degree of economic co-operation between the Irish states.[1] All of these factors suggest that it is worthwhile to look at both together, when unemployment is the central concern.

At the same time, this perspective does not imply a commitment to their political unity. Rather, it is a recognition of common problems, particularly with respect to unemployment and their common location on the periphery of the EC. In any case, those most determined to create a single state within

---

[1] see Teague, P. (1989), Economic Development in Northern Ireland: has Pathfinder lost its way?, *Regional Studies*, 23, pp. 63-9.

Ireland are not primarily driven by economic arguments. Certainly, it is difficult to see how Northern Ireland could sustain either its financial incentives to industry or its relatively high social spending without continued subvention by the British exchequer. As Kennedy comments:[2]

> Both an 'independent' Ulster and a 'united' Ireland are non-viable constitutional options except under conditions of continuing external benefaction (the begging bowl scenario) or a catastrophic decline in living standards (a working class nightmare).

Comparing the Irish Economies

Table 8.1 provides a summary of basic indicators comparing the Irish Republic, Northern Ireland and the UK. The Irish Republic has a population more than twice as great as Northern Ireland's, but it is more geographically dispersed. Both have similar proportions of their populations of working age, though with marked differences in the young and old components. Northern Ireland has higher birth and death rates, while infant mortality is also greater, a reversal of previous trends.

These economies exhibit both similarities and differences. Each has similar percentages of employees engaged in industry, though with very different proportions in agriculture and services. The Irish Republic only really began to seriously industrialise after Partition - agriculture, therefore, continued to play a more significant role in its economy. Curiously, the operation of the Common Agricultural Policy helped sustain agricultural employment by, in effect, offering subsidies to inefficient agriculture. Fiscal policies have had a similar result. Without a significant shift in either of these, it is unlikely that the role of the Irish Republic's agriculture in sustaining employment will fall to Northern Ireland levels.

There has been some debate about the significance of the very high service content of employment in Northern Ireland. Some economists argue that the advanced economies are destined to see services displace manufacturing as the engine of economic growth,[3] in which case Northern Ireland would be some distance along the road. However, the alternative view is that the loss of manufacturing is inevitably associated with economic decline: deindustrialisation.[4] Certainly in the case of Northern Ireland, there has been a dramatic fall in manufacturing employment. Many of the lost jobs have been replaced by public sector employment rather than business services or the new technologies of communication and co-ordination. By the early 1990s, public service employment constituted around 42 per cent of all employees in the region.

---

[2] Kennedy, L. (1989), *The Modern Industrialisation of Ireland 1940-1988*, The Economic and Social History Society of Ireland, Ireland, p.50.

[3] Neuburger, H. (1982), 'Does manufacturing deserve special status?,' in Currie, D. and Sawyer, M. (eds.), *Socialist Economic Review*, Merlin, London.

[4] Coates, D. and Hillard, J. (1986), The Economic Decline of Modern Britain, *op.cit.*

Table 8.1 Basic Comparative Indicators, the Irish Republic,
Northern Ireland and the UK, 1988

	Irish Republic	N.Ireland	UK
Population, (000s)	3,538.0	1,578.1	57,065.6
Persons per Sq. Km.	51.4	111.8	233.8
Population % under 15 (1987)	28.7	25.2	18.
over 65 (1987)	10.9	12.1	15.5
Birth Rate per 1,000	15.3	17.6	13.8
Death Rate per 1,000	8.9	10.1	11.3
Infant Mortality per 1000 (1987)	7.9	9.5	9.3
Employment (1989)			
Agriculture	15.5	5.7	2.2
Industry	28.8	29.3	32.6
Services	55.8	65.0	65.1
Unemployment rate. (1989)	17.1	17.3	7.3
GDP per head (EC12 = 100)	65.0	80.0	107.0

Note: Figures relate to 1988 unless otherwise stated.

Source: Regional Trends (1991), table 14.1

The existence of a very large public sector has implications for the whole economy. The region's Department of Economic Development argued in the late 1980s that Northern Ireland lacked an enterprise culture.[5] In a sense, the public sector was 'crowding out' entrepreneurial development by providing secure and relatively well-paid employment for those who might otherwise have initiated private businesses. This thesis became a key assumption for policy development in the 1990s. During the 1980s, the Irish Republic negotiated a painful transition from a highly indebted economy. Without an external benefactor, increased public spending had to be financed by borrowing. When governments felt they were no longer able to manage public debts amounting to 113 per cent of GNP, public expenditure in general, and social expenditure in particular, were much reduced.

---

[5] Department of Economic Development, Northern Ireland (1987), *The Pathfinder Process*, Belfast.

Both economies have similar levels of unemployment which is about 70 per cent higher than the average for the European Community. However, the entry of Greece to the Community in 1981 and the more recent arrival of Spain and Portugal in 1985 increased the unemployment average within Europe. Unemployment in the Irish states was thus drawn closer to a European average without any resolution of their respective problems.

There are also clear differences in the respective levels of GDP per head, implying a better position in Northern Ireland. However, this is largely illusory. Around 60 per cent of GDP in Northern Ireland has been generated by public expenditure, of which about two-fifths consists of British Exchequer subvention. Without that annual subsidy, which has risen to around £1.8 billion, Northern Ireland's GDP figure would be undoubtedly lower, by about 25 per cent, thus giving an adjusted GDP per head ratio of about 60.

In many respects, Northern Ireland is more like the Irish Republic than the UK. The latter is a much larger entity with considerably greater population density than both Irish states. The structure of the UK population is also different with relatively less dependent children and a greater proportion of its population over 65. Equally, it has a substantially lower unemployment rate, a greater GDP per head and an employment structure that differs from those in the Irish states.

Nevertheless, there are severe limitations to a 'snap shot' picture of the two areas. Accordingly, these indicators are examined in further detail with particular reference to changes over time.

Employment

Between 1982-88 the total numbers at work in the Irish Republic dropped by an average of 10,000 per annum. This was reflected in the large rise in unemployment from 11.4 per cent in 1982 to 17.7 per cent in 1987, improving to a rate of 16.6 per cent in 1988. Northern Ireland also experienced a consistent rate of growth in unemployment up until 1986, followed by decline between 1986 and 1990. Thereafter, reflecting the severe recession in the British economy, unemployment began to grow again.

Table 8.2 compares employment and unemployment in the two Irish economies. In the Irish Republic, changes in the structure of employment in the 1980s have been significant. The long-term decline in agriculture continued, while there was a growth in services. Both manufacturing and construction registered falls in employment. Employment in construction by 1987 had dropped to 41 per cent of its 1980 level. This trend was partly influenced by decreases in public capital expenditure. In the period 1981-87, manufacturing's share of total employment fell from 22 per cent to 19 per cent, similar to that in Northern Ireland. This was about a fifth of all employment compared to around a quarter in Britain. Both Britain and Northern Ireland showed a high share in the services sector - at 68 per cent it was considerably greater than the 57 per cent in the Irish Republic. Nevertheless, the service sector in the Irish Republic has been growing in relative importance. In the 1970s it accounted for 77.8 per cent of net new jobs created outside agriculture. While agriculture and related industries are more important in terms of jobs in Northern Ireland than in Britain, they are of even greater significance in the Irish Republic. In 1987 agriculture accounted for 11 per cent of GDP in the Irish Republic and employed 15 per cent of the total employed. Moreover, a fifth of the manufacturing sector was devoted to the food processing industry.

Table 8.2   Civilian Workforce and Unemployment, Irish Republic and Northern Ireland, 1985-1990

	Civilian Labour Force (000s)		Employed (000s)		Unemployment Rate	
	IR	NI	IR	NI	IR	NI
1985	1,305	693.0	1,079	563.7	17.3	16.3
1986	1,308	695.6	1,081	561.5	17.4	17.6
1987	1,312	697.8	1,080	563.7	17.7	17.5
1988	1,310	695.5	1,091	571.7	16.7	16.3
1989	1,292	686.6	1,090	572.4	15.6	15.7
1990	1,303[1]		1,120		14.0	15.7

Notes: [1.] Figures for June
          The 1990 figures for the Irish Republic are estimates.

Sources: Economist Intelligence Unit, (1991), *op.cit.*, pp.13 & 42; Eurostat
          (1991), *op.cit.*, table 3.30

In the period 1979-87, manufacturing employment in Northern Ireland slumped by over 45,000.[6] Since the mid-1980s, there has been a net loss of over 5,000 manufacturing and 3,000 construction jobs, a drain only partially compensated by a consistent increase in service employment. The effect was that by 1988 there were nearly 3,000 jobs fewer than five years previously. However, between June 1988 and June 1991 the number employed increased by over 8,000 and those self-employed by over 3,000. All of the increase took place in services, with manufacturing and construction shedding 6,000 jobs, as can be seen in table 8.3. Approximately 50 per cent of total employment in the manufacturing sector in Northern Ireland is still represented by 'traditional' sectors such as shipbuilding, textiles, clothing and tobacco industries and, until the recent spate of redundancies, employment in

---

[6] Northern Ireland Economic Council (1989), *Economic Strategy: Overall Review*, Belfast.

both Harland and Wolff, and Short Brothers and Harland accounted for about 10 per cent of the total.

Table 8.3 Employment Trends in Northern Ireland, 1981-91				
Years (June)	Manufacture	Construction	Services	Total
1981	123,000	28,300	325,200	506,920
1982	111,550	28,750	328,900	499,760
1983	106,900	28,250	331,050	497,650
1984	107,230	26,970	333,310	498,040
1985	108,070	27,100	339,210	504,590
1986	104,810	24,550	343,800	502,510
1987	103,370	25,840	347,080	505,050
1988	105,550	26,360	357,640	518,050
1989	106,310	25,990	366,550	527,410
1990	104,890	25,940	371,140	530,330
1991	102,400	23,350	372,460	526,370
Source: Policy, Planning and Research Unit, Economics Division (1991), Monthly Economic Report, November, table 3				

However, in employment terms, services was by far the most dynamic sector. It is notable that public services still represents nearly half of total service employment in Northern Ireland. Growth in critical private sector areas, such as banking, insurance and business services, has been modest. On the other hand, in the Irish Republic between 1981-87 the share of total employment represented by the 'Commerce Insurance and Finance' component of its service sector rose from 18 per cent to 20 per cent. The change in services employment during the 1980s can be seen in table 8.4.

Table 8.4 Employment Change in the Service Sector, Northern Ireland, 1981-90			
	1981	1990	% Change
Distribution	20,300	21,700	+7
Retailing/ Repair	42,200	52,050	+23
Hotels & Catering	12,350	19,900	+61
Transport	10,872	11,850	+9
Communications	9,150	8,550	-7
Banking & Insurance	11,100	11,850	+7
Business Services	14,750	22,450	+52
Public Admin.	51,200	55,750	+9
Sanitary Services	3,850	7,900	+105
Education	56,150	57,550	+2
Health	45,950	48,350	+5
Other Services	41,100	50,500	+23
Sources: Northern Ireland Annual Abstracts of Statistics, 1984 and 1991			

Unemployment Patterns: Northern Ireland

Northern Ireland shows a persistently worse unemployment rate than the UK as a whole. It also has a higher share of its male unemployment in the long-term category (over 52 weeks duration) compared to Britain - 59.2 per cent compared to 44.6 per cent in July 1988.

Reflecting the job shake-out in the 1980s, unemployment in Northern Ireland substantially increased during the decade. Between 1979 and 1981 unemployment rose by over 60 per cent and continued to increase until 1986, when the official unemployment rate reached 18.1 per cent.[7] This represented a total of 127,800 unemployed people, over 70 per cent of whom were men. Between then and 1990, unemployment fell by over 30,000. However, this apparent reduction in unemployment has to be seen in the context of the labour market effects of motivation programmes such as Restart, and availability for work tests on the number of unemployed claimants and in rule changes which disqualified under 18-year-olds from benefit. There were over 33,000 people in government employment and training schemes in 1990, a substantial increase since 1979.[8] Even so, unemployment once more began to rise and by October 1991 stood at 101,441.[9]

The severity of the unemployment problem is indicated by long-term unemployment figures shown in table 8.5.

Table 8.5	Duration of Unemployment in Northern Ireland, 1981 and 1990					
	1981		1990		% Change	
	Males	Females	Males	Females	Males	Females
Up to 6 months	30122	18671	21583	12208	-3	-3
6 months to 1 year	18631	7667	10364	4265	-4	-4
1 year to 2 years	13625	4452	10485	3360	- 2	-3
2 years +	12831	2090	31330	5881	+44	+81
All	75209	32880	73762	25714	-2	-2
Sources:	Northern Ireland Annual Abstract of Statistics, 1982 and 1990					

---

7 Northern Ireland Economic Council (1989), *Autumn Economic Review*, Belfast.

8 Northern Ireland Economic Council (1991), *Autumn Economic Review*, October, Belfast, table 5.3.

9 Economics Division, Policy, Planning and Research Unit (1991), *Monthly Economic Report*, Department of Finance and Personnel, Northern Ireland, November.

Between 1981 and 1990, unemployment fell for both men and women. However, the percentage declines were greatest for the groups with low unemployment duration. The very long-term unemployed category (two years +) saw very substantial increases. Thus, unemployment was recomposing over the decade with greater proportions falling into the longer term category. As indicated in Chapter Two, duration of unemployment is a crucial variable in determining the poverty of the unemployed. Moreover, prolonged absence from the labour market is associated with less job search activities and greater reluctance by employers to offer jobs. By 1990, 57 per cent of men and 37 per cent of women had been out of work for at least a year. Changes in the unemployment count in 1982 excluded some unemployed women from the register, so the 1990 figure undoubtedly under-represents their experience of long- term unemployment.

The uneven spatial distribution of unemployment in Northern Ireland was also exacerbated over the 1980s. The analysis of change in this respect is difficult because of the redesignation of 'travel to work' areas. Two such areas, Armagh and Downpatrick, which existed in 1981, had disappeared by 1990. The former was incorporated in Craigavon and the latter in Belfast. Moreover, Magherafelt did not exist in 1981 but appeared in the 1990 data. It appears that this was formerly part of the Londonderry travel to work area.[10] Thus, to make a comparison over time, some data aggregation is required for each year. This exercise reveals that while unemployment fell by just over 5 per cent between September 1981 and July 1990, areas like Ballymena and Enniskillen enjoyed substantially greater falls - 70 per cent and 15 per cent respectively. By contrast, Londonderry and Newry saw significant increases in their numbers unemployed - 15 per cent and 11 per cent. Arguably, such spatial differentiation reflects a further unequal division in the distribution of employment and unemployment within the region.

Unemployment in Northern Ireland cannot be addressed without attention to the differential rates experienced by the two religious communities. Few now contest the basic proposition that unemployment is twice as high amongst Catholics as amongst Protestants. What is fiercely disputed is the explanation for this disparity. One view sees it as an inevitable outcome of deliberate Unionist government policy to implement discriminatory employment practices in the public sector and to recommend a similar disposition to its brethren in the business community. Leading Unionist figures such as Brookeborough and Craigavon are quoted as openly advocating this ploy as a means of containing a whole community

---

[10] Information from the Statistics Branch, Department of Economic Development, Northern Ireland.

characterised as 'disloyal' on the basis of their religion.[11] From such a perspective, the mechanisms deployed for this purpose included:[12]

ensuring industry was located in places inaccessible to Catholics;

refusing to select Catholics who applied for jobs;

companies establishing reputations as being unreceptive to Catholic recruitment, so that Catholics come to perceive the futility of job applications;

by-passing public processes of selection, so that informal networks, including the channels of the Orange and Masonic Orders, substitute as recruitment agencies.

In addition to such factors as the location of jobs and job losses, and the procedures of selection and promotion, another device seen as curtailing Catholic employment is intimidation in the workplace itself.[13] Thus, discrimination can be overt or covert: it can be intentional or the legacy of pro-active policies of the past. Whatever the form it takes, it persists, remaining the most significant determinant of religious distinctions in the labour market.

An alternative perspective explains the differential unemployment rates largely in terms of factors inherent in the Catholic community itself. Included in these would be higher population growth rates, lower social status, bigger family size and a disjuncture between its geographical distribution and job location.[14] The obvious corollary of such interpretations is that resolution of religious inequalities in the labour market is the responsibilty of the victimised community.

The variation in fertility rates between the two communities is a long-standing issue of contention. The rate in Northern Ireland as a whole is greater than that in Britain, and within Northern Ireland, Catholic fertility rates have traditionally exceeded those of Protestants. Arguing that this inevitably results in high labour market entry and surplus labour supply in the Catholic community, Compton has suggested that this accounts significantly for the 'extra' unemployment suffered by Catholics.[15] But Eversley disputes its importance, pointing out that the inconsistencies of the differential rate historically had no notable impact on the disparities in unemployment: 'The further we go back in the post-war evolution of the Northern Ireland

---

[11] Farrell, M. (1976), *Northern Ireland: The Orange State*, Pluto Press, London.

[12] Rowthorn, B. and Wayne, N. (1987), *The Political Economy of Northern Ireland*, Lawrence & Wishart, London.

[13] Rolston, B. and Tomlinson, M. (1989), *Winding Up West Belfast*, Obair, Belfast.

[14] Compton, P. (ed.) (1981), *The Contemporary Population of Northern Ireland and Population Related Issues*, The Queen's University, Belfast.

[15] *Ibid.*

population the smaller the share of Catholics in both the child and the adult working age groups; yet the excess unemployment was always there.'[16]

A different emphasis on the fertility factor highlights the link between higher Catholic fertility rates generating Protestant fears of being overwhelmed by its religious and political foes, fears which in turn give rise to prejudice, which itself is the foundation of discriminatory employment practices. But however much this may explain the process, it cannot be used to justify it.

The argument for greater Catholic labour mobility as a means of reducing the unemployment gap is based on the particular geography of jobs in Northern Ireland. It reflects the economic partition of the region between the relatively prosperous East, centred around Belfast, and the depressed West, where Catholics are concentrated. Finding themselves in such a disadvantaged area, Catholics, it is said, should be enterprising enough to move to areas where jobs exist. There are a number of problems with this argument. It fails to distinguish between 'undevelopment' as an inevitable, if unfortunate, outcome of 'natural' market determinants of industrial location, and 'under-development' as a function of deliberate neglect by capital and state. Moreover, it does not explain why even in the prosperous East, the concentrated areas of worst unemployment, like West Belfast, contain predominantly Catholic populations.[17]

Another issue raised by those who regard the problem as fundamentally one of supply is that of the 'skills mismatch', whereby Catholic education is said to fail to develop the necessary aptitudes for a technology-intensive economy. Traditional concentration on the Arts and Humanities displaced the emphasis that should have been attached to engineering and scientific skills. The problem with this diagnosis is that the unemployment differential preceded the more recent period when an increasing bifurcation of the labour market has demanded high-tech skills. Also, despite an increasing convergence in educational patterns between the two communities in recent years, the differential in unemployment remains considerable. Lastly, there is a higher unemployment rate amongst qualified Catholics than amongst their Protestant counterparts.

The inequalities have also been apparent in employment patterns. Successive Fair Employment Agency (FEA) and Fair Employment Commission (FEC) reports[18] have testified to an imbalance in the labour forces both of whole industrial sectors and particular significant firms. Not only are Catholics under-represented generally but there is also a progressively decreasing representation the further one looks up the hierarchy

---

[16] Eversley, D. (1989), *Religion and Employment in Northern Ireland*, Sage Publications, London, p. 221.

[17] Gaffikin, F. and Morrissey, M. (1990), *Northern Ireland: The Thatcher years, op. cit.*

[18] See for example, Fair Employment Agency (1983), *Report of an Investigation by the Fair Employment Agency into the Non-Industrial Northern Ireland Civil Service*, Belfast.

of supervisory and managerial grades. Eversley again disavows the explanation of location: 'Even in the more heavily Catholic areas, Catholics got less than their proportional share of managerial, professional and supervisory positions, men and women alike. In predominantly Protestant areas, their share was even smaller.' [19]

Even during the boom years of the 1960s, the differential experience of unemployment did not significantly alter. Certainly, when the Protestant labour market tightened, there were better prospects for Catholics. But this still left them vulnerable if only on the basis of the practice of 'last in first out'. Nor did the advent of transnational capital in the 1950s and 1960s make an appreciable difference. Apparently, despite often bringing in their own senior management, these firms tended to reproduce existing employment patterns. Figures from the 1990 Labour Force Survey[20] suggest that this remains at least partly the case. The larger employers tend to be transnational in character. Yet, the share of male employees who were Catholic was 43 per cent in workplaces with fewer than 25 employed, but 34 per cent in workplaces with 25 or more employed.

The 1990 Labour Force Survey offers the most up-to-date review of the employment and unemployment patterns between the two communities. According to its figures, Protestants accounted for 44 per cent and Catholics for 56 per cent of the total unemployed. The rate of unemployment among Catholic males was twice that of Protestant males (22% and 11% respectively), though the gap for females was less marked (10% and 7% respectively). The difference in male unemployment rates was greatest in the 25-39 age group (with Catholics at a rate of 21% and Protestants at 9%) and was lowest in the 16-24 age group (with Catholics at 24% and Protestants at 15%).

A comparison of 1989 and 1990 figures shows that of those in employment in 1989, a slightly higher proportion of Protestants (94%) than of Catholics (91%) remained in employment a year later. In addition, of those unemployed in 1989, a significantly higher share of Protestants had found work (35%) compared to Catholics (21%). This is reflected in the data for length of time seeking employment. The percentage of Catholics looking for work after one year or more was 61, whereas the comparable figure for Protestants was 48.

At odds with this picture of severe and persistent Catholic disadvantage is the data for employment when set alongside that for the economically active. Of all economically active males, 59 per cent were Protestant and 41 per cent were Catholic. Of the total number of males in employment, 62 per cent were Protestant and 38 per cent were Catholic. Expressed in these terms, the jobs disparity is much less severe.

---

[19] Eversley, D., *op.cit.*, p.228.

[20] Statistics and Social Division, PPRU (1991), *1990 Labour Force Survey: Religion report*, PPRU Monitor 3/91, Belfast.

To what extent does the Labour Force Survey bear out the arguments of the main protaganists? Amongst the economically active, while females from both communities had similar levels of qualifications, the share of Catholic males with no qualifications (51%) was considerably higher than the share of Protestant males (39%). This would seem to lend some weight to the argument of those who explain the unemployment disparity in terms of differential educational attainment. On the other hand, the share of Protestants and Catholics attaining higher education qualifications was about the same (12% and 11% respectively). Yet, arguably, this similarity is not reflected in terms of employment. Another interesting difference is both communities' perception of employment prospects. Of the economically inactive, a higher share of Catholics (16%) than of Protestants (10%) gave the lack of available jobs as the reason for not seeking work.

The over-representation of Catholics among the unemployed would seem to be multi-causal in terms of the interaction of both supply-side and demand-side factors. The existence of supply-side factors, such as higher fertility or differential educational qualifications, does not invalidate the operation of the many forms of discrimination. Nor does it allow for any complacency about the effectiveness of anti-discrimination legislation.

Patterns of Unemployment: The Irish Republic

As in other market economies, unemployment in the Irish Republic was consistently higher in the 1980s than in the previous decade. Its unemployment rate rose from 7.14 per cent in 1979 to 17.51 per cent in 1987. It then fell to 14.72 per cent by 1991, but this was more than double the 1979 rate.[21] The characteristics of unemployment in the latter half of the 1980s is given in table 8.6. The numbers unemployed remained above 200,000 for the entire period and the unemployment rate was the second highest in the EC. The unemployment rates for women and young people were higher than the general rate although these groups constituted about a third of the total unemployed. Yet during this period, the Republic's economy grew rapidly with GDP per head increasing by 40 per cent between 1985 and 1989. However, in recent years, the Irish Republic has relied on export-led growth, and the general recession at the end of the 1980s shrank its export markets. By October 1991, the unemployed numbered 264,600, while employment had fallen by 5,000 over the year. Manufacturing output and retail sales remained static and agricultural output had fallen by nearly 3 per cent.[22] Economic growth reduced unemployment to the levels of the 1970s.

---

[21] Anderton, R., Barrell, R. and in't Veld, J.W. (1991), 'Macro economic convergence in Europe', *National Institute Economic Review*, no. 138, November, table 5.

[22] Tansey, P. (8/12/1991), 'Profile of an economy in decline', *Sunday Tribune*.

Indeed, it would appear that the unemployment base stayed around 200,000 with significant rises during recession.

Table 8.6 Unemployment in the Irish Republic, 1985-90				
	Number (000's)	Rate	% Women	% <25 Years
1985	240	18.2	35.0	38.2
1986	239	18.0	35.1	36.1
1987	230	17.4	34.7	34.3
1988	208	16.0	34.6	31.7
1989	202	15.6	35.9	32.0
1990	239	18.2	34.2	38.5
Note:	The unemployment rates do not correspond completely with those above since the former are derived from OECD data.			
Source:	Eurostat (1991), op.cit., tables 3.21 and 3.22			

As in Northern Ireland, the rise in unemployment was accompanied by more rapid growth of the long-term group, who were 35 per cent of all unemployed in 1980, rising to 45 per cent in 1988.[23] Between April 1981 and April 1991, the number of long-term unemployed males increased by 237 per cent and of females by 442 per cent.[24] There was thus a similar recomposition of unemployment, with a substantial bias towards the longer term categories. The social costs and difficulties of re-integrating the long-term unemployed into the labour market have been indicated earlier.

Some analysts suggest that the Irish Republic's experience of unemployment in the 1980s was largely the result of earlier economic mismanagement. Despite upward pressure on labour supply due to increasing participation and a high natural population growth rate in the 1970s, expansionary public policies contained the rise in unemployment. Unfortunately, such policies were financed by foreign borrowing. When it was considered necessary to contain the debt/GNP ratio and, hence, introduce deflationary policies, these coincided with an international downturn. The unemployment impact was all the greater. As Barry and Bradley commented: '....the unemployment of the 1980s has been to a significant extent a consequence of the fiscal mismanagement of the 1970s, when inappropriate policies were pursued, the tax base eroded, and the national debt built up.'[25]

The examination of unemployment in the Irish Republic must also take into account its patterns of emigration. The migration of population from

---

[23] Blackwell, J. (1990), 'The EC social charter and the labour market in Ireland', in Foley, A. and Mulreany, M. (eds.), *The Single European Market and the Irish Economy*, Institute of Public Administration, Dublin, p.352.

[24] Calculated from *Statistical Abstract (1986)*, CSO, and *Statistical Bulletin (1991)*, vol. 66, no.4, December, Stationary Office, Dublin, tables 8 and 8.21.

[25] Barry, F. and Bradley, J. (1991), 'On the causes of Ireland's unemployment', *The Economic and Social Review*, vol. 22, July, p.278.

Ireland, particularly to Britain, has been an established pattern since the 19th century and continued after independence in this century. However, during the 1970s economic growth and increased employment produced net immigration. The harsher economic climate of the 1980s once again saw the outward movement of population. Net emigration averaged 14,400 per year between 1981-86 and 35,000 per year between 1986-89.[26] Critics have argued that this process reduces the skill base of the labour market, since the most mobile are frequently the young and highly skilled. Certainly, the proportion of those with higher education degrees who emigrated increased from 8.4 per cent in 1980 to 29.4 per cent in 1988. It has been contended that the greater facilitation of labour mobility within the European Single Market will exacerbate the trend, particularly with anticipated falls in the Community's population aged 15-25. The Irish Republic will continue to have large numbers in this age group, the majority of whom will be better educated than potential migrants from the Southern periphery of the EC.[27] However, the UK remains the major location for Irish migrants and high levels of unemployment there may inhibit emigration there.

Comparative Living Standards and Poverty

Any consideration of personal disposable income in Northern Ireland must take into account the region's net fiscal transfers from the UK Exchequer. Similarly, the figure for the Republic in 1985, given in table 8.7, reflects something of the high levels of public borrowing during this period.

Table 8.7 Personal Disposable Income per Capita in Ireland and the UK, 1985	Exchange Rate Conversion to Sterling	Purchasing Power Parity for Private Consumption
Irish Republic	2869	2708
N. Ireland	3538	3538
UK	4221	4211
Ratios:		
Irish Republic/UK	68.1	64.3
N.Ireland/UK	84.0	84.0
Irish Republic/N. Ireland	81.0	76.5
Source: Kennedy, K. et al. (1988), table 6.3		

Both sustained income levels that would otherwise have been unattainable. The two measures of living standards were based on different criteria. In the

---

[26] Blackwell (1990), *op.cit.*, p.352.

[27] See Sexton, J. (1990), 'The labour market implications of the completion of the internal market', in Foley and Mulreany, *op.cit.*, pp.348-9.

first, personal disposable income per capita was converted to sterling. On this basis, while Northern Ireland had a lower standard than the UK, the Republic fell even further behind. The gap widened when consideration was given to the spending power of these income levels. A higher cost of living in the Republic reduced the value of personal income further in relation to Northern Ireland.

In the debate about comparative standards, the relative benefit of the respective social welfare infrastructures to the citizens of each, is a crucial issue. Comparisons between the two welfare states in Ireland is difficult because of their different structures, different allocation of services between central and local government and the voluntary sectors, and different distribution of finances. Studies in the mid-1980s indicated that Northern Ireland devoted a higher proportion of GDP to social spending and, in areas like housing and health, offered more comprehensive provision.[28] Between 1984 and 1989, expenditure on health, education and social welfare in the Irish Republic averaged 27.3 per cent of GDP. In the same period, expenditure on health, education and social security in Northern Ireland averaged 36 per cent of GDP. Since GDP per head in Northern Ireland is greater than in the Irish Republic, these figures suggest that the former enjoyed higher social expenditure.[29]

While Northern Ireland was partially insulated from the public expenditure restraint practiced in Britain, particularly with respect to housing, it suffered disproportionately from social security reforms. The Irish Republic's social welfare provision also suffered the consequences of fiscal retrenchment, as government reduced the Public Sector Borrowing Requirement from 16 per cent of GNP to 3.5 per cent between 1984 and 1989.

Northern Ireland has been traditionally regarded as the UK's poorest region. During the 1980s, it had the lowest GDP per head, the greatest levels of dependency on social security and the highest unemployment. In addition, average earnings were lower than in British regions, with greater recourse to Family Income Supplement and Family Credit. Thus, the working poor were a substantial segment of all those in poverty. While there was some convergence of average household income with some declining British regions over the decade, in terms of general poverty characteristics, Northern

---

[28] See *'Administration'* (1985), Journal of the Institute of Public Administration of Ireland, vol. 33, no. 3. This issue was devoted entirely to a comparison of social policy in the Irish Republic and Northern Ireland.

[29] Figures taken from Economist Intelligence Unit, *Country Profile 1990-91, Ireland; the Northern Ireland Annual Abstract of Statistics (1990)*; and Eurostat (1991), *Basic Statistics of the Community*, Brussels.

Ireland remained at the bottom of the UK regional distribution.[30] Recent material from the Child Poverty Action Group has confirmed this position.[31]

There is also considerable evidence to link unemployment with poverty in the region. Harris's analysis of 1981 Family Expenditure Survey data concluded that: 'In Northern Ireland, the (*ceteris paribus*) effect of being unemployed increases the probability of being in poverty by over 60 per cent.'[32] Northern Ireland's Continuous Household Survey confirms the low levels of income of the unemployed. Indeed, 20 per cent of households with an unemployed head had an annual income of less than £2,000, and 68 per cent had an income less than £5,000 in 1989/90.[33]

It has been estimated that in the Irish Republic in 1980 875,000 persons were in poverty, using a poverty definition of 140 per cent of basic benefit levels. Of these, 460,000 were children. The percentage of the unemployed who fell below this threshold was 60.4, by far the highest for any of the household groups identified.[34] Different definitions of poverty give different figures. Using the EC definition of poverty, households with an unemployed head accounted for 34 per cent of all households whose income fell below 50 per cent of the mean in 1987. This was considerably higher than in 1973 when 10 per cent of such households had an unemployed head. Thus, there was a significant recomposition of poverty over the period. As the Combat Poverty Agency argued: 'The growth of unemployment is perhaps the single most important factor influencing this change'.[35] More recent evidence suggests a deterioration in the position of the unemployed:[36]

....in 1990 the income of a single unemployed person in receipt of Unemployment Benefit was equivalent to only 27.1% of that of the average worker whereas in 1987 it was 29.6%. The position of married people on Unemployment Benefit compares more favourably: in 1990 an unemployed person with two children received 52% of average earnings but, again, the gap here has been widening in the last number of years the proportion being 59% in 1982 and 54.5% in 1987.

---

[30] See Gaffikin, F. and Morrissey, M. (1990), *op. cit.*

[31] Oppenheim, C. (1991), *Poverty: The facts*, CPAG, London.

[32] Harris, R.I.D. (1990), 'Income', in Harris, R.I.D., Jefferson, C.W. and Spencer, J.E. (eds.), *The Northern Ireland Economy*, Longman, London, p.240.

[33] *PPRU Monitor* (1991), 'Continuous household survey: Preliminary results for 1989/90', Department of Finance and Personnel (NI), Belfast, October, table 14.

[34] Roche, J.D. (1984), *Poverty and Income Maintenance Policies in Ireland*, 1973-80, Institute of Public Administration, Dublin, pp.75-9.

[35] Policy and Practice (1991), *Urban Poverty: the economy and public policy*, Combat Poverty Agency, Dublin, p.19.

[36] Combat Poverty Agency (1991), *Making social rights a reality*, Dublin, p.1.

The Irish Republic thus presents a cogent example not just of the relationship between unemployment and poverty but of a country with increasing unemployment even though replacement ratios are falling.

Public Spending

In Northern Ireland, public spending, excluding social security, had a 1.3 per cent real annual growth rate in the five years up to 1989. In contrast, the UK saw an annual average decline of about 0.5 per cent. However, the emphasis accorded different programmes changed significantly over the period. Agriculture, Industry, Energy, Trade and Employment, and Housing all saw significant reductions.[37] Other programmes, such as Education, Health and Personal Services, and Law and Order were then taking up a greater share of total spending. The Northern Ireland Office committed itself to holding public expenditure in the region at around that level until 1992. In fact, additional allocations were made in 1989-90 and 1990-91.

In the early 1980s, the Irish Republic saw a significant increase in government spending as a share of GNP. However, since 1987, this trend has been set in reverse. Partly, this has been a result of lower expenditure on social security with a reduction in claimants and more stringent criteria for eligibility. Partly, it is because of emigration. But the major factor has been government concern to reduce public indebtedness.

Previously, governments borrowed to help finance trading deficits only to be faced with significant interest payments on the debt incurred - a dilemma confronting many industrialising countries of the Third World. At the end of 1988, the National Debt in the Republic totalled IR£24.6 billion, representing 113 per cent of GNP, nearly twice the EC average of 60 per cent. Estimations for 1989 indicated that nearly a third of taxation revenue would be devoted to debt service.[38] It is expected to be a continued drain on economic resources into the 1990s; one estimate suggests that annual debt servicing will remain above IR£1 billion per year up to 1999.[39]

The issue of public indebtedness has been a long-standing focus of policy concern, and has been responsible under the tenure of the Haughey government for severe fiscal restraint and related expenditure reductions in areas of social consumption such as health. This, in turn, has contributed to a deflation in domestic demand and has decreased potential levels of employment in what are labour-intensive services.

---

[37] The Northern Ireland Economic Council (1989), *Economic strategy: Overall review*, Belfast.

[38] The Government of Ireland (1989), *Ireland: National Development Plan, 1989-1993*, Dublin.

[39] Economist Intelligence Unit (1991), *Country Profile 1991-92, the Irish Republic*, London, p.34.

Northern Ireland does not have to face the same problem. It is difficult to obtain precise and meaningful data on Northern Ireland's export performance; at any rate its trade deficit would be compensated by fiscal transfers from Britain. It should be said that by the mid-1980s, per capita public expenditure in Northern Ireland exceeded that in Britain by over 27 per cent, with only about 54 per cent of this financed by tax revenue from Northern Ireland.[40]

Economic Integration and Unemployment

Since the partition of Ireland, there has been an ongoing debate about its consequences. In general, the tone of the debate has been political, focusing either on the denial of aspirations to unity as expressed in the results of the 1918 General Election, or on the rights of a majority in the North East to have their own semi-autonomous state. These contrasting political positions have tended to be supported by a variety of economic arguments.

On one hand, it is claimed that partition generated considerable negative consequences for both economies: the inhibition of trade; the extra costs of establishing two separate administrative systems; and the failure to gain from economies of scale in areas such as energy and transport. In addition, areas along the new border became peripheralised to each separate economy and thus suffered considerable underdevelopment. Equally, it is contended that Northern Ireland would have gained from a larger market for its manufactured goods, while the South would have obtained a more developed industrial infrastructure and a larger fiscal base. Finally, the division of the island created a historic grievance, continued tension and crisis in the North and the distortion of Southern politics.

On the other hand, proponents of partition focus on the existing uneven economic development within Ireland and the integration of the industries of the Northeast into the British economic system. To cut these industries off from their natural markets and traditional sources of new capital, possibly behind tariff barriers, would have meant their destruction. The link between Northern Ireland and Britain has thus been of considerable advantage to the former, particularly since the British exchequer was prepared to underwrite subsidies to declining industries in the shape of the Loans Guarantees Act and to finance the development of a welfare state. Certainly, the political tensions are real, but, it is pointed out, an all-Ireland political entity might have suffered equal tensions resulting from the grievances of loyalists.

Moreover, much of the industrial change experienced by Northern Ireland since partition was not due to its insulation from the South but rather to changes in global demand for specific products. Since linen was a much less

---

[40] Canning, D., Moore, B. and Rhodes, J. (1987), 'Economic growth in Northern Ireland: Problems and prospects', in Teague, P. (ed.), *Beyond the Rhetoric*, Lawrence & Wishart, London.

versatile fabric than cotton, international demand for the products of the Northern Ireland linen industry virtually collapsed in the 1930s and was only temporarily rescusitated by the Second World War. The Belfast shipyards have historically been vulnerable to shifts in global demand for shipping and were negatively affected by the huge investments in shipbuilding made by the Pacific basin economies after World War II. This vulnerability was later mirrored in artificial fibres, a sector attracted by the drive for inward investment in the 1960s. Thus, many of the most significant developments in the Northern Ireland economy have been independent of its constitutional status and its relationship with the Irish Republic.

This theme was echoed in the submission of Charles Carter to the New Ireland Forum. He suggested that the economic problems of Northern Ireland should be seen more in the context of the international flow of mobile capital and the state of the British economy, than in the relationship between the region and the rest of Ireland. Indeed, given the seriousness of these problems, the region would continue to require heavy public expenditure, in part subsidised by the British Exchequer. While this could be reasonably expected within a unitary state committed to similar standards of provision for all citizens, it could not be guaranteed under different constitutional arrangements:[41]

> The proposition that it is necessary, for reasons of past history, to make large transfers to another State (which is not suffering Third World poverty) would be vulnerable to the very first round of budgetary cuts. Indeed, no British government is in a position to make long run promises of aid; Parliament will defend its right to vote money a year at a time.

There is no single, incontestable interpretation of the economic effects of Partition nor are the potential benefits of a change in Northern Ireland's constitutional status immediately clear. Much of the debate assumes an advantage will be gained by the ending of violence and political crisis. However, the continued, albeit impotent, opposition of Unionists to the Anglo-Irish Agreement suggests that they are far from even beginning to contemplate a constitutional relationship with the Irish Republic. Decisions to institute such a relationship would therefore have to be taken over their heads. Undoubtedly, they would retain a substantial capacity for destabilising any new arrangement. The alternative of mass emigration would be politically, morally and economically unacceptable. With regard to unemployment, the essential question of this long-lasting debate is whether enhanced economic co-operation would enhance job creation to the extent of reducing the numbers unemployed in both states.

Recently, the degree of economic exchange between the states has been fairly low - in 1988 Northern Ireland accounted for only 3.8 per cent of the Republic's imports and 6.2 per cent of its exports. As a percentage of total trading activity, cross-border trade in Ireland declined between 1980 and

---

[41] Carter, C. (22/10/1983), 'Submission to the New Ireland Forum', *Irish Times*.

1988.[42] These figures compare with Britain's share of the Republic's imports and exports - 38.2 per cent and 29.2 per cent, respectively, in 1988.

Britain has always been a more important trading partner of the Irish Republic than Northern Ireland. Nevertheless, the Republic has succeeded in diversifying its trade away from a single dominant partner. In 1924 Britain provided nearly 70 per cent of the Irish Republic's imports and received over 40 per cent of its exports. By 1980, while still the Republic's largest single trading partner, Britain had substantially declined in significance and accounted for 46.7 per cent of Republic's imports and 35.8 per cent of its exports. More recently, the rest of the EC has become the Republic's most important market. As mobile capital located there to gain entry to EC markets, this development is unsurprising.

Some critics of development policy in Northern Ireland have argued for the need for a single development strategy across the two states.[43] In the context of the European Single Market, the two states of Ireland may suffer in common the problems of peripheralisation. Each competes with the other for mobile investment and tourism, while some areas like energy policy would gain from economies of scale. Both have Objective I status as regions most deserving of EC structural funds, although the Irish Republic does rather better in this respect, receiving IR£7.1 billion between 1973 and 1986 compared to Northern Ireland's £1.4 billion. This has been attributed to a lack of concern by the British government to promote Northern Ireland at Brussels, since it constitutes only 2.4 per cent of the UK population. The corollary is that the interests of Northern Ireland would be better represented if it were the responsibility of the government of the Republic. However, this must be qualified by the recognition that EC receipts to Northern Ireland are considerably less than the subsidy provided by the British government. At the same time, the EC looks with particular favour at proposals designed to overcome the marginalisation of border areas. Ireland offers substantial opportunity for the development of such proposals and there is scope for greater co-ordination of both governments' activities in this respect.

Also in the recent period, the two governments have reformed their industrial development policies along similar lines. In the Republic, an Industrial Policy Review group, established to reassess the statutory agencies' responsibilities for industrial promotion, reported its conclusions in January 1992. Its proposals included:
• the need to split development effort into two components - one concerned with the attraction of overseas investment, the other responsible for Irish-owned companies;

---

[42] Harrison, R.T. (1990), 'Northern Ireland and the Republic of Ireland in the Single Market', in Foley and Mulreany, *op.cit.*, table 18.7.

[43] Freeman, J. et al. (1989), *The Irish economies: A common future?*, Amalgamated Transport & General Workers Union, Belfast.

- a shift of financial assistance from firms targeted at fixed-asset subsidies to more repayable alternatives, particularly in the form of state equity participation;
- an emphasis on industrial sectors with most growth potential and the encouragement of 'clusters' of similarly oriented firms. Overseas promotion would focus on these sectors in order to exploit national competitive advantage and develop lucrative world markets. Engineering, telecommunications, chemicals and food were among those suggested;
- clustering policy should also be concerned with the industrial linkages between domestic and multinational firms;
- in terms of agricultural reform, the diminution of subsidy should be used as an opportunity to exploit Ireland's 'green' image in an ecology-conscious era. Link-ups with multinationals should offer the most likely prospect of modernising the food industry and securing access to overseas markets.

The report also called for a reorganisation of existing training structures, a broadening of the fiscal base through the abolition of relief and allowances, a reconsideration of the 10 per cent manufacturing industry tax rate, measures to improve the physical infrastructure and a regionalised economic support structure to encourage local initiative.

In Northern Ireland, while the reformed industrial development strategy has been considerably more market-oriented, it is also focused on growth sectors and improved competitiveness. Similarly, grant aid for capital acquisition has been replaced with a system of incentives to assist research and development, design, quality assurance and marketing.[44] There is considerable similarity in both approaches and it might be possible to develop a common industrial development policy from this basis.

The inter-governmental conferences established by the Anglo-Irish Agreement have focused primarily on political and security issues, but within their terms of reference are economic and social issues. If British and Irish governments are determined to co-ordinate policy effort towards Northern Ireland, the tackling of unemployment might be a key theme. Moreover, in 1991 the dramatic rise in unemployment levels in the Irish Republic has prompted calls to establish an Unemployment Forum, modelled on the New Ireland Forum, but focusing on ways to tackle unemployment. One of the sponsoring bodies, the Irish National Organisation of the Unemployed, operates on an all-Ireland basis. Thus, there is now a greater concern with unemployment than there has been for at least a decade.

These developments suggest that more attention should be paid to co-ordinating economic development within Ireland. The gains are liable to accrue in the longer rather than shorter term, but may be significant nevertheless.

---

[44] See, The Northern Ireland Economic Council (1991), *Economic Strategy in Northern Ireland*, Belfast, July.

9. Overview and Conclusions

Previous chapters examined data on the patterns of unemployment within two of the three global economic blocs - the US and the EC - described as the market economies. There has been less attention paid to Japan, partly because of its exceptionally low levels of unemployment and partly because its aggressive export performance and high levels of domestic market protection (often called 'mercantilist') imply that, in terms of government management of the economy, it operates on almost pre-capitalist principles.[1] Certainly, the countries reviewed constitute a valid sample of market economies. They include five of the G7, and vary between advanced industrial economies, like the United States and West Germany, and the late developing economies of Portugal and Greece. The case studies focused on economies in transition: the UK whose approach to unemployment underwent radical shifts in the 1980s; and the Irish economies, undergoing an almost unique mixture of decay and development.

With the exception of the US all these countries suffered higher unemployment in the 1980s than in the previous decade. In 1990 West Germany's unemployment was seven times higher than in 1971. In France it trebled over that period, and in the UK and Italy it doubled. Even Japan's unemployment was twice as high, although it still remained lower than that of any other major economy.[2]

Yet the 1980s was also a period of substantial economic growth. For most countries, the effects of the 1979 oil shock had dissipated by 1982. Thereafter, GDP and employment grew at rates only marginally below that in previous boom periods. Annual GDP growth in the 12 countries which make up the EC averaged 2.3 per cent between 1981-90 compared to 3 per cent in 1971-80. In the UK, the respective growth rates for each period were 2.6 per

---

[1] *The Economist* has frequently used the term mercantilist to describe Japanese economic policy, while Brian Reading in *Japan: The coming collapse* (1992), Weidenfeld & Nicholson, London, uses the phrase 'neo-feudal Japanese corporatism'.

[2] OECD (1991), *Economic Outlook*, July, table R.19.

cent and 1.9 per cent and in West Germany, 1.7 per cent and 2.2 per cent.[3] If economic performance in 1981-82 is discounted, the majority of these economies were growing faster in the 1980s than the overall average for the 1970s. A slowdown in GDP growth alone fails to explain the higher unemployment rates.

In fact, only the US had a strong negative correlation between GDP and unemployment. Within the European Community, economic growth tended to create jobs for those who were not already registered as unemployed. For example, 60 per cent of the jobs growth in the UK occurred in part-time employment. The majority of such new jobs were taken up by women although in the UK, the unemployment rate for women was substantially lower than for men. This does not imply that non-registered women should be prevented from taking up work, but it explains the paradox of job creation which fails to reduce unemployment. In the Irish Republic similar problems existed. While emigration reduced unemployment totals, new jobs frequently went to potential migrants rather than those on the unemployment register.

Regarding patterns of unemployment, the OECD commented:[4]

Average unemployment in the OECD area did not fall below 6 per cent in the 1980s despite the sustained expansion through most of the decade; for the European Community, the unemployment rate remained over 8 per cent....The projected moderate recovery would probably be sufficient to stabilise the rate of unemployment, but not bring it down; at the end of 1992 the unemployment rate in the OECD area could still stand at 7 per cent.

Economic prediction is notoriously unreliable, but the evidence of the last decade suggests that unemployment will remain high into the 1990s. In January 1992, unemployment in the US had climbed back up to the level of six years previously. By then, private borrowing by households and non-financial corporations had reached almost $500 billion. The federal deficit amounted to a further $300 billion. GDP growth was a mere 0.7 per cent in 1991 and the dollar continued to fall against both the Yen and Deutschmark.[5] The seriousness of the trading deficit prompted President Bush to visit Japan to complain about trading imbalances and the loss of US jobs, while the stricken car industry began to implement a wave of factory closures and redundancies. Since the beginning of the decade, the US economy has suffered the hangover of the 1980s' budgetary and trading deficits. At the

---

[3] Commission of the European Communities (1991), *European Economy: Annual economic report, 1990-91*, Brussels, table 10.

[4] OECD (1991), *op. cit..*, p.x.

[5] Harris, A. (1991), 'The economic consequences of Mr. Reagan', in *The World in 1991*, Economist Publications.

same time, the federal government has failed to develop a coherent strategy for redressing the situation.

Supply-side solutions, like interest rate reductions, have failed to pump-prime growth because debt-burdened consumers and corporations have been reluctant to increase their exposure. The 'peace dividend' has proved elusive since it was those faster growing companies which benefited most from defence expenditure and which need to shed labour through restructuring for alternative products. Moreover, the research and development effort required to generate new, saleable products will not be met through federal funding, unlike defence projects. The uncertain performance of the US economy does not seem to be temporary.

Nor does a rapid European recovery seem within easy reach. Even the engine of the European economy, Germany, has slowed under the impact of reunification. The OECD predicts that GNP growth there will fall to 2.2 per cent in 1992 compared to 4.5 per cent in 1990, domestic demand will fall from 5.1 per cent to 2.5 per cent and its $57.2 billion trading surplus of 1989 will slump to $11.1 billion.[6] In 1991, Germany transferred £60 billion to the former East Germany, almost equivalent to that area's GDP. German trade unions have complained that the tax and interest rate burdens of reunification have been disproportionately borne by their members. In 1992 the public sector unions broke the government's pay guidelines through the most widespread series of strikes since 1974. Were such pay increases implemented, the Bundesbank would further raise interest rates and inhibit new growth in the economy. This, in turn, would affect other economies in terms of their exports and their currencies through the Exchange Rate Mechanism.[7]

Even if the optimistic predictions of the Cecchini report regarding the benefits of a single market in Europe are realised, the resultant jobs increase will be geographically concentrated, while the EC peripheries will continue to experience acute underdevelopment. Moreover, economic integration will be associated with the creation of a European Central bank whose proposed constitution is modelled on the Bundesbank. The primary function of the latter had been to squeeze inflation out of the German economic system, whatever the wishes of particular governments. European financial policy is thus likely to also have a distinctive anti-inflationary rather than full employment orientation. Further, the disciplines of the European Exchange Rate Mechanism mean that significant reductions in unit labour costs, rather than currency devaluation, will be required to restore export competitiveness for the weaker EC members. Under a European single currency, this discipline would be more intense. Accordingly, in the frailer European economies, firms will be sensitive to labour costs and, all things being equal are more likely to shed labour than expand employment. This will be

---

6 OECD (1991), *op. cit.*, p. viii.

7 *Ibid.*

particularly true of weak regions. Thus, the dynamics of the European economy and the key developments in economic management are unlikely to substantially reduce its very large numbers of unemployed - around 15 million in 1990.

Previous chapters have also demonstrated a close relationship between unemployment and poverty. Studies in both Europe and the United States have demonstrated that the unemployed figure prominently among the poor. However, the unemployed are not a homogeneous group and poverty tends to be assumed as a characteristic of households rather than individuals. Nevertheless, the presence of unemployed members still reduces aggregate household income. European data indicate both the existence of a substantial number of households with more than one unemployed member and that partners of unemployed heads of households are less likely to be in employment than where the head of household is in full-time work. It is thus unlikely that income from other household members compensates for the loss of income suffered by a majority of the unemployed.

Within the ranks of the unemployed, certain key groups suffer even greater poverty risk. In Europe, unemployment rates for women tend to be higher than for men, although women still constitute a minority of all unemployed. It cannot be assumed that unemployed women are simply re-absorbed into households and, are in some sense, more cushioned from the poverty impact of unemployment. The proportion of households headed by women has steadily increased so that the male-dominated nuclear family is decreasingly the norm. Not only do women feature more prominently among the poor, but the interaction of family, state and economy reinforce that condition.[8] Within families, women frequently have the responsibility of managing budgets without having control over resources, while suffering from unequal patterns of household consumption. Women also tend to receive less compensation than men in state support schemes, frequently because their participation in secondary labour markets with lower earnings reduces their insurance contributions. Finally, women's participation in labour markets is often on unequal terms: they have more experience of part-time employment; in general, they occupy lower status occupations; their career patterns are disrupted by child bearing; and their average earnings remain below the levels for men. Thus, their greater exposure to unemployment is merely one aspect of a conjunction of factors that determine the seriousness of their poverty.

In the US there has been considerable attention given to female heads of households in the underclass debate. Essentially, underclass theories argue that insufficient attention has been paid to family and culture in the generation of poverty. Certain groups within the US are held to have a greater cultural propensity towards single parenthood and this contributes significantly to their inclusion in the underclass. The poverty levels of black

---

[8] Millar, J. and Glendinning, C. (1987), *Women and Poverty in Britain*, Wheatsheaf Books, Brighton.

households with a female head is offered as statistical support for this analysis.

It is interesting that the US and Europe have seen such divergent positions in the analysis of women's poverty, although Murray has argued that Britain is experiencing a growing underclass.[9] In Europe, the debate over the feminisation of poverty has been conducted in terms of the effect on women of the interaction of key social and economic structures. In the US, the emphasis has been on the personal and familial characteristics of women themselves. While these approaches reflect differing adherences to pathological and structural aspects of poverty, some theorists take the view that an overemphasis on one to the neglect of the other leads to an incomplete theory of poverty.

Another group which has been severely affected by unemployment is young people. With the exception of West Germany, unemployment rates among young people are higher than those among older age groups for the entire EC. Easy assumptions that young people are cushioned by their families are inappropriate. In any case, since Eurostat data uses 25 years as the age threshold, many of these young people are themselves the heads of multiple member households. The contraction of unemployment compensation for the young in particular, to instill greater motivation to work, has engendered migration and homelessness.

By far the greatest risk of poverty is suffered by the long-term unemployed where a combination of demoralisation, benefits erosion and social exclusion form the basic framework of their lives. The 1980s saw a recomposition of unemployment with an ever increasing proportion falling into the long-term category. The resistance of unemployment to economic recovery is largely explained by the low labour market opportunities for this group. To reintegrate the long-term unemployed into the labour market, the current orthodoxy proposes a range of measures to reduce social benefits dependency and improve labour market prospects. If the latter fail, however, the contraction in benefits would mean a further reduction in disposable income.[10] This group represents the real test of European social policy in the 1990s. Programmes to assist this group are small-scale and are frequently informed by supply-side assumptions about the nature of unemployment. The Social Charter is primarily targeted at those in employment rather than the long-term unemployed. It remains to be seen whether the EC or any of its member states will be able to resolve the problem. In the US, the long-term unemployed fall almost outside the benefits system. The pressure to reduce budget deficits has disproportionately hit social programmes, particularly welfare programmes. Thus, a greater concern for fiscal rectitude and the predominance of supply-side ideologies about the unemployed indicate that their condition will deteriorate rather than improve in the medium term.

---

[9] Murray, C. (1990), The Emerging British underclass, *op. cit.*

[10] See for example, OECD (1991), *op.cit.*

At the same time, the preoccupation with unemployment should not conceal the plight of other groups on the margins of the labour market. The importance of seasonal employment in some regions and the growth of part-time work generally suggest the existence of groups for whom unemployment is not a chronic condition, but who nevertheless suffer extensive deprivation. There is growing concern about the prevalence of child labour in late developing economies such as Portugal. There, rapid inflation and low wages have driven many families to put their children in the labour market at whatever terms and under whatever conditions can be found. Yet, Portugal signed the Social Chapter accompanying the Maastricht Treaty, which commits it to improving working conditions. Whether the reality of increased competition for jobs will permit such improvements is questionable.

Finally, the legitimate concern about poverty and unemployment in the market economies must be put in the context of 1 billion people living at or below subsistence levels in the Third World. Only when substantial redistribution is effected both within and between countries, will the prospect exist of a new political and social order which incorporates some principle of social justice. However, in the recent period egalitarian objectives are held to be incompatible with economic efficiency. Even in Sweden the political charge of excessive social expenditure within an ailing economy brought down the Social Democratic government. The crisis of Keynesianism there was merely delayed for a decade. Can full employment be achieved along with economic competitiveness? Can an advanced welfare state positively redistribute resources without engendering a fiscal crisis for government?

Options in Tackling Unemployment

The 1980s saw an attempt by Western governments to reclaim some of the ideological tenets of *laissez-faire* economics. In most respects, the results were hardly edifying. In the UK since 1979, taking average annual figures, the inflation rate has been 7.5 per cent, growth has been 1.7 per cent, and unemployment has been 2.5 million. The record of the previous Labour government (1974-79), with 15.6 per cent inflation, 2.1 per cent growth, and 1 million unemployed compares favourably, even though it was hampered by the acute escalation of oil prices, did not enjoy the bonanza of North Sea oil and the benefit of falling world commodity prices. But Britain under the Tories saw the elevation of a strategy to defeat inflation, over one to combat unemployment. Certainly, the experience of the US over this period has been different, as indicated earlier. While its capacity to generate new jobs, and thereby contain unemployment, was partly attributable to a more flexible labour market, it also owed much to the 'military Keynesianism' endorsed under Reagan.

In Britain, despite Margaret Thatcher's advocacy of the virtues of hard work and thrift, housing policy's emphasis on home ownership encouraged prospective buyers to view housing as a form of capital investment rather than accommodation. The inference was that quick money could be made on escalating housing prices. In this respect, the policy infringed two central tenets of Thatcherism: that wealth should be generated through effort rather than speculation; and that inflation was the central economic evil rather than a boon to house buyers. Once the housing bubble burst, with many casualties in terms of repossession and homelessness, a government which extolled the efficacy of markets felt compelled to intervene with a series of measures designed to limit repossessions. Here the disparity in both countries between the persistent rhetoric of the free market and the periodic intrusion of pragmatic politics needs to be highlighted.

As a new decade starts in the deepening gloom of recession, there remains scepticism about both the priority attached, and the policy instruments available, to tackle unemployment in both countries. Striking similarities abound in their predicaments. Both have been governed by conservative parties for a considerable period; both of those parties changed their leader to one less doctrinally attached to the New Right project of the 1980s; and in both cases, the parties of the left have felt obliged to retreat from their orthodoxies to accommodate, to some extent, the agenda set by neo-conservatism.

Economically, both are faced with problems of sluggish growth, budgetary and trading deficits, and rising unemployment. Much of their economic buoyancy in the late 1980s was linked to a credit boom, which has now come to grief. As the figures from the OECD in Table 9.1 illustrate, the consumption indulgences of the last decade have seen personal debt rise sharply as a share of household disposable income, particularly in Japan, the US and the UK.

Table 9.1	Personal Debt as a percentage of Household Disposable Income, Selected Countries, 1980 and 1990	
	1980	1990
US	0.80	1.03
UK	0.57	1.14
Japan	0.77	1.17
Germany	0.15	0.18
France	0.62	0.78
Italy	0.08	0.13•
Canada	0.87	0.94
Note:	* 1989	
Source:	The Guardian (30\12\1991)	

In addition to national and personal debt, corporate debt in both countries also multiplied, as companies sought a quick alternative to organic development in a rush of acquisitions and mergers, and speculative investments in the booming property market. The crash of this extravaganza in the US, exemplified by the Savings and Loans and 'junk' bond scandals, was mirrored in the UK. The corporate icons of Thatcherism - Saunders of Guinness, Asil Nadir of Polly Peck, Goodman of International Leisure Group, Walker of Brent Walker, and the leading jeweller Ratner - were all displaced from eminent positions. Together with the collapse of the Bank of Credit and Commerce International and the Maxwell empire, these men symbolised the vagaries of a recovery based on over-extended loans and a vulnerable retailing and property expansion.

The legacy of this period has inevitably impeded reflationary potential. Governments were initially compelled to raise interest rates to rein in the over-heating and inflationary pressures. As banks have had to make unusually high provisions for bad debts resulting from company insolvencies and property collapses, to be offset against their operating profits, a more circumspect lending policy has been adopted. Debt repayment obligations have discouraged further spending by consumers and investment by business. The reality of recent unemployment, or the fear of it, has further chastened the consumer.

While both the US and UK share much of this history, each is now pursuing a different exit from its calamities. The US slashed its interest rates as the key device to minimise the impact of a new recessionary dip. By contrast, in the UK, while headline inflation dropped from 11 per cent to around 4 per cent, interest rates fell from 15 per cent to 10.5 per cent, leaving a 'real' interest rate of 6.5 per cent, higher than at any time since the 1930s. Given the weakness of economic activity, this bodes ill for the stimulation of new demand. Nor has it assisted the mortgage burdens, which have generated defaults on repayment and subsequent repossession which, in turn, have depressed further a housing market whose inflated value in the 1980s formed the collateral for so much extravagant borrowing.

The reason for this monetary tightness in the face of a downturn is, of course, tied to the disciplines of the ERM, as previously mentioned. The decision of a reluctant Margaret Thatcher to join can be understood as a resignation to Britain's inability to contain inflation without the help of the Bundesbank. As things stand, this means that priority will always be given to inflation over unemployment. The 1980s in the UK seemed to confirm that unemployment significantly below 2 million cannot be achieved without triggering an inflationary spiral. Leading economists such as Gavin Davies confess they know of no solution to this trade-off.

The options available, even had Labour formed a government in Britain, are thus severely constrained. The effect of closer monetary union in Europe would be to compel a convergence in economic policy amongst the contending parties in Britain. Of course, some argue that Labour could devalue, or it could realign sterling with the other European currencies, in effect a devaluation. Advocates of this policy argue that by raising output relative to domestic demand, devaluation boosts exports and limits imports, thereby supporting domestic production and improving the considerable trading deficit. At the same time, by offering more comfortable accommodation within the ERM, it permits interest rates to fall, stimulating investment and job growth in the process.

There are several problems with devaluation. Even in the short term it might give rise to higher interest rates, as the price to be paid to offset the shock to the financial markets and reclaim the confidence of speculators. It might 'import' inflation, an important consideration given the changed pattern of corporate ownership in Britain. Many foreign multinationals depend on imported components, in what are often mainly assembly-based operations. In this industrial structure, devaluation no longer offers an unproblematic stimulus to exports.

Nor do tax cuts offer an easy option. In Britain, a cut of 1p in the pound off income tax deprives the Exchequer of some £2 billion. Tax reduction, used as an instrument of demand-management, would have to be more extensive than a 1p concession. Given the creaking social and physical infrastructure in the UK, there must be doubt as to whether reducing the tax base further will not imply the need for more public sector borrowing as indicated by the 1992 budget statement. This scenario could also send negative signals to the international money markets, affecting the exchange rate, and again requiring higher interest rates to contain any run on sterling which would cancel any reflationary impact of the original tax cuts.

Thus, while the policy orthodoxies of the 1980s have hardly been successful, even on their own terms, they have nevertheless established parameters which radical opposition parties would find difficult to overturn. In any case, France's ailing Socialist government is likely to move further to the right in pursuit of a further term of office. In some countries, such as the Irish Republic and Italy, social democratic parties have only won power in coalition with more conservative, and usually more dominant, partners and thus have rarely been in the position to embark on ambitious social programmes. In countries with highly advanced social welfare structures, such as Belgium, excessive external debt is creating pressure for cutbacks.

This has been reinforced by the devaluation of the idea of economic planning, generally provoked by the extreme difficulties faced by the economies of Eastern Europe and the former Soviet Union. All of the central claims of superiority of the command economy - full employment, superior social welfare infrastructures and greater egalitarianism - have proved illusory.

In fact, the West won the Cold War. Decisions in the late 1970s to embark on ever more expensive weaponry development, forced the Soviet Union to abandon its command planning. While the need for reform was recognised by Gorbachev and translated into his 'peace offensive', the Communist Party of the Soviet Union (CPSU), proved incapable of implementing the necessary economic restructuring. The efficacy of central planning in extensive industrialisation, albeit with enormous social costs, failed dramatically when the economy needed to intensively industrialise. The bureaucratic and hierarchical structures of the CPSU proved inadequate to either recognise or respond to this challenge. After six years in power, Gorbachev's domestic achievements were minor compared to his international impact.

In one sense, his successors have inherited an even greater crisis. They have moved to marketisation in the midst of extensive shortages, a profound lack of confidence and the possibility of a slowdown in the internal trade of the new Commonwealth. Since these economies were previously integrated and highly interdependent, the expansion of their internal trade is a key condition for development. While such problems are being resolved, and there may well be recourse to new forms of authoritarianism as popular opposition to simultaneous price rises and income falls grows, a former superpower has become a recipient of food aid. While such aid is clearly necessary, it would be unfortunate if a major share of funds earmarked for the Third World were to be redirected towards the North. Indeed, some redirection has already occurred. This danger is particularly acute given the fact that should the former command economies effect a successful market transition, they will be attractive locations for profitable investment with their low labour costs coupled, in global terms, with highly educated workforces and, ultimately, new and large consumer markets.

One key result of the current difficulties in such countries has been a renewed confidence in market supremacy. During the 1960s, the idea of the mixed economy based on Keynesian demand management was seen as the perfect compromise between the *laissez-faire* economy of the US and the Soviet command economy. On one hand, it gave considerable freedom to market forces and, on the other, the nationalisation of key industries and infrastructure created an appropriate base for economic planning. This economic 'mix' underpinned governments' commitment to full employment through the management of aggregate demand. Moreover, its advanced welfare state was held to offer social support and effect the kinds of redistribution necessary to promote a modest degree of egalitarianism. This was in contrast to the rigidities of the command economy and the weakness of social support within the *laissez-faire* economy. However, today the market economy is seen as avoiding the inflationary pressures implicit in Keynesian demand management and the supply-side obstructions caused by bureaucratic central planning. It thus appears to represent the ideal compromise of the 1990s. In turn, this further inhibits the range of policy options considered necessary to tackle unemployment. Thus, while the 1980s were not successful, given the levels of unemployment in the market economies, there are few remaining policy options.

Even with its economic deficiencies, the capitalist system of the West has become universal. The unemployment debate, if it is to be realistic and of practical benefit to the unemployed, has to accept the durability and pre-eminence of capitalism for the foreseeable future. Policy alternatives have to be constructed within this framework. As Leadbeater argues:[11]

---

[11] Leadbeater, C. (1991), 'Marketing the World', *Marxism Today*, January.

The culmination of the decade in which capitalism was re-energised came in 1989 with the collapse of planning and communism in the face of markets and capitalism. Socialism's 80-year threat to capitalism had been decisively defeated. It was indisputably capitalism's decade.

This has not ushered in a new non-ideological age. Many socialists remain unwavering in their criticism of capitalism, despite the collapse of the command economies. For them, the failures of Stalinism, or indeed Leninism, have not invalidated the basic premise of class conflict nor the need to construct an egalitarian social and economic order. They continue to respond to an imperative to find forms of political expression and economic organisation that can deliver this objective. Similarly, sections of the New Right shrug off the difficulties experienced by the market economies. For them, Reagan embraced only the supply-side component of their economic prescriptions, Britain abandoned sound money policies in the mid-1980s, and Europe was too locked into corporatism to make the transition. Accordingly, they hold to the prospect of the 'nightwatchman state', parsimonious in its economic and social interventions, and enjoying both non-inflationary growth and general prosperity.

For the foreseeable future however, pragmatism within the framework of marketisation would seem to be the dominant tendency. This does not imply that only a single set of policies are on offer. Liberal economic policies have been associated both with historic high levels of unemployment and the erosion of social support for its victims. As already indicated, with respect to economic growth its long term record has been less impressive than the Keynesian decades.[12] Moreover a hard belief in the market's capacity to sustain equilibrium carries with it the assumption that unemployment is essentially voluntary. Yet a decade of market dominance in the UK, for example, with the introduction of many disincentives to the unemployed, has not eliminated unemployment.[13] The alternatives of social democracy and corporatism can co-exist with the market economy, but can full employment be reinstated as a central policy goal?

Back to Full Employment?

Despite its deficiencies, the best prospect for the jobless and the poor remains social democracy. Social democratic regimes may have been converted to liberal economics, but this was with reluctance and without the market evangelism of the New Right. Unfortunately, in response to the New Right

---

[12] See for example, Keegan, V. (4/11/1991), 'Batting for Britain means keeping score accurately', *The Guardian*.

[13] Davies, G. (1989), 'Governments can affect employment: a critique of monetarism, old and new', in Shields, J. (ed.), *Conquering Unemployment: the case for economic growth*, Macmillan in association with the Employment Instiute, London.

offensive, social democracy has collapsed into technocratic, market-dominated strategies, with correspondingly low priorities for any social agenda that implies increasing expenditure or taxation. Social democracy in France and Britain have been key examples of this tendency. The key issue will then be whether it can regenerate itself within an inimical global economy.

One key failing of social democracy lay in the tension between social concern and economic management. On one hand, even upporters frequently charged that its social concern was largely cosmetic and readily downgraded during periods of economic difficulty. On the other, its critics argued that this social commitment generated both fiscal crisis, and structural imbalance, undermining competitiveness and jettisoning prospects for sustainable growth.

Moreover, in some countries such as the UK, the Republic of Ireland and France, the corporatist style of social democracy was frequently elitist, whereby leaders of industry and trade unions were recruited by government in a consensus at the top, with scant regard for participative democracy or accountability. In any case, this approach often failed to deliver, since industrial confrontation at the micro-level could jeopardise these macro-agreements. In other countries, such as Germany, it is difficult to assess whether corporatism was an important condition of economic growth or whether economic growth could afford to accommodate corporatism. But in general, the limits of social democracy lay in its inability to adequately manage its social and economic agenda while, at the same time, delivering participative democracy.

The style of contemporary politics may be working in the opposite direction. Political parties increasingly make use of sophisticated polling and other techniques to elicit the concerns of the floating voter who can be decisive in determining particular election outcomes. This may offer a brief advantage to a specific political party, such as the Republicans in the US in 1988. However, whatever attractive innovations of policy are so generated, contending parties will soon employ similar techniques and consequently appropriate similar policies. The end result is that a brief period of policy differentiation is replaced by policy convergence which not only limits real opportunities for participation in policy formation, but also demotes those issues which are not being registered by polling techniques as matters of immediate concern. This is exacerbated by the role of the media in presenting complicated political issues in appropriately packaged sound bites and photo-opportunities. The electorate thus becomes spectators rather than participants in the political process.

Yet democratic issues may have taken on a new urgency in the 1990s. The political defeat of Eastern European regimes and the dismantling of the Soviet Union has been widely interpreted as a major advance not just for marketisation, but for democracy. Governments which have consistently applauded the advance of democracy in the East may themselves become vulnerable to democratic demands in the West. This could create some space for the generation of a new politics which could reinvigorate social democracy beyond its traditional concerns.

Such a political movement may be consonant with an economic movement for 'bottom-up' development. One of the central challenges to the economic orthodoxies of the 1980s consisted of community economic development supported by sympathetic local states. This was the case in the UK, in parts of Northern Italy, in the Basque region of Spain and in certain Lander in West Germany. Such projects were underpinned by academic research, which emphasised the significance of locality in economic development. This did not disavow the relevance of general structural forces, but still asserted the uniqueness of place. Thus, local people may be best placed to understand that uniqueness and to prescribe the most appropriate forms of regeneration.

Finally, if a post-Fordist scenario has any meaning, it implies more than production and marketing strategies. Central to the concept is the elevation of consumer sovereignty and the sanctification of consumer choice. The implication is that economic power is more devolved to the consumer, whose needs have to be precisely serviced. This points to a more disaggregated form of economic development, where people have greater leverage on the corporations whose products they consume. In addition, it is sometimes argued that the fall in the real costs of information technology hardware and software creates easier entry points in some kinds of services for the self-employed, small businesses and co-operatives.

However, the picture is not entirely rosy. The consequences of political change in Eastern Europe have been more problematic than was anticipated. Poland was one of the first to make the transition to a market economy. The state sector shrank by 20 per cent in 1991, unemployment rose to 12 per cent and welfare support was steadily eroded. In 1992, following a series of strikes and street demostrations, the Prime Minister, Jan Olszewski, announced the return to a more interventionist policy: '....the gains from the market reform strategy launched in 1989-90 have been more modest than originally predicted while social costs and burdens have proved to be greater than expected.'[14]

The revolutions in the Eastern bloc since the late 1980s have not just been driven by a popular anger against a bureaucratic and incompetent economic system, which failed to deliver efficiency and prosperity. They were also engendered by a political impulse to reclaim a suppressed sense of nationality. While much of this rediscovery of ethnic and cultural roots might be understandable, the repercussions have, in places like Georgia and Yugoslavia, included convulsive assertions of identity and territory. The substitution of a contrived and enforced homogeneity among the diverse peoples of Eastern Europe by an authoritarian and militaristic nationalism could hardly be considered an advance for civilisation.

---

[14] Quoted in Borger, J. 'Poland retreats from rapid market reform', *The Guardian* (6/2/92).

In place of these fragmentations, which accentuate social cleavage and disrupt economic co-operation, the challenge is to accommodate a form of devolution which is both democratic and operable. The interdependence of the modern world calls for a reconceptualisation of national sovereignty. However, the consensual reconstitution of appropriate cross-national relationships in much of the Eastern bloc, as in Yeltsin's project for a new Commonwealth, is proving easier to visualise than to execute.

The pressures for political devolution or separatism are not exclusive to the former Communist countries. The Scottish, the Basques, to say nothing of the protagonists in Northern Ireland, are all pressing at this particular door. Distinguishable from these movements is the emerging force of the Ultra Right, exemplified by Le Pen's National Front in France. Intent on exploiting the popular unease about economic prospects in the 1990s, these groups attempt to amplify racial distinctions by suggesting that problems such as unemployment are attributable to migrant labour. In short, the resurgence towards greater autonomy for ethnic and religious groups is problematic both in the rationale and the delivery of its objective.

These political segmentations may also be seen as congruent with the market fragmentations derivative of post-Fordism. As earlier mentioned, this supposed new age of production is one response to the demand from the modern sophisticated customer for greater diversity and speciality. Reflecting a desire to reassert individuality in an atomised world, the post-Fordist era promises to put a premium on purchaser determination of design, style and product. Its capacity flexibly and efficiently to service fluctuations in fashion heralds, for the New Right, the only permissible political control over markets: consumer sovereignty. However, the claim that this commodification of choice and decision is democratic is illusory. It ignores the exclusion of many social groups, whose limited purchasing power effectively disenfranchises them. It also underestimates the extent to which demand is generated and manipulated by slick marketing and advertising, and subsequently controlled by oligopolistic suppliers.

The global reach of transnational corporations imposes severe constraints on participative forms of democratic control. There is a formidable argument that the imperfect, but only, means of regulating such enterprises lies in supranational structures. The challenge to construct a political system capable of checking global economic power, while simultaneously being accessible to grassroots involvement, remains relevant to the left. In meeting it, the left will be obliged to redefine itself. The current temptation for this political position is either to immunise itself against the radical fall-out of post-communism, pretending that this collapse is transient, or to assume the denunciation of the penitent, and disown the whole egalitarian project. The problems of capitalism, starkly evident in unemployment, poverty and Third World exploitation, still call for redress. But the advocates of change can no longer credibly displace painful, gradual, and compromising engagement by the hollow rhetoric of revolution.

The EC, post-Maastricht, will be a significant arena for this political contest. The existing constraints of the European Exchange Rate Mechanism on national governments' room for manoeuvre in economic policy will be intensified as the Community moves towards monetary union. In areas such as exchange rates, borrowing, interest rates and ultimately taxation, national governments' capacity for independent decision making will be severely limited. As Grieve Smith argues: 'The EMU Treaty, like the De Lors Report, is essentially based on monetarist concepts from the early 1980s. With its prescription for an independent Central Bank and restrictions on budget deficits, it reflects a reaction to the inflationary conditions of the 1970s rather than an attempt to tackle the unemployment problem of the 1990s'.[15]

This not merely reduces the ability of electors to influence policy but, with the political discontent so created, there is a greater movement towards a nationalistic, right-wing politics. Italy has seen the strengthening of its fascist and right-wing regionalist tendencies. In Germany the disenchantment with Kohl's Christian Democrats has not translated into additional support for the SPD but, instead, a surge of support for neo-Nazism. The hegemony of the Conservative party in Britain with its election to a fourth term of office is the major exception to trends in European politics.

Additionally at the level of EC structures, the Council of Ministers has been remodelled on the basis of qualified majority voting. This both shifts power to the larger EC countries and reproduces the limited power of the European parliament. Because of this, the democratic deficit within the Community will be even more pronounced.

The most fertile engagement for this new political terrain may lie in the deceptively simple concept of democracy. The transformations in Eastern Europe, despite their uncertain results, make it difficult to dismiss efforts to extend democracy in the West. Even conservative parties have mooted citizen and public client charters in recognition of their popular appeal, although this attempted appropriation may deform the genuine potential of such charters. In opposition to such developments, an alternative and pluralistic concept of democracy can be articulated, particularly since the term carries a legitimacy which communism can no longer claim. This democratic process may take many forms: the restructuring of electoral systems and the affirmation of citizen rights; political devolutions from centralised states; advances in regional autonomy; facilitations of local economic development; and real public participation in planning. These could complement the strengthening of minority rights and the affirmation of equal employment strategies.

One of the shortcomings of social democracy's response to the assault of the New Right has been its reluctance to claim this wider agenda. Instead, it has presented itself as the more humane, but more efficient, manager of the status quo. Thus it embraces markets, preaches fiscal rectitude, promises to

---

[15] Grieve Smith, J. (1992), *Full Employment in the 1990s*, The Institute for Public Policy Research, London, p.63.

reconstruct the supply-side, but continues to assert a marginally more ambitious social agenda. Curiously, just as the impulse to democratise strengthens, the platforms of political parties converge, real choice is minimised and political debates degenerate into personalised rhetoric.

There are also acute dangers in attempting to mobilise political support on the proposition of superior economic performance. In the 1980s, conservative governments successfully absolved themselves from this responsibility by claiming the supremacy of the market. If social democracy becomes locked into a set of performance principles, it faces the threat of being further undermined, if these do not succeed.

The position advocated here is that a concern with a broadly conceived process of democracy represents a better alternative than a narrow preoccupation with technocratic efficiency. Moreover, this notion of democracy has little in common with conventional representative democracy which can engender tyrannies over minorities - the lack of concern of the employed for the unemployed or of the full-time white male core worker for the black peripheral female worker. It should be admitted, however, that a programme which is premised on a prime value like democracy, is open to the charge that other prime values could have equal status - for example, liberty or even security.[16] At the same time, any attempt to integrate a value system with a political perspective may be vulnerable to this criticism. There may be greater drawbacks either in disavowing any values or in articulating such a wide set of values that the end result is an evocation of purely situational ethics. Equally, if this concept of democracy is regarded as a process in thinking as well as action, it would be subject to self analysis, reform and organic development. Thus, it would not be given to the determinism and reductionism that has characterised many sections of the left.

Social democracy has, then, to offer a broader, more pluralistic vision of social change based on a radical democratisation. But this cannot occupy only the political terrain. In the US one can find structures to accommodate devolution, legislation to ensure freedom of information, all the appearances of pluralism, and radical affirmative action programmes. However, economic power rests almost exclusively with a set of multinational corporations. Thus there remains a crucial argument of economic democracy of a form that markets do not provide. As indicated in previous chapters, there exist endemic conditions of market failure. The intended and unintended consequences of market operations have been a threat to the global ecology. The global dominance of markets has generated acute imbalances between First and Third Worlds represented in 1 billion living at subsistence level and an international debt crisis. Moreover, market perspectives and speculative impulses are prone to be short-term without consideration of longer-term

---

[16] Donnison, D. (1991), *A Radical Agenda: After the new right and the old left*, Rivers Oram Press, London.

consequences. All of these factors demand levels of regulation and intervention that can be precisely described.

Some have argued not for the opposition of public and private sectors but a recognition of their interdependence since the state both creates and sustains markets. The notion of a free market may thus be a contradiction in terms. Markets should therefore be designed to maximise social good. Moreover, there are key areas of the public sector where equity and efficiency are not incompatible, for example in education and training. The key challenge is to find the precise form of interdependence which maximises the potential of state intervention and market operation.[17] With the OECD's 1992 Employment Outlook pointing to around 30 million unemployed in the industrialised countries and calling for more active labour market policies to address the problem, the dominance of free market thinking about labour markets may be decisively on the wain.[18] Simultaneously, the New Keynesians have developed a set of microeconomic analyses which suggest that greater coordination between employers and trade unions in wage bargaining and substantially greater investment in training could do much to relieve unemployment.[19]

Such ideas are not entirely novel. They have been articulated in economic debates for decades. However, integrating economic ideas about the necessity for market regulation in a way that is democratic and participative, rather than corporatist, could have a contemporary relevance.

In particular, this is relevant to unemployment and the prospect of a return to full employment. One of the themes of this book has been the trade-off between unemployment and inflation, between egalitarianism and economic efficiency and the general disposition of governments in the 1980s to tolerate higher unemployment as the price for containing inflation. However, unemployment did not merely increase in this decade, but the rates between different countries also diverged. Some countries managed unemployment better than others, but there are different interpretations about why this was so. Therborn attributes high unemployment entirely to a lack of political will. Yet that kind of political will was most lacking in the US whose unemployment record in the 1980s was better than Europe's. Whether this was due to its proclaimed labour flexibilities or a consumer indulgence bolstered by unprecedented levels of credit, is disputable. Moreover, both the US and Britain created many jobs but mainly in the low productivity, low pay ends of the service sector; the issue should be not just the quantity but the quality of the jobs created. Within Europe, Germany's growth and export performance limited its unemployment rise, though guest workers encountered much greater difficulties.

---

[17] See Blackstone, T. et al, (1992), *Next Left: An agenda for the 1990s*, The Institute of Public Policy Research, London.

[18] OECD (1992), *Employment Outlook*, Paris.

[19] See Teague, P. (1992), *New Keynesianism and the Labour Market*, University of Ulster.

The approach to unemployment should therefore embrace a specification of the conditions and circumstances of the necessary interventions in markets by a democratising state, and a willingness to adopt the best practices of those countries which have least suffered mass unemployment. Economic conditions may suggest that the achievable goal in the medium term is 'fuller' employment than is currently the case rather than full employment. A decade of market commitment has graphically indicated the real costs of free market operations. Resolving such costs may be conceived both negatively and positively. The former includes compensation for those damaged by market operations, in particular displaced workers. This does no more than ameliorate detrimental market effects without promoting the kind of market evolution that would minimise such effects in future. For example, Belgium offers relatively generous income support to its unemployed without being able to significantly reduce unemployment. While this form of compensation makes the condition of unemployment more tolerable, it does not address the wider personal and social consequences of joblessness, and ultimately generates fiscal problems in the form of excessive public debt.

A preferable alternative is to respond positively to market exigencies through systems of industrial support, suitably designed and targeted to promote growth and competitiveness, and to alleviate spatial and social imbalances. The latter can be justified as much in terms of efficiency as equity, to which the congested, overheated regions of Europe and the US bear testimony. In turn, these systems need to be coordinated with an appropriate commitment to quality training and education to produce a multi-skilled and knowledge-intensive labour force. With respect to unemployment, the key idea is of an investment in the unemployed which would have four components: adequate compensation to avoid poverty; training linked to available jobs and job creation; monitoring and support of job search activities; and, crucially, the participation of unemployed people in the running and development of such programmes.

The difficulty of affirming this kind of model as a universal set of imperatives is that it may be said to be insensitive to cultural diversity. The role of culture in economic development has been subject to intense, but inconclusive, debate. For example, Rostow's thesis on modernisation suggested that an important pre-condition of development was the diffusion of modern ideas, such as rationality, and the dismantling of traditional cultures.[20] Yet Japan's traditional culture has been adapted rather than abandoned, to facilitate what is by any standard a highly dynamic economy. Similarly, the growing cultural diversity of the US did not prevent rapid economic development in the 1980s. On the other hand, Solow speculates that the cultural homogeneity of the Nordic countries may have been the significant factor in their relative containment of unemployment in the

---

[20] Rostow, R. R. (1960), *The Stages of Economic Growth: A non-communist manifesto*, Cambridge University Press, Cambridge.

1980s.[21] Culture may thus be important in economic development, but precisely how is open to question.

However the approach advocated here is that diverse industrial cultures, most of which have tolerated high unemployment and marginalised the unemployed, could develop more positively if this radical democracy was their prime value. The 1990s will be a difficult decade for the unemployed in the market economies. There are no easy solutions, but at least this approach would ensure that the issue remained central to the political and economic agenda. The tragedy of the 1980s was not just the growth of unemployment and the marginalisation of the unemployed, but also the devaluation of unemployment as a social concern.

---

[21] Solow, R. (1991), 'Unemployment as a social and economic problem', in Cornwall, J (ed.), The Capitalist Economies: Prospects for the 1990s, *op. cit.*

Bibliography

Books

Aaronovitch, S., Smith, R., Gardiner, J. and Moore, R. (1981), *The Political Economy of British Capitalism: A Marxist Analysis*, McGraw Hill, London.

Abalkin,L. (1988), *USSR: Reorganisation and Renewal*, Progress Publishers, Moscow.

Adnett, N. (1989), *Labour Market Policy*, Longman, London.

Allen, J. and Massey, D. (eds.) , (1988), *The Economy in Question*, Sage Publications, London.

Armstrong,P. Glyn,A. and Harrison,J. (1984), *Capitalism Since World War II*, Fontana, London.

Artis, M.J. (ed), (1989), *Prest and Coppock's The UK Economy*, Weidenfeld and Nicholson, London.

Ashton, D.N. (1986), *Unemployment under Capitalism*, Wheatsheaf Books, Brighton.

Auletta, K. (1982), *The Underclass*, Random House, New York.

Barrett Brown, M. et al. (eds.), (1978), *Full Employment*, Spokesman, London.

Bettleheim, C. (1978), *Class Struggles in the USSR, 1923-1930*, The Harvester Press, Sussex.

Blackaby, F. (ed.) (1979), *De-industrialisation*, National Institute of Economic and Social Research and Heinemann, London.

Blalock, H. (1967), *Toward a Theory of Minority Group Relations*, John Wiley New York; Barton,

Bleaney,M. (1985), *The Rise and Fall of Keynesian Economics*, MacMillan, London.

Bluestone, B. and Harrison, B. (1982), *The Deindustrialisation of America: Plant closings, community abandonment, and the dismantling of basic industry*, Basic Books, New York.

Bosanquet, N. and Townsend, P. (eds.), (1980), *Labour and Equality*, Heinemann, London.

Bowen, W. (ed.), (1965),*Labor and the National Economy*, Wiley and Sons, New York.

Braverman, H. (1974), *Labour and Monopoly Capitalism,* Monthly Review Press, London.

Brett, E.A. (1985), The World Economy Since the War: The Politics of Uneven Development, MacMillan, London.

Brown,J.C. (ed.), (1984), *Anti-Poverty Policy in the European Community*, Policy Studies Institute, London.

Brown, M. (ed.), (1988), *Remaking the Welfare State: retrenchment and social policy in America and Europe*, Temple University Press.

Caves, R. and Krause, (1980), *Britain's Economic Performance,* Brooking's Institute, Washington.

Cliff,T. (1974), *State Capitalism in Russia*, Pluto, London.

Coates D. Johnston G. and Bush R. (eds.), (1985), A Socialist Anatomy of Britain, Polity, London.

Coates, D. and Hillard, J. (eds.), (1986),The Economic Decline of Modern Britain, Wheatsheaf Books, Brighton.

Cohen, S. and Zysman (1987), Manufacturing Matters : The myth of the post-industrial economy, Basic Books, New York.

Cornwall, J. (ed.), (1991),*The Capitalist Economies: Prospects for the 1990s*, Edward Elgar,Aldershot.

CSE London Working Group (1980), *The Alternative Economic Strategy: A labour movement response to the economic crisis*, CSE Books, London.

Curwen, P. (1990), *Understanding the UK Economy*, MacMillan, London.

Currie, D. and Sawyer, M. (eds.), (1982), *Socialist Economic Review*, Merlin, London.

Cutler,T. Haslam,C. Williams,J. and Williams,K. (1989), *1992: The struggle for Europe*, Berg, New York.

Danziger, S.H. and Portney, K.E. (eds.), *The Distributional Impacts of Public Policies,* MacMillan,London.

Dahrendorf, R. (ed.), (1989), *Competing Visions for 1992*, IEA, London, pp.41-2.

Daniel, W.W. (1990), *The Unemployed Flow*, Policy Studies Institute.

Deacon, B. (1983), *Social Policy and Socialism*, Pluto Press, London.

Deakin, N. (1987), *The Politics of Welfare*, Methuen, London, p.37.

Design, K. (ed.), (1989), *Combating Long-Term Unemployment: Local\EC Relations*, Routledge, London.

Dilnot, A. and Walker, I. (eds.), *The Economics of Social Security*, Oxford University Press, Oxford.

Donaldson, P. (1986), *Worlds Apart*, 2nd edition, Penguin Books, Middlesex.

Donnison, D. (ed.), (1991), *Urban Poverty: the economy and public policy*, Combat Poverty Agency, Dublin,.

Donnison, D. (1991), *A Radical Agenda: After the new right and the old left*, Rivers Oram Press, London.

Eatwell J. et al. (eds.), (1990),*Social Economics*, MacMillan, London.

Eatwell, R. (1979), *The 1945-1951 Labour Governments,* Batsford, London, p.25.

Ei-Agrad, A.M. (ed.), (1982), *The Economics of the European Community*, Philip Allan, Oxford.

Ellwood,D. (1988), Poor Support : Poverty in the American family, Basic Books, New York.

Eversley, D. (1989), *Religion and Employment in Northern Ireland*, Sage Publications, London.

Fallon, P. and Verry, D. (1988), *The Economics of Labour Markets*, Philip Allan, Oxford.

Farrell, M. (1976), *Northern Ireland: The Orange State*, Pluto Press, London.

Fields, G.S. (1980), *Poverty, Inequality and Development*, Cambridge University Press, Cambridge.

Fishman, B. and Fishman, L. (1969), *Employment, Unemployment, and Economic Growth*, Thomas Crowell, New York.

Foley, A. and Mulreany, M. (eds.), (1990), *The Single European Market and the Irish Economy*, Institute of Public Administration, Dublin.

Freeman, R. and Holzer, H. (eds.), *The Black Youth Unemployment Crisis*, University of Chicago Press, Chicago.

Galbraith. J. (1988), *The Great Crash 1929*, Penguin, Middlesex.

Gaffikin, F. and Morrissey, M. (1990), *Northern Ireland: The Thatcher years*, Zed Books, London.

Gamble, A. (1988), *The Free Economy and the Strong State*, MacMillan.

George, S. A. (1989), *A Fate Worse than Debt*, Penguin Books, Middlesex.

George,V. and Manning,N. (1980), *Socialism, Social Welfare and the Soviet Union*, Routledge & Kegan Paul, London.

Grahl,J. and Teague, P. (1990), *1992: The big market*, Lawrence & Wishart, London.

Green, F. and Sutcliffe, B. (1987), *The Profit System*, Penguin, Middlesex.

Hagstrom, J. (1989), *Beyond Reagan: The new landscape of American politics*, Penguin Books, New York.

Hall,S. and Jacques,M. (eds.), (1989), *New Times*, Lawrence and Wishart, London.

Harris, N. (1986), *The End of the Third World*, Penguin Books, London.

Harris, R.I.D., Jefferson, C.W. and Spencer, J.E. (eds.), *The Northern Ireland Economy*, Longman, London.

Harrison, B. and Bluestone, B. (1988),*The Great U-Turn: Corporate restructuring and the polarizing of America*, Basic Books, New York.

Held, D. et al., (eds.), (1985), *States and Societies*, Blackwell, Open University, Oxford.

Hitiris, T. (1991), *European Community Economics*, Harvester Wheatsheaf, London.

Hudson, R. and Williams, A. (1986), *The United Kingdom*, Harper & Row, London.

Hughes, J. and Perlman, R. (1984), *The Economics of Unemployment: A comparative analysis of Britain and the United States*, Harvester Press, Wheatsheaf Books, London.

Hunt,E.K. and Sherman,H.J. (1986), *Economics: An Introduction to Traditional and Radical Views*, 5th edition, Harper & Row, New York.

Jenkins, C. and Sherman, B. (1979), *The Collapse of Work*, Methuen, London.

Jencks, C. and Peterson, P. (eds.), (1991), *The Urban Underclass*, The Brookings Institute, Washington DC.

Jones, C. (ed.), (1988), *The Reagan Legacy: promise and performance*, Chatham, New Jersey.

Keane,J. & Owens,J. (1986), *After Full Employment*, Hutchinson, London.

Kennedy, L. (1989), *The Modern Industrialisation of Ireland 1940-1988*, The Economic and Social History Society of Ireland, Ireland.

Keynes,J.M. (1983 edition), *The General Theory of Employment, Interest and Money*, Volume VII of The Collected Writings of John Maynard Keynes, MacMillan, London.

Le Grand, J. and Estrin, S. (eds.), (1989), *Market Socialism*, Clarendon Press, Oxford.

Lekachman, R. (1982), *Greed is not Enough: Reaganomics*, Pantheon Books, New York.

Levitan, S. and Shapiro, J. (1987), *Working But Poor: America's contradiction*, John Hopkin's University Press, Baltimore.

Lynn L (Jr.). and Mc.Geary, M. (eds.), (1990), *Inner City Poverty in the United States*, National Academy Press, Washington DC.

Mandel,E. (1978), *Late Capitalism*, Verso, London.

Markovich, D. and Pynn, R. (1988), *American Political Economy*, Brooks\Cole Publishing Company, California.

Massey, D. and Meegan, R. (1982), *The Anatomy of Job Loss: The How, Why and Where of Employment Decline*, Methuen, London.

Merritt, G. (1982), *World Out Of Work*, Collins, London.

Millar, J. and Glendinning, C. (1987), *Women and Poverty in Britain*, Wheatsheaf Books, Brighton.

Morris, D. (ed), (1985)*The Economic System in the UK*, Oxford University Press, Oxford.

Moynihan, P.(ed.), *On Understanding Poverty: perspectives from the social sciences*, Basic Books, New York.

Murray, C. (1984), *Losing Ground*, Basic Books, New York.

Murray, C.(1990), *The Emerging British Underclass*, Welfare Series no.2, Health and Welfare unit, IEA, London.

Myrdal, G. (1965), *The Challenge of Affluence*, Basic Books, New York.

O'Higgins,M. and Jenkins, S. (1988), *Poverty in Europe*, Centre for Analysis of Social Policy, Bath University, Bath.

Palmer, J. (1988), *Trading Places*, Radius, London.

Philpott, J. (ed.), (1990), *Trade Unions and the Economy: Into the 1990s*, Employment Institute, London.

Pinder, J. (1991), *European Community: The building of a union*, Opus, Oxford University Press, Oxford.

Poulantzas, N. (1979), *Fascism and Dictatorship*, Verso, London.

Rajan, A. (1990), *A Zero Sum Game*, The Industrial Society Press, London.

Ricketts, E. and Sawhill, I. (1986), *Defining and Measuring the Underclass*, Urban Institute, Washington DC.

Rolston, B. and Tomlinson, M. (1989), *Winding Up West Belfast*, Obair, Belfast.

Rostow, R. R. (1960), *The Stages of Economic Growth: A non-communist manifesto*, Cambridge University Press, Cambridge.

Rowthorn,B. (1980), *Capitalism, Conflict and Inflation*, Lawrence & Wishart, London.

Rowthorn, B. and Wayne, N. (1987), *The Political Economy of Northern Ireland*, Lawrence & Wishart, London.

Samuelson, P. (1973), *Economics*, 9th edition, McGraw Hill, New York.

Savage, S. P. and Robins L. (eds.) (1990), *Public policy under Thatcher*,

Macmillan, London.

Sawhill, I. (ed.), (1988), *Challenge to Leadership*, Urban Institute, Washington DC.

Shields, J. (ed.), (1989), *Conquering Unemployment, The case for economic growth*, Macmillan in association with the Emploment Institute, London.

Sinfield,A. and Showler, B. (eds.), (1981), *The Workless State*, Martin Robertson, Oxford.

Sinfield, A. (1981), *What Unemployment Means*, Martin Robertson, Oxford.

Smith, K. (1986), *The British Economic Crisis*, Penguin, Middlesex.

Sullivan, A. (1990), *Urban Economics*, Irwin, Boston.

Swann, D. (1984), *The Economics of the Common Market*, Pelican, Middlesex.

Teague, P. (ed.), (1987), *Beyond the Rhetoric*, Lawrence & Wishart, London.

Therborn, G. (1980), *The Ideology of Power and the Power of Ideology*, Verso, London.

Therborn, G. (1986), *Why some peoples are more unemployed than others*, Verso, London.

Todaro, M.P. (1981), *Economics for a Developing World*, Longman, Harlow.

Todaro, M.P. (1985), *Economic Development in the Third World*, 3rd Edition, Longman, London.

Townsend,P. (1979), *Poverty in the United Kingdom*, Penguin, Middlesex.

Walker, R. Lawson, R. and Townsend, P. (1984), *Responses to Poverty: Lessons from Europe*, Heinemann Educational Books, London.

White,M. (1983), *The Long Term Unemployed and Labour Markets*, Policy Studies Institute, London.

Williams, T. and Kornblum, W. (1985), *Growing Up Poor*, Heath, Lexington.

Wilson, W.J. (1987), *The Truly Disadvantaged: The inner city, the underclass, and public policy*, University of Chicago Press, Chicago.

Worswick, G.D.N. (1991), *Unemployment: A problem of policy*, Cambridge University Press, Cambridge,

Young, H. (1990), *One of Us*, Pan Books London

Articles

Anderton, R., Barrell, R. and in't Veld, J.W. (1991), `Macro economic convergence in Europe', *National Institute Economic Review*, no. 138, November.

Ascherson, N. (3/11/1991), 'Punishment for the poor, not the apparatchiks', *The Independent on Sunday.*

Atkinson,J. and Gregory,D. (1986), 'A flexible future: Britain's dual labour force', *Marxism Today*, April, pp. 12-17.

Barry, F. and Bradley, J. (1991), `On the causes of Ireland's unemployment', *The Economic and Social Review*, vol. 22, July.

Begg, I. and Mayes, D. (1991), 'Social and economic cohesion among the regions of Europe in the 1990s', *National Institute Economic Review.* November.

Benjamin, D.K. and Kochin, L.A. (1979), 'Searching for an explanation of unemployment in interwar Britain', *Journal of Political Economy*, vol.82, no.3, June, pp.441-478.

Brummer, A. (21/3/1992), 'Problems remain no matter what the political flavour', *The Guardian.*

Borger, J. (6/2/92), 'Poland retreats from rapid market reform', *The Guardian.*

Desai, M. and Shah, A. (1988), 'An Econometric Approach to the Measurement of Poverty', *Oxford Economic Papers.*

Dodall, G. (1974), 'White gains from black subordination in 1960 and 1970', *Social Problems*, 22, pp.162-83;

The Economist (30/3/1991), 'America's wasted blacks'.

The Economist (4/4/1992), 'New Deal Chic'.

Elliot,L. and Kelly,R. (28/10/1991), 'Europe stands breathless as the German engine hits the buffers', *The Guardian*.

Edsall, T. and Edsall, M. (1991), 'Race', *The Atlantic Monthly*, vol.267, no.5, May.

Faire,A. (1983), 'Ten Years of Crisis for the Advanced Capitalist Economies', in *World View 1983*, Pluto Press, London.

Farley, J. (1987), 'Disproportionate black and hispanic unemployment in US metropolitan areas: the roles of racial inequality, segregation and discrimination in male joblessness', *American Journal of Economics and Sociology*, April, vol. 46, no.2.

Gans, H. (1990), 'Deconstructing the underclass: the term's dangers as a planning concept', *American Planning Association Journal*, no. 271, Summer.

The Guardian (19/11/1991), 'Fear of fortress Europe'.

Hakim,C. (1987), 'Trends in the Flexible Workforce', *Employment Gazette*, London, November.

Harris, A. (1991), 'The economic consequences of Mr. Reagan', in *The World in 1991*, Economist Publications.

Hutton, W. (4/5/1992), 'Taking the yellow brick road to ruin.' *The Guardian*.

Jones, J.P. and Kodras J.E. (1990), Restructured Regions and Families: The feminisation of poverty in the US, *Annals of the Association of American Geographers*, Vol.80, No.2, pp.163-183.

Kain. J. (1968), 'Housing segregation, negro employment, and metropolitan decentralisation', *Journal of Economics*, vol.82.

Kasarda, J. (1990), 'Structural factors affecting the location and timing of urban underclass growth', *Urban Geography*, vol.11, no.3, pp. 234-64.

Keegan, V. (4/11/1991), 'Batting for Britain means keeping score accurately', *The Guardian*.

Leadbeater, C. (1991), 'Marketing the World', *Marxism Today*, January.

McLaughlin,E. (1991), 'Work and welfare benefits: social security, employment and unemployment in the 1990s', *Journal of Social Policy*, Vol. 20, Part 4, October, pp.485-508.

Marshall, A. (12/4/1992), 'Maastricht begins to split at the seams', *The Independent on Sunday*.

Massey, D. and Eggers, M. (1990), 'The ecology of inequality: minorities and the concentration of poverty', 1970-1980, *American Journal of Sociology*, vol.95, March, 1153-88.

Millar, J. and Glendinning, C. (1989), 'Gender and Poverty', *Journal of Social Policy*, 18, 3, pp.363-381.

Moore, T. and Laramore, (1990), 'Industrial change and urban joblessness: An assessment of the mismatch hypothesis', *Urban Affairs Quarterly*, vol.25, no. 4, June, pp. 640-58.

Nathan, R. (1987), 'Will the underclass always be us?' *Society,* March-April.

Nathan, R. and Lego, J. (1986), 'The changing size and concentration of the poverty population of large cities, 1970-1980', memorandum, Princeton University.

The Nora-Minc Report (1978), quoted in, 'The next French revolution', *New Scientist*, June.

Peel,Q. (22/10/1991), 'Germany given recession warning,' *Financial Times*,

Piachaud, D. (10/10/1981), 'Peter Townsend and the Holy Grail', *New Society*.

Piachaud, D. (1987), 'Problems in the definition and measurement of poverty, *Journal of Social Policy,* 16, 2.

Ruggles, P. and Marton, W. (1986), 'Measuring the size and characteristics of the underclass', mimeo.

Stoesz, D. and Karger, H. (1991), The corporatisation of the United States welfare state, *Journal of Social Policy*, vol. 20, part 2, April, pp.157-71.

Teague, P. (1989), Economic Development in Northern Ireland: Has Pathfinder lost its way?, *Regional Studies*, 23, pp. 63-9.

Tiebout, C. (1956), 'A pure theory of local expenditures', *Journal of Political Economy*, 64, October, pp. 416-24.

Tienda, M. and Lii, D (1988), 'Minority concentration and earnings inequality: Blacks, Hispanics, and Asians compared', American Journal of Sociology, vol.93, pp.141-65.

Tienda, M. (1990), 'Welfare and work in Chicago's inner city', *The American Economic Review*, pp. 372-7.

Tipping, B. (1982), 'Scrounging in Northern Ireland: The beginnings of an investigation', *The Economic and Social Review*, vol.13, no. 3, Dublin.

Tisdall, S. (24/1/1992), 'Black America waits for a rallying call', *The Guardian*.

Travis, A. (13/12/1991), 'PM backs aid plan to stem home losses', *The Guardian*.

Townsend, P. (1991-92), 'Hard Times', *European Labour Forum*, no.6, Winter.

Unemployment Unit & Youth Aid (1991), 'Actively seeking work', London, November.

Walker, M. (30\1\1992),'Pay-later US budget takes first steps towards reform', *The Guardian*.

Walker, M. (6/5/1992), 'Less welfare, more wafare', *The Guardian*.

Wilson, W.J. (1991), 'Studying inner city social dislocations: the challenge of public agenda research', *American Sociological Review*, vol. 56.

Reports

ACARD (1979), *Joining and Assembly: The impact of robots and automation*, HMSO, London.

Blackstone, T. et al, (1992), *Next Left: An agenda for the 1990s*, The Institute of Public Policy Research, London.

Brandt Report (1980), *North-South: A Programme for Survival*, Pan Books, London.

Budget of the US Government, Fiscal Year 1992 (1992), US Government Printing Office, Washington DC.

Bureau of Labor Statistics (1990), *Unemployment Rates*, Department of Labor, Washington DC.

Cambridge Econometrics (1991), *Regional Economic Prospects*, Cambridge, January.

The Cecchini Report (1988), *1992: The benefits of a Single Market*, Wildwood House Ltd., Aldershot.

Combat Poverty Agency (1991), *Making social rights a reality*, Dublin.

Commission of the European Communities (1988), *Social Europe*, Brussels.

Commission of the European Communities (1988), *1992: The European social dimension*, Brussels.

Commission of the European Communities (1989), *Employment in Europe*, Brussels.

Commission of the European Communities, (1990), *Eurobarometer: The perception of poverty in Europe*, March, Brussels.

Commission of the European Communities (1990), *The European Labour Market*, Brussels.

Commission of the European Communities (1990), *European Economy*, Brussels, December.

Commission of the European Communities (13/2/1991), *Final report of the second European poverty programme*, Brussels.

Commission of the European Communities (1991), *The Regions in the 1990s*, Brussels.

Commission of the European Communities (1991), *European Economy*, no.50, December, Brussels.

Commission of the European Communities (1992), *From the single act to Maastricht and beyond*, Brussels.

Compton, P. (ed.) (1981), *The Contemporary Population of Northern Ireland and Population Related Issues*, The Queen's University, Belfast.

Council of Economic Advisers (1984), *Economic Report to the President*, Government Printing Office, Washington DC.

Council of Economic Advisers (1987), *Economic Report to the President*, Government Printing Office, Washington DC.

Council of Economic Advisors (1988), *Economic Indicators*, Government Printing Office, Washington DC.

Council of Economic Advisers (1990), *Economic Report to the President*, US Government Printing Office, Washington DC.

Council of Economic Advisers (1991), *Economic Report to the President*, U.S. Government Printing Office, Washington DC..

Counter Information Services Report No.23 (1978), The New Technology, and The Advisory Council for Applied Research and Development, *The Application of Semi-Conductor Technology*, HMSO, London.

Department of Economic Development, Northern Ireland (1987), *The Pathfinder Process*, Belfast.

EC (1973), *Treaties Establishing the European Communities*, Luxembourg.

EC (1990), *Poverty in Europe: Estimates*, The Institute of Social Studies Advisory Service, Rotterdam University, Rotterdam.

Economics Division, Policy, Planning and Research Unit (1991), *Monthly Economic Report*, Department of Finance and Personnel, Northern Ireland, November.

Economist Intelligence Unit (1991), *Country Profile 1991-92, the Irish Republic*, London.

Espoir Ltd. (1980), *Europe Against Poverty*, Bath.

Eurostat (1988), *Long-term unemployment,* Brussels.

Fair Employment Agency (1983), *Report of an Investigation by the Fair Employment Agency into the Non-Industrial Northern Ireland Civil Service*, Belfast.

Freeman, J. et al. (1989), *The Irish economies: A common future?*, Amalgamated Transport & General Workers Union, Belfast.

The Government of Ireland (1989), *Ireland: National Development Plan, 1989-1993*, Dublin.

Grieve Smith, J. (1992), *Full Employment in the 1990s*, The Institute for Public Policy Research, London.

Junankar, P.N. (ed.), *Very Long Term Unemployment*, Commission of the European Communities, Brussels.

McCormick, B. (1991), *Unemployment Structure and the Unemployment Puzzle*, Employment Institute, London.

Manley Report (1985), *Global Challenge: From crisis to cooperation: breaking the north-south stalemate*, Pan Books, London.

The Northern Ireland Economic Council and the National Economic and Social Council (1988), *Economic Implications for Northern Ireland and the Republic of Ireland of Recent Developments in the European Community*, Belfast & Dublin.

Northern Ireland Economic Council (1989), *Economic Strategy: Overall Review*, Belfast.

Northern Ireland Economic Council (1989), *Autumn Economic Review*, Belfast.

Northern Ireland Economic Council (1991), *Autumn Economic Review*, October, Belfast.

OECD (1984), *Employment Outlook*, Paris.

OECD (1985), *Quarterly labour force statistics*, no. 4.

OECD (1988), *Employment Outlook*, Paris.

OECD (1991), *Economic Outlook*, July.

Office of the US Trade Representative (1984-85), *Annual Report of the President of the United States on the Trade Agreements Program*, Washington DC.

Oppenheim, C. (1991), *Poverty: The facts*, CPAG, London.

Piachaud, D. (1991), *Unemployment and Poverty*, Campaign For Work, research report, London, vol.3, no.3, May.

Policy and Practice (1991), *Urban Poverty: the economy and public policy*, Combat Poverty Agency, Dublin.

PPRU Monitor (1991), *Continuous household survey: Preliminary results for 1989/90*, Department of Finance and Personnel (NI), Belfast, October.

Policy Studies Institute (1981), *Micro-Electronics in Industry: the extent of use*, PSI, London.

Roche, J.D. (1984), *Poverty and Income Maintenance Policies in Ireland, 1973-80*, Institute of Public Administration, Dublin.

Room, G., Laczko, F. and Whitting, G. (1987), *Action to combat poverty: The experience of sixty five projects*, Working Papers Evaluation Section, no. 9, December, Centre for the Analysis of Social Policy, University of Bath, Bath, p.4.

Statistics and Social Division, PPRU (1991), *1990 Labour Force Survey: Religion report*, Belfast, PPRU Monitor 3\91.

Shields, J. (ed.), *Conquering Unemployment: the case for economic growth*, Macmillan in association with the Employment Instiute, London.

Social Trends, (1989) HMSO, London.

Unemployment Unit and Youth Aid, December (1991), *Working Brief.*

United Nations Organisation, Secretariat of the Economic Commission for Europe (1987), *Economic Survey of Europe, 1986-87*, Geneva.

The World Bank (1991), *Poverty: World Development Report 1990*, published for the World Bank by Oxford University Press, Oxford.

Index